*Standing on New Ground*

# Standing
# on New Ground
## Women in Alberta

EDITED BY   CATHERINE A. CAVANAUGH
AND RANDI R. WARNE

**ALBERTA NATURE AND CULTURE SERIES**
*John E. Foster and Dick Harrison*
*General Editors*

THE UNIVERSITY OF ALBERTA PRESS

The University of Alberta Press
141 Athabasca Hall
Edmonton, Alberta, Canada  T6G 2E8

Copyright © The University of Alberta Press 1993

ISBN 0–88864–258–X

**Canadian Cataloguing in Publication Data**

Main entry under title:
Standing on New Ground: Women in Alberta

(Alberta nature and culture series)
ISBN 0–88864–258–X

1. Women—Alberta. 2. Women—Alberta—History.
I. Cavanaugh, Catherine Anne, 1945– II. Warne, R.R.
(Randi Ruth), 1952– III. Series.
HQ1459.A4S83 1993    305.4'097123    C93–091885–1

Cover illustration
Annora Brown, *Wild Sunflowers*. Oil on canvas. (Courtesy
The University of Alberta Central Collection and used
with permission of Morley Brown.)

Printed on acid-free paper. ∞
Printed and bound in Canada by Quality Color Press Inc.,
Edmonton, Alberta, Canada.

# CONTENTS

Alberta Nature and Culture Series offers informed commentary on Alberta and its people, past and present, and on related national and international issues. It brings together specialists from a range of disciplines in the Arts, Humanities, Social and Natural Sciences with writers and researchers from the wider community. The first title in the series is *Buffalo*.

# ACKNOWLEDGEMENTS

When we were invited by the General Editors of the Alberta Nature and Culture Series to put together a volume of collected works focussing on women in Alberta we readily agreed. The series' mandate is to provide an interdisciplinary forum for works of general interest to a wide readership. This approach appealed to our own commitment to feminist activism and the subject of this special issue reflected our shared scholarly interest in prairie women. We also welcomed the opportunity to continue our collaborative work which began in 1988 with an exhibition and video celebrating the sixtieth anniversary of the Persons Case and featuring the "Famous Five" Alberta women who successfully brought the action to the Privy Council in England in 1929.

We wish to thank our General Editors, John Foster and Dick Harrison, for having had the idea in the first place and then generously supporting us at every stage of preparation and publication. Also a very special thank you to the women at The University of Alberta Press, especially Norma Gutteridge, Mary Mahoney-Robson, and Kerry Watt. Our editor, Barbara Demers, came highly recommended and then far exceeded her own reputation. Thank you Barbara for your professional dedication and enthusiastic support.

Our gratitude to the University of Alberta, the Historic Sites and Archives Services, Cultural Facilities and Historic Resources Branch, Alberta Community Development, and the Alberta Foundation for the Arts, a beneficiary of the Lottery Fund of the Government of Alberta, for their financial support.

We dedicate this volume to all Alberta women; past, present and future.

*COMMITTED TO THE DEVELOPMENT OF CULTURE AND THE ARTS*

# INTRODUCTION

*Standing on New Ground: Women in Alberta* continues a conversation about the place, history, and endeavours of women in Alberta. It is a prairie piece, acknowledging the impact of geography, settlement patterns, and aspirations for the future which continue to characterize the Canadian West. At the same time, it affirms Alberta's uniqueness as a province with a distinctive political mix, economic base, and ideological diversity embodied in both its history and its contemporary realities. *Standing on New Ground* collects recent works of academic and independent researchers in an accessible and varied volume; its purpose will be achieved if readers become more aware of women's experience in Alberta, and even more so if further discussion is sparked, and new voices join the conversation.

The papers in this volume range from explorations of the experiences of early women missionaries and settlers of European descent to contemporary efforts to shape Alberta's social and cultural landscape. A primary concern of the authors is the place Alberta women have occupied in and outside public institutions, both formal and informal. Within this broad framework important questions are raised about the perceived and actual role of women in the "public sphere"— a separate and primary domain occupied by men with authority over women's "private sphere." Alberta came into existence at a time when relations between women and men were widely defined by the socially constructed concept of the companionate marriage, which assumed cooperation between women and men while each asserted authority over their separate and complementary spheres of influence. Separate spheres technically granted women an equal share of power based on the division of authority by gender. In practice, however, it was separate and hierarchical. The domestic sphere occupied by the woman/wife/mother was deemed important but subordinate to and supportive of the public sphere of the man/husband/father. While many women accepted these definitions of gender and their attending roles, others rebelled against them. Furthermore, gender roles were more permeable than separate spheres would suggest. The private and the public were often conflated as women actively made their own lives and communities through their day-to-day work, civic and political action, and community building.

Alberta women have a long history of activism. While our presence in the prairie west predates the establishment of the province of Alberta in 1905, the turn-of-the-century agrarian frontier provided Euro-Canadian women with a unique opportunity to intervene to redraw social divisions toward greater equality between men and women. References in the literature to women cutting their hair and donning "men's" trousers upon their arrival in the West are suggestive of the transformative influence of the frontier.[1] More generally, the "pioneering partnership" between women and men forced by necessity to share the burdens of settlement in a harsh and often unforgiving environment gave support to women's claim to full citizenship.[2]

Over time, the opportunity of the frontier, real or imagined, was muted, and divisions along gender lines were more sharply drawn. The resulting tensions between appearance and reality, image and experience which are explored here partly reflect the relative speed with which the Alberta frontier developed into a modern urban culture which in itself generated new reforms. Thus, the twentieth century which began with the "woman question" is ending with a similar though more wide ranging debate about women's place within the institutional life of the province. During the early decades of the century, the total exclusion of women from public life encouraged a specific focus on inclusion through the vote and other legislative reforms. Women have learned in the intervening years that other barriers exist to "personhood" such as the "glass ceiling," the "double-day," and the devaluation of women's traditional experiences. In large part this discussion reflects the extent to which provincial women have rebelled against and continue to resist a restrictive ideal of their "proper place," establishing new positions of authority for themselves and in the process reconstructing the prevailing views of womanhood and manhood. Alberta women have often been at the forefront of this change. For example, five women from Alberta, Emily Murphy, Louise McKinney, Henrietta Muir Edwards, Nellie McClung, and Irene Parlby, challenged the exclusion of women from the Senate and won constitutional recognition of women as "persons" in 1929. Nevertheless, the traditional assumption of a dependent, supporting, and subordinate womanhood persisted in Law long after the concept of partnership had redefined gender relations in public discourse. This disjunction was graphically illustrated in the 1970s when Iris Murdoch, a southern Alberta farmwoman, failed in her divorce action to win a share in the family farm she had helped to build. When, in 1974, the court ruled against Murdoch because her labour was "just about what the ordinary rancher's wife does" women across the country organized a successful campaign for legislation guaranteeing a wife's interest in family assets.[3] Under the new rules of law women moved from being viewed as matrimonial property to becoming equal owners in matrimonial property.

From midcentury significant social and economic changes together with women's evolving activism have substantially broadened the context in which women's struggle for equality has taken place. As the population of Alberta has become more culturally and ethnically diverse, new voices have brought a more varied perspective and a wider scope to women's organized reform. Today, these struggles are as diverse as reproductive rights, band status for native women married to non-natives, and refugee status based on state-sponsored violence against women. Resistance to sex discrimination continues in the context of shifting gender identities.

The works presented here capture some of the important developments in the lives of Alberta women. In particular they show how women have attempted to influence, use, and transform formal and informal institutions or, alternatively, to create counter-institutions to more effectively meet women's needs and advance their agendas. This exploration reveals much that is particular about women's experience in Alberta as well as suggesting ways in which it is continuous with other prairie cultures.

The prairie provinces hold a special place in Canadian culture as the site of intentional, structured "nation-building." Vast expanses of land, a relatively open (though sex-specific) homesteading policy, and unabashed government propaganda drew settlers from both the Old World and the New. No less than Saskatchewan and Manitoba, Alberta saw enthusiastic efforts in this regard. Envoys from the dominant Anglo-Celtic culture took it upon themselves to "civilize" both the region's original inhabitants and the many immigrant peoples who came west in the early years of this century to start a new life. In "'Lighting the Pathways for New Canadians': Methodist and United Church WMS Missions in Eastern Alberta, 1904–1940," Michael Owen explores the particular efforts of the Woman's Missionary Society of the Methodist Church to "Christianize" and "Canadianize" the Ukrainians of Alberta. There are at least two stories here to tell. Owen focusses on the so-called "civilizers" rather than on those who served as objects of their perhaps well-meaning but culturally imperialistic ministrations. His study illuminates the contradictions, both in action and in theory, experienced by WMS women in working toward the organization's stated goals.

This exploration supports recent scholarship[4] which suggests that, in the end, the constructive achievements of providing educational and medical services were much more successful than missionary attempts at proselytism, either religious or cultural. Spurred on by assumptions of cultural superiority, missionaries provided needed and valuable social services to struggling immigrants facing immense hardships in a harsh and unfamiliar land. They were responsible for bringing medical services to outlying areas, and while their efforts to provide educational opportunities for young immigrants undoubtedly reflected their concern to impart to "New Canadians" a particular vision of Canadian life, they nevertheless offered the opportunity for education which could provide an entree into a better life. Nor were the Ukrainians who were the target of WMS efforts duped by their agenda. Ultimately, as Owen points out, the Woman's Missionary Society was forced to recognize that its overt assimilationist efforts among Ukrainians in western Canada were ineffective.

Owen's study reminds us of the complex nature of social change, and the often contradictory elements which inform its progress. It also encourages further study to elicit the voices of those who resisted efforts to shape them into an alien reality in order to hear their experience and perceptions of their accommodation to their newly adopted land.

The task of "civilizing" the frontier was taken seriously by women of the dominant culture. During the early decades of this century women reformers increasingly worked through middle-class volun-

tary clubs and organizations. The "club movement" was an attempt
to respond more effectively to the scale of modern industrial life and
its attendant social and economic change. This movement is usually
seen as an urban phenomenon; however, in Catherine Cole and Ann
Milovic's study "Education, Community Service, and Social Life: The
Alberta Women's Institutes and Rural Families, 1909–1945," we are
reminded that rural Alberta provided fertile ground for women's voluntary associations as well. The success of the province's women's
clubs owed much to the harsh conditions faced by many women living on isolated homesteads. Women's Institutes along with other
clubs and associations offered a means of overcoming the isolation of
the prairie and building crucial social and political networks which
often afforded women influence beyond what their numbers alone
would allow. Indeed, by the 1920s Alberta women had gained a reputation as effective organizers. In a tribute to Alberta women, Mrs.
McCorquodale, editor of the High River *Times*, said that she "would
have no difficulty recognizing the Alberta women in Heaven. . . . with
pencils and notebooks, they would be in little groups beside the river
of life putting the finishing touches to resolution B72894 urging that
more rural children be taken into the Heavenly Choirs."[5]
   Established in Alberta in 1909 under the auspices of the provincial
government, the nonsectarian, nonpartisan Alberta Women's Institutes (AWI) enjoyed an unrivaled popularity. Known as the rural
women's university, the AWI quickly established itself as the primary
vehicle for the dissemination of information—touching on every
aspect of rural women's lives from child care to farm and home management to legislative reform.[6]
   Women's clubs and organizations have been seen as important to
the development of women's networks and served as vehicles of entry
into the mainstream of public life.[7] By focussing on the relationship
between the AWI and rural families, Cole and Milovic suggest a more
complex relationship between women's clubs and female solidarity. If,
as the authors argue, family and club life were closely intermingled,
then clubs would be less effective in providing an alternative for criticizing women's traditional role within the family. In the case of the
AWIs, however, the promotion and education of women as farm pro-
ducers may have reinforced the notion of economic partnership.
   Despite their apparent influence we know surprisingly little about
the early history of women's organizations. Did they, as Cole and
Milovic suggest, play an important, formative role during the years of
settlement and community building? In order to answer this question

we need to know much more about the membership as well as the specific programs and activities of various organizations. Who were its members, its leaders, and what was their underlying philosophy? Did they promote class, ethnic, and religious divisions, acting as lay missionaries preaching the gospel of the dominant Anglo middle-class, or did they appeal to a wide spectrum of society and therefore act as a mediating influence between social groups? What was the relationship between women's social activities and women's political activism? What strategies did they use to win community support?

Important clues about women's lives are not only conveyed in the record of women's organizations. Individual women too perceived and documented their frontier. One of these women was Jessie Burk Umscheid, who grew up on her family's farm near present-day Milo. Umscheid's vision of herself is the subject of Barbara Evans's article, "'We Just Lived It As It Came Along': Stories From Jessie's Albums." Using photographs taken by Umscheid between 1917 and 1922, Evans explores several themes first raised in her film *Jessie's Albums*. Jessie's pictorial history begins when she is fifteen years old and reflects her youthful optimism. Her intention is to capture the day-to-day life of women at work, at play, and in rare moments of solitary reflection. The result is a pictorial record that stands in marked contrast to the stiff, contrived photographs typical of professional photographers of the period. There is a compelling immediacy in Jessie's images which seems to collapse time by drawing the viewer into the action.

As Evans points out, Jessie's youthful vision challenges the view of pioneer farm women as socially isolated and burdened by the demands of family and hard physical labour under harsh frontier conditions. This study also raises questions about the construction of memory and the selection of perspective. By her own admission, Jessie intended to capture the positive moments of living life "as it came along." There is no dark side to Jessie's photographs, which end with the Depression because "[w]e didn't think it was anything too nice to take pictures of." By editing out the negative images, Jessie constructed an uplifting vision of her life that sustained her through hard times. Evans reminds us of the subjectivity and purposefulness of memory and how it informs our understanding of the past. Her article also underscores the importance of who has control of the means of representing the past.

Lassiter and Oakes's article, "Ranchwomen, Rodeo Queens, and Nightclub Cowgirls: The Evolution of Cowgirl Dress," illustrates how powerful "official" images can be, creating the impression of a reality which is in fact at significant variance with lived experience. "Cowgirl dress" has typically suggested a certain freedom and liberality of movement without challenging dominant conceptions of "femininity." As Lassiter and Oakes point out, this popular image has undergone a number of changes throughout the years. Finding its origin in the garb of ranchwomen who came west to homestead in the mid- to late-nineteenth century, the popular form of cowgirl dress evolved in relation to a variety of cultural factors and emphases. Of particular significance was the popularity of Hollywood westerns in the 1940s and 1950s. Cowgirls kept the basic form of the practical attire worn by earlier generations of "rodeo girls" but embellished it through the use of seductive fabrics like satin and an overall concern for glamour and femininity reminiscent of Hollywood starlets. The emergence of the image of the "urban cowboy" brought another transformation in cowgirl dress, as designer blue jeans, fancy boots, and skin-tight shirts came into vogue.

According to Lassiter and Oakes, however, the popular image of cowgirl dress had little to do with the realities of women living the ranching life. Far from the sporty, romantic, or frankly sexual image portrayed through the stereotype, ranching women continued to adopt functional attire—sturdy "work pants, work shirts, and a well-worn Stetson." Their historical overview gives rise to intriguing questions about the relation between popular culture and practical realities, and the power of that culture to make genuine innovations in dress (themselves reflective of certain social changes) conform to dominant notions of appropriate gender representation.

Nanci Langford's article, "'All That Glitters': The Political Apprenticeship of Alberta Women, 1916–1930," shifts our attention to the formal area of legislative politics. Here too the tensions between image, myth, and reality are brought to bear. As conventional wisdom would have it, women's political activism culminated with the achievement of suffrage in 1916 only to disappear until the emergence of the women's movement of the 1960s. Langford shows that in fact the postsuffrage years were important and productive both for the gains provincial women made and for the critical lessons they learned.

The period 1916–30 marks the entrance of women into the legislature and cabinet and the achievement of much social legislation backed by the new woman voter. However, Langford notes that these victories were often far from complete. In contrast to the heady days of 1916, when Alberta women won the right to vote in provincial and municipal elections and on school matters, the 1920s saw the collapse of the suffrage coalition and an increasingly conservative climate which eroded support for women's reform agenda. In the face of growing divisions within their own ranks and renewed opposition from outside, reformers began to reassess the significance of equal voting rights as well as their organizational strategies for change.

Langford shows that the critical accomplishment of winning the vote was only the first step to women's full and equal inclusion with men in the political life of Alberta. Thus, while 1916 marks the end of women's formal exclusion from equal citizenship, the immediate postsuffrage period marks the beginning of the struggle to win full inclusion in the political process; as voters, members of political parties, legislators, and cabinet ministers. As provincial women took up that struggle they learned that the achievement of formal equality was insufficient in itself to achieve widespread social change. Indeed, having won the vote they found that they had lost a powerful strategic advantage. While lobbying and moral suasion were effectively applied by Alberta suffragists prior to achieving the vote, they carried less force once it could be said that women had the necessary tool to effect the changes to the social order that they advocated. Different strategies and stances would be required to achieve their goals in the postsuffrage world.

A more complete understanding of the lessons of women's "political apprenticeship" could provide significant insights into the contemporary struggle for political and social equality. Indeed, a central question for feminists today is whether women are most effective as agents of change working within or outside of existing structures and institutions.

In her study, "A Few Good Women: Female Legislators in Alberta, 1972–1991," Linda Trimble asks the question: Do women make a difference in political office? Using Alberta Hansard she examines the impact women have had on political discourse within the provincial legislature. At the heart of Trimble's study is the question whether women's issues can be effectively represented within existing political structures. The answer, of course, has important implications for how women organize for legislative change.

By tracking debates on so-called women's issues over the past twenty years, Trimble identifies a number of encouraging trends. Despite significant barriers to women's full participation in the legislature, she concludes that women—given sufficient numbers—can make a difference to both the tone and the substance of debate. However, the difference that women make depends upon several critical factors. First and foremost is the number of women elected as members of the Legislative Assembly. Trimble argues that a "critical mass" is necessary before women begin to have an influence on the kinds of issues brought before the legislature and the framework for the subsequent debates. Second, she concludes that women make a difference when they are prepared to break the rules. Her study shows that as the number of women MLAs has increased they have been most effective in representing women's interests when they cooperate across party lines, work consensually, and pursue "issue-oriented discourse."

According to Trimble, one of the most significant changes affecting the representation of women in the Alberta legislature is the increased presence of women within the ranks of the opposition. She points out that opposition women in particular have played a crucial role in advancing the debate on women's reproductive, economic, and social choices. This study raises an intriguing question of what might be called the "feminization of opposition" in Canadian politics. Any conclusion must await closer analysis of trends in other provincial legislatures and the national parliament as well as comparative studies of nonparliamentary systems of government such as in the United States. If Trimble's results can be applied to other jurisdictions then parliamentary structure may offer Canadian women an effective forum for change.

The political apprenticeship of some of the women currently holding political office in Alberta began in the late 1960s and early 1970s at a time when the contemporary women's movement erupted in a widespread critique of the narrow confines of women's domestic role within the family. Initially, women struggled to establish an identity separate from the family and challenged the fantasy of "happiness ever after" that surrounded a domesticity which cast women as the emotional centre of the ideal household. As one early feminist wrote: "Our window on the world is looked through with our hands in the sink and we've begun to hate that sink and all it implies—so begins our consciousness."[8] What began as a rebellion against women's confinement within the family, "dusting her life away," led to a widespread questioning of women's role outside the home; in the paid labour force, in the professions, and in the boardrooms and the legislatures of the nation.

The promise of women's rebellion was liberation from the assumption of their domestic destiny to an assumption of freedom to choose their destiny. For many middle-class women in the 1960s the route to independence was through higher education. *The Report of the Royal*

*Commission on the Status of Women in Canada,* published in 1970, showed a dramatic rise in the number of women enrolled in Canadian universities beginning in 1960–61. The report noted that between 1955–56 and 1966–67 female participation rates had quadrupled while the male rate had doubled.[9] At the same time, the number of women enrolled in graduate programs was less than it had been four decades earlier in 1921.[10] In "From Friedan to Feminism: Gender and Change at the University of Alberta, 1960–1970," Elaine Chalus examines the impact of these changes on undergraduates at the University of Alberta during the 1960s as revealed through the student newspaper, *The Gateway,* and the activities of the "Wauneitas," an all-women's club.

According to Chalus, during the early years of the decade, societal assumptions of women's domestic destiny determined the acceptability and judgments about their right and ability to participate in postsecondary education. Women were not taken seriously as scholars. Their participation was largely limited to faculties such as Education and Household Science which reinforced notions of women's domestic function. While undergraduate men were expected to prepare for future careers in the professions it was widely assumed that undergraduate women would equip themselves to be better wives and mothers. Indeed, it was commonly believed that the primary objective of most "freshettes" was a "MRS" not a BA or MA. By the midsixties women were beginning to challenge these social conventions by demanding greater personal freedom and an end to sex segregation. Chalus finds that change for University of Alberta women was gradual but significant throughout the 1960s. The debate, which ranged from "free love" to child care to combining career and family, was full of contradictions and, not surprisingly, gave rise to tensions that sometimes erupted in open hostility toward women, particularly feminist women.

Chalus makes a convincing case for the need to return to the origins of the contemporary women's movement, both within universities and outside them, in order to assess its meaning in our lives today. In particular, her study raises questions about the influence of the 1960s generation of women in shaping feminism during the subsequent decades and how feminism made a difference in their own lives and the lives of their daughters.

One of the features of current feminism is a commitment to broadening horizons and the range of choices available to girls and women as they shape their own lives. If institutional structures have proved a barrier, education has been seen as a means of gaining entry to and transforming those structures. Women educators have undertaken a special responsibility to make educational institutions accountable to their own ideal of open access. As Chalus shows, however, access alone is insufficient; advocacy is often necessary.

At the University of Alberta direct action was taken to advocate women's entry into the scientific professions. Through an initiative taken by the late Dr. J. Gordin Kaplan, WISEST (Women in Scholarship, Engineering, Science and Technology) was established in 1982. Its mandate was to "increase the percentage of women in decision-making roles in all fields of scholarship."

Margaret-Ann Armour offers a description of WISEST and the various programs it has sponsored to encourage female participation in the fields of science, technology, and engineering. One such program provides girls and women with "hands on" experience of what scientists or engineers do in their daily work, familiarizing them with what might otherwise seem an alien discipline. Other initiatives include an annual conference at which high school and university women have the opportunity to meet with women in nontraditional careers and ask them questions about their work. They also learn about how these women manage competing demands of family and personal life, given current societal expectations. Overall, WISEST initiatives are successfully reaching an increasing number of girls and women, building toward the association's goal of bringing female perspectives and agendas into science's historically male preserve.

This collection illustrates that existing structures are not always sufficient to address issues which women would want to bring to the fore. New organizations are required. One of these, as we have seen, is WISEST; another is the Women's Program and Resource Centre established on the University of Alberta campus as a subunit of the Faculty of Extension in 1981.

Pat Rasmussen, a former director of the Women's Program, "tells the story" of its inception, development, and intended goals over a ten year period. She documents the framing of the program's mandate to include a strong community development perspective and social change agenda, and the modification of some of its specific goals and practices over time. Despite constraints facing the program, many important resources have been made available to women. Especially useful has been the establishment of a data base system funded by the Secretary of State in 1986–87. "Womansource" lists the program's myriad books, offprints, bibliographies, and binder materials, allowing users to access essential but otherwise difficult-to-obtain materials on women.

Rasmussen's study illuminates the considerable practical difficulties, such as the reality of project-by-project funding, which have served equally with a prejudicial environment outside the program to make its successful operation such a challenge. "Telling Our Story" raises important questions about the relation of physical space/location and an institution's philosophy, the relationship and positioning of women's groups vis à vis one another, and the tradeoffs involved in being an "alternative" institution within a larger system. Too, it highlights the tensions between some feminist objectives and the ability of existing institutions to embody radical change. Can effective social change be brought about within established institutions? If so, what are the costs?

We conclude this volume with Patricia Roome's "Remembering Together: Reclaiming Alberta Women's Past." As the range of contributions above indicate, women in Alberta have engaged numerous structures, formal and informal, in their struggle for identity and equality. However, this collection tells but one small part of the story. There is a much larger tapestry within which these explorations figure. The voices which are missing from this essentially white, northern Euro-American Protestant conversation are lifted up in "Remembering Together." Roome provides an accessible yet detailed literature review which illustrates the breadth of the subject matter and the amount of work which remains to be done. In mapping this territory, Roome notes differences in interpretation, developments in perspective, and representative scholars in the field. In particular, we are called to attend to the missing voices of native, Metis, and Ukrainian women. Recent literature dealing with these excluded women raises important questions about the power dynamics which gave rise to their exclusion. Roome also points out that even a woman of relative ethnic, class, and urban privilege "could not speak loud enough to be heard by future generations." Elsie Park Gowan is an Alberta playwright whose works have only now been rediscovered. "Remembering Together" underscores the essential task of continuing to retrieve the lives of all Alberta women. As the various pieces in this volume illustrate, we need to be continually aware of the contexts of women's lives and the opportunities and barriers they experienced as a result.

The studies here show that even in the land of fresh beginnings the ground was not neutral ground. Inherited prejudice and power shaped the cultural agenda. The dominant culture continued to reshape the new vision according to its own mythology. Yet the West did create spaces for women to see themselves in new ways. Through political activism Alberta women have intervened to claim existing cultural structures as rightfully their own. They have struggled to shape their own ground through access to institutions in order to change them. Yet, thus far, it could be argued, the best that has been achieved is access. The ground is never simply won. Today women find themselves fighting many of the same battles their foremothers did.

One strategy from the past which women are reclaiming is advocacy through woman-specific groups and organizations. While integration on the same basis as men is essential, the lack of neutral ground requires a safe and specific place from which women can act. This collection identifies some of those places; others remain to be explored.

*Standing On New Ground* provides a critical perspective from which to consider women's experience in and of Alberta. It invites further exploration, and the charting of new and fresh directions from the vantage point of women's history, experience, and aspirations.

*Catherine A. Cavanaugh* is completing a Ph.D. dissertation on Irene Parlby, an Alberta pioneer, founding member and president of the United Farm Women of Alberta, and Minister Without Portfolio in the United Farmer's government from 1921 to 1935. Cathy's recent article "The Limitations of the 'Pioneering Partnership': The Alberta campaign for 'Homestead' Dower 1909–1925" appears in *Canadian Historical Review* 124, no. 2 (June 1993). She is a tutor at Athabasca University, an Alberta-based distance, open university with students across Canada.

*Randi R. Warne* completed her Ph.D. in Religion and Culture at the University of Toronto in 1988. Her dissertation, entitled "Literature As Pulpit," an analysis of the religion, feminism, and social activism of Nellie L. McClung, will be published by Wilfrid Laurier University Press this year. In addition to several articles on McClung and on religious social activism in Canada, she has published in the area of feminist methodology. Randi has taught religion and culture, social ethics, and women and religion in several contexts, including the University of Lethbridge and the University of Alberta. Most recently, she has been program director at St. Stephen's College at the University of Alberta. She is currently president of the Canadian Society of Church History. As an actor, Randi performs dramatic monologues in the character of Nellie McClung across the country.

Notes
1. One example is Helen Shaw who cut off her "lovely golden hair" shortly after arriving in the Northwest in 1883. See Emma Curtin, "Two British Gentlewomen," *Alberta History* (Autumn 1990), p. 12. When Mollie Dorsey Stanford arrived in the Colorado Territories in the 1860s she borrowed a riding habit and went riding across the plains. Pronouncing it a "delicious sport," she wrote, "I felt like a bird uncaged." Quoted in Carl N. Degler, *At Odds: Women and the Family in America* (New York: Oxford University Press, 1980), p. 46. Susan Jackel, ed., *A Flannel Shirt*

and Liberty (Vancouver: The University of British Columbia, 1982) concludes that the psychological impact of the unoccupied space of the frontier was experienced as liberating by British emigrant gentlewomen in the Canadian West. Eliane Leslau Silverman, "Women's Perceptions of Marriage on the Alberta Frontier," *Building Beyond The Homestead*, David C. Jones and Ian MacPherson, ed. (Calgary: The University of Calgary Press, 1985), pp. 49–64, reminds us of the limitations of this interpretation which probably applies to British middle class women in particular.

2. Prairie reformers frequently based their claim to rights for women on the "pioneering partnership" and it is worth noting that when he introduced the new suffrage bill in 1916 Premier Sifton declared that by their heroic pioneering work provincial women had earned "an unalterable right by eternal justice to be placed on an equality with men." Quoted in Catherine Lyle Cleverdon, *The Woman Suffrage Movement in Canada* (Toronto: University of Toronto Press, 1950), p. 73.

3. *Reports of Family Law* 13 (Toronto: Carswell, 1974), pp. 185–209.

4. See for example, Ruth Compton Brouwer, *New Women of God: Canadian Presbyterian Women and India Missions, 1876–1914* (Toronto: University of Toronto Press, 1990), and Leslie A. Flemming, ed., *Women's Work for Women: Missionaries and Social Change in Asia* (Boulder: Westview Press, 1989).

5. Nellie McClung, *The Stream Runs Fast* (Toronto: T. Allen, 1945), p. 185.

6. Shelly Anne Marie Bosetti, "The Rural Women's University: Women's Institutes in Alberta 1909–1940" (M.Ed. thesis, University of Alberta, 1983) examines the educational role of the AWI.

7. Karen J. Blair, *The Club Woman As Feminist: True Womanhood Redefined, 1868–1914* (New York: Holmes & Meier, 1980).

8. Sheila Rowbotham, *The Past Is Before Us: Feminism in Action Since The 1960s* (London: Penguin, 1990), p. 1.

9. *Report of the Royal Commission on the Status of Women in Canada* (Ottawa: Information Canada, 1970), p. 169.

10. Ibid.

MICHAEL OWEN

# "Lighting the Pathways for New Canadians"

## Methodist and United Church WMS Missions in Eastern Alberta, 1904–1940

"[O]ur work among the Austrian people . . . [is] to make them *Christian* and *Canadian*. . . . [A] good Canadian is a Christian," stated Edith Weekes Leonard in *The Austrian People*, published by the Woman's Missionary Society of the Methodist Church. Leonard, a missionary at Wahstao and Kolokreeka, small settlements near Smoky Lake, Alberta, between 1905 and 1910, believed wholeheartedly in the goal of the Methodist missions among the Ukrainian people settled in Alberta to create "good Canadians." "Here," she continued, "is the sufficient and complete justification for our whole work, comprising day school, night school, Sunday school, sewing-meetings, evangelistic visiting, caring for children in the mission homes, visiting the sick and helping those who need help in business transactions. In a word, here is the justification for our life among the Austrian people."[1]

Leonard revealed much about the work and the motivations of the women who devoted their lives to the Alberta missions of the Methodist (later United) Church's Woman's Missionary Society. Leonard's description of the work among Ukrainian immigrants shows us these paragons of Christian Canadianism at their best and worst. Leonard's ignorance of the national origins of many of the new immigrants, lumping Austrians, Russians, Ukrainians, and Poles into one great national conglomeration, was shared by most Canadians of the era. She adhered to the view of middle-class Protestant Canadians that there was one manifestation of Canadian nationality: that of the dominant evangelical Protestants of Anglo-Celtic heritage. Leonard's description of Methodist missions among the "Austrians" illustrated well the multitude of activities through which she and her companions attempted to bring New Canadians their understanding of Canadian nationalism and Protestant Christianity. By the 1930s, the emphasis had shifted, but only slightly. In its 1934 report, the board of Home Missions informed United Church members that "the missionary enterprise is an endeavour of idealists to produce through the religion of Jesus Christ a Canadian Christian citizenship out of the many varied and mutually contributing cultures." While paying lip-service to Canada's multicultural society, the board argued that "in immigrant areas of the Western plains," missionaries still worked to overcome "issues created by mistaken Government policies in establishing colonies and endeavoured to create on the part of the people an attitude of receptivity to the Gospel of Jesus Christ *as we understand it.*"[2]

Although they agreed with these views, WMS missionaries were generally more positive toward the New Canadians and their contribution to Canadian life. While providing a range of religious and social services to New Canadians, these women came to an awareness and an understanding, albeit limited, of the value of the New Canadian to Canada. While subscribing to prevalent opinions of the non-Anglo-Celtic immigrants as irreligious, corrupted, and corruptible, intemperate and unhygienic, they also argued against these notions and claimed instead that the New Canadians were deeply religious and committed to their new nation. In this paper, I explore the often conflicting opinions, attitudes, and motivations of these women missionaries among the Ukrainian settlers of northeastern Alberta. I note their insensitivity to the religious and cultural traditions of the New Canadians and acknowledge their unstinting attachment to their church and its self-imposed mission to protect Canada from all that it perceived as non-British and non-Christian. Nevertheless, these women were often motivated by kindness and empathy for the plight in which many New Canadians found themselves. Through this study, I hope to recover some Alberta women's experience in the first decade of the twentieth century.[3]

Background to Missions in Alberta

In the period 1890 to 1930, Canadians viewed non-Anglo-Celtic immigrants with a mixture of foreboding and pride. The Anglo-Celtic majority, Protestants and Catholics alike, believed immigration was the only way in which the prairies could be populated and Canada could assume its rightful place as the leader of the British Empire.[4] Yet their vision of Canada was threatened by European immigrants who settled in cities, in resource towns of western Canada, and "en bloc" in Manitoba, Saskatchewan, and Alberta.[5] In a 1925 pamphlet printed in honour of the Methodist Woman's Missionary Society's work, Mrs. W.H. Graham captured the view of the majority middle-class Canadians toward non-British immigrants and the churches' task in protecting the nation while uplifting these New Canadians:

> These European folk[s] who have come in response to a hearty invitation constitute a problem all their own. . . . [T]hey settle in drifts on our wide provinces, and in the downtown areas of our cities. . . . [Their] mass ideals are not high, customs are crude, superstition is rife. Canadian liberty is not sufficient to lift them from these lower levels. It must be imbued with something higher. Only Christ can make Christians, only a knowledge of the ideals of Jesus can give true freedom. . . . Unfortunately these new-comers from Central Europe have been allowed to segregate themselves in solid communities, where they maintain their old-world customs, and fail to come in touch with Canadian ideals and ways of living. . . .[6]

New Canadians appeared impervious to the efforts to build a nation in the West—a nation that would be imbued by evangelical Protestant principles and a commitment to a British heritage.

To overcome this apparent threat to Canada's destiny, mainline Protestant denominations initiated evangelical, educational, and medical missions among New Canadians. Although New Canadians, or "foreigners" as they were commonly called, belonged to Christian churches, few Protestant denominations accepted their traditions as legitimate expressions of Christian faith. Among church societies that developed and financed missions to New Canadians was the Methodist Woman's Missionary Society (WMS). Its missions to Ukrainians of Alberta had three purposes: to bring to the immigrants a "true" understanding of the saving gospel of Jesus Christ as one's personal saviour and as interpreted by these Protestant denominations; to bring to the immigrants educational, medical, and social services that were otherwise unavailable in remote locations; and to save Canada for Christ by converting new European immigrants to the twin gospels of evangelical (Protestant) Christianity and Canadian nationalism.

## Wahstao, Kolokreeka, and Edmonton—Centres of Christianity and Canadian Nationalism

Dedicated to saving Canada and Ukrainian settlers for Christ, Methodist women missionaries served as evangelists, teachers, nurses, doctors, and social workers because of their abiding faith in Christianity as an evangelical religion. As staunch Canadian nationalists, these women believed in a Canadian morality and Canadian character defined within the frame of liberal Protestant Christianity. In their service to the immigrants, Methodist (and United) Church women missionaries brought to their work the belief that they served both God and the nation by teaching the New Canadians about Jesus Christ as a personal saviour, the errors of non-Protestant churches, and the need to subscribe to the principles of personal hygiene, temperance, political purity, and Sabbath observance. Apparently, few understood that many immigrants subscribed to similar principles, although with different interpretations of what was and was not possible in their new environment.

The Woman's Missionary Society opened its first mission to Alberta's Ukrainian immigrants in 1904 when Reta Edmonds and Jessie Munro undertook a long and arduous journey to Wahstao (near present-day Smoky Lake) over a trail filled with stumps, ruts, sloughs, and swarms of mosquitoes. In the next twenty years, WMS missions expanded to Kolokreeka, Smoky Lake, Pakan, Lamont, Chipman, Radway, Bonnyville, and Edmonton. These women missionaries to the Ukrainian communities in the Smoky Lake-Lamont-Pakan region—teachers, nurses, evangelists—believed completely in the task that the society had set for them.[7] From their perspective, they "grasped the torch of enlightenment and held it high. . . . They lived among the settlers, learned their language, shared their hospitality, won their confidence, allayed their suspicions, and interpreted Christian Canada." They believed that they "exemplified the best of Canada, and . . . , with God's help, they could build a Canada in which He would have dominion, and the day would dawn when those immigrants would no longer be 'strangers and foreigners' but good fellow-Canadians."[8]

To achieve these goals of Canadianizing and "Christianizing" Ukrainian immigrants, Methodist women missionaries employed a variety of strategies: Sunday schools, home visits, evening schools for adults and young people for instruction in English, and "private" schools, when public schools in the district were few and open only irregularly. Sunday schools were a prominent aspect of Protestant churches' religious education for children and youth. Respecting this tradition, Edmonds and Munro, for example, had gathered three boys and one girl into a Sunday school in their tent even as their mission buildings were under construction. They also held itinerant Sabbath schools and services in the homes of settlers whenever possible. Although attendance at home-based Sunday schools fluctuated greatly, with just one or two families present, the women missionaries were "very hopeful of good" from this work. Distributing New Testaments and tracts to the boys and girls, they revelled in the achievements of the older children who earned Bibles "by memorizing verses" while younger children received "a copy of Matthew as soon as they can read even a very little." They judged Ukrainian children's Bible reading "very favourably with that of Canadian children of the same school standard."[9] While they emphasized English-language instruction, often telling Bible stories "for the whole school in English before the classes begin,"[10] some employed the language of the people to teach gospel lessons. At Kolokreeka, where a Sunday school was opened in 1909, the missionaries conducted the Bible teaching "almost entirely . . . in Russian" supplemented by "a little English . . . each day, so that in five Sundays they have learned nearly thirty words."[11] These English language stories had a threefold purpose: improving English skills of the children, transmitting to the children the teachings of the church, and, covertly, transmitting to the home an understanding of both Canadian morality and Protestant evangelism.

While Sunday schools occasionally became the nuclei of separate congregations,[12] thereby providing women missionaries with a sense of accomplishment, more often they became lightning-rods of denominational and ethnic conflict. When local priests objected to Ukrainian settlers sending their children to the Methodist Sunday schools, attendance dropped off quickly. In 1909, Ethelwyn Chace reported on the "checkered career" of the Bavilla Sunday School. Closed for one month "in the depth of the winter," attendance varied from twenty-five to one. "This last was on a day immediately following a visit of the Greek Orthodox priest to the church four miles distant. This coincidence," Chace argued, "is suggestive. The following Thursday, at our annual picnic, that school was represented by a full score, every [sic] smallest child of whom walked four miles each way." Priestly intervention, real or fancied, was anticipated by the missionaries. Edith Weekes, then at the Kolokreeka, reported on the success of one Sunday school until mid-March 1909, "when just one boy came, instead of fifteen, because of the mandate of the priest." Children returned gradually until July when another decline occurred, "fol-

lowed by a complete cessation. . . ." Three years later, there was "no
regular Sunday School at [Kolokreeka], because of the direct opposition of the Greek Catholic priest," claimed Phoebe Code. She kept the
mission house open for nearby settlers who joined the missionaries
"in singing, Bible study and conversation, as opportunity affords."[13]
In spite of the opposition, these women persevered. Sunday schools
remained open, even for one or two faithful followers. The missionaries attributed more to the priest's intervention than to the settlers'
own preference for familiar and traditional forms of worship and
social intercourse. Optimistically underestimating the influence of the
priest who "had not made any serious difference in our work," except
that the people attended the "Ukrainian" church more often on Sundays and church holidays, Ella MacLean stated that missionaries did
not encroach "on priestly territory, for the priest does not visit the
homes."[14] Weekes felt "no difference in the attitude of the people
toward us; they are as friendly as before, and we believe it is only the
rush of work that shuts us from their homes." However, homes were
shut to Methodist women because of the priests' opposition. They
"rejoiced" at the opposition. Alice Stanford believed that "the greatest
darkness is before the dawn" and was not discouraged.[15] Chace took
it "as a tribute to our influence and as a more hopeful sign than passive indifference."[16]

Yet not all the opposition to the Methodist women's work came
from the priests. Opposition, however muted and not obvious to the
missionaries, came from the people themselves and, in the 1920s and
1930s, from indigenous communist and Ukrainian national move-
ments.[17] WMS women, ironically, did not recognize the importance of
religion as a component of Ukrainian nationalist sentiment. But opposition of the nationalist movement, Margaret Addison claimed, forced
the WMS "to rethink our missionary work." They challenged "our
every motive and our work, it is they who say that we are no longer
needed. Are we ready to step out?" Ukrainian Canadians questioned
the missionaries' "right to claim that our church offers more opportunity for Christian living than does theirs."[18] The results of any self-
inquiry by the women missionaries were not detailed in their reports.

Religious enthusiasm permeated all WMS missionaries' contacts.
Sunday schools and church services were clearly evangelical. Social
activities and community work also had evangelical overtones. Alice
Stanford romantically described the weekly "sewing meeting" held at
Wahstao in 1911–12. "Such chattering, laughing, and hushing of babies!
The work-hardened fingers could only hold the largest of needles, but

the women were quite willing to sew the stiffest of squares, if only they were bright and pretty." The conversation at sewing meetings held in the mission house or homes of the women, with missionaries bringing quilting squares and supplies, always turned to the gospel. Apparently Ukrainian women "eagerly" listened "to the simple gospel story" and sang hymns, demonstrating that "evidences of real heart interest were never wholly wanting . . . ."[19] Men also showed "genuine interest" by asking "many very earnest questions . . ."[20] Although WMS missionaries used these meetings for evangelism, Ukrainian women used them for the equally important reason of social meeting. The men may have been present to oversee the women and their relations with the Methodist interlopers.

The most promising institutions, in the missionaries' view, were the school homes. WMS missionaries believed unfalteringly in the power of the public school to Canadianize the New Canadians.[21] Reflecting on opposition encountered to their evangelism, Chace emphasized "the strategic importance of the Public School. If the worst should come . . . that homes should be shut against us, that our Bible talks should be hindered, that our Sunday schools should be depleted . . . the Public School is, humanly speaking, the surest weapon that can be used against ignorance and bigotry."[22] Evangelistic meetings and night schools for adults had some efficacy, but to WMS missionaries the future lay in educating the children, "capturing" them for Christ and Canada, and training them to be the leaders of the future. Through children the "influence of Canadian ways and Christian teaching" would permeate the home, the children providing the link between parents and teachers. E.J. Kerr, associate field secretary of the WMS, viewed Ukrainian work in Alberta as most promising since the opening of a government school at Wahstao in 1907. Under the direction of a teacher, also a WMS missionary, children made "rapid progress, many of them reading the English Bible fluently and intelligently." However, the public school system, effectively controlled by provincial authorities, did not spread widely throughout eastern Alberta until the 1920s and 1930s. Moreover, when available, public schools were open only sporadically. Therefore, while Methodist missionaries supported the public school system, they formed private schools to meet an apparent demand for education from settlers and because children made better progress in acquiring the English language and other skills necessary for integration into Canadian society if their attendance was more regular. Before government day schools opened in the Wahstao district in 1907, the WMS had operated a school for the children of the district.[23] Kerr reported that "teaching of the public school from May to November [and] a private school in the Home during the winter" comprised a major activity of the women missionaries.[24] These private schools provided children with educational benefits and, from the missionaries' perspective, superior care in a "Christian" home environment. Missionaries praised Ukrainian children's ability to learn and parents who took advantage of opportunities for children to attend school regularly. To Dell Young, teacher at Wahstao in 1911–12, "the work is most encouraging, as the children make good progress, in spite of the difficulty of learning a new language. It surprises one to see how quickly even the little ones pick up English. Of course we allow *only* English spoken in the school. The children are almost invariably quick to learn, their desire to learn accounting for their rapid progress."[25] Such progress, again from the missionaries' perspective, demonstrated the efficacy of these services in promoting the assimilation of the Ukrainian Canadians.

The Wahstao "School Home" was representative of Protestant educational facilities for Ukrainian children. In the Wahstao district, public schools were built at Bavilla and Provischena in 1906, but opened only during the summer. Mission workers firmly believed that Ukrainian children would be served better if schools were open for longer periods, especially in the winter. The school homes, missionaries believed, met these educational and spiritual needs of the children.

There are fifteen or more children who would come to us for the winter if we had the accommodation. Four will be the most we can possibly take, unless we extend our building. We need a school room and children's dining room on the ground floor and bedrooms upstairs. Although Public Schools will soon be built, these are but for the summer months; and cannot in any case take the place of a boarding school. The school might not be entirely self-supporting for a time, for cash with our people is scarce, but there are other ways in which they could help, and as they came to know more of the benefits of such a school, we feel confident each would try to contribute his share. This work was not planned for in the beginning but it seems to have opened up before us, and now that we have a small Christian community to draw from, we are not so much afraid of the priest spoiling the plan.[26]

By the 1920s the Wahstao School Home had an enrolment of thirty students, with a staff of four.

The Wahstao "School Home," and school homes at Kolokreeka and Radway, served both as residences for students and as "schools." The curriculum at all Methodist and United Church-operated mission schools followed the prescribed Alberta Department of Education guidelines, suitably modified to meet the needs of children and the goals of the mission. In 1918 Miss Robinson, a native Albertan who had been trained at the WMS Training School in Toronto, asserted that students in the boarding home received "instruction along the lines provided by our public school curriculum[,] . . . lessons in domestic science—laundry, etc.—and most important of all lessons in the life of Christ."[27]

But the school home, stressed Alice Stanford, teacher at Wahstao in 1912, gave missionaries advantages for nation-building and conversion that were not available in the public school. The school home gave the missionaries unrestricted access to and control over the children. This influence was essential since WMS missionaries "firmly believe[d] that much of the hope of this work lies in the children whom we have come in closest contact with in the home, and that the sooner provision is made for keeping more children constantly in the house, the better for them and for all the future of this neighbourhood."[28] To Dell Young, the school home was primarily a religious initiative: "Two of the children staying with us have already given themselves to Christ, and only those living with them can realize how much this means. Two little girls, who left us last spring . . . , were influenced and greatly interested." At Kolokreeka, where seven children sojourned for different periods of time during the same year, the home is "not only a school for English education but a place where the spirit of Jesus Christ . . . make[s] itself felt in the lives of the children."[29] In the school homes, missionary-teachers rarely missed opportunities to further religious as well as nation-building goals. Religious holidays were celebrated by concerts. Local clergy, especially Protestant Ukrainian ministers such as Mr. T. Hannochko, assisted the WMS workers and provided services to the mission every Sunday evening. Such services, especially when provided in Ukrainian by a Ukrainian convert to Methodism, greatly enhanced the efficacy of the mission and its religious and nationalistic goals.

Sunday schools, where the missionary held sway, often created a demand for school homes. For example, in 1905, one year after the opening of Wahstao, Edith Weekes began Sunday schools between Smoky Lake and Pakan in settlers' homes. Soon, according to the missionaries, a demand developed for a "Home and School." A site was located north of Smoky Lake at Kolokreeka. Ella MacLean and Edith

Weekes superintended the construction of a new building and opened this mission on 31 December 1909. Kolokreeka was not a pretentious building, having a basement, a kitchen, a dining-sitting room, pantry, three small bedrooms, and two dormitories with room for eight children in each. Like Wahstao, Kolokreeka had Sunday schools, Sunday services, and evening English classes for adults. Missionaries held Sabbath schools and services in points outside Kolokreeka. Kolokreeka, however, was primarily a "school home," that is, the mission was a private school for children from families outside the settlement who wished their children to obtain an education but did not wish to send them to Edmonton. Mission staff, some of whom were trained teachers, served as teachers in the school, and used the prescribed Alberta curriculum, and "Christian" reading materials—the Bible and Methodist magazines. By 1914, Kolokreeka had some thirty-one boarders in its dormitories with thirty more students in the day school. Fifteen years later, attendance remained stable at twenty-four pupil-boarders, most under the age of twelve years. Mission staff taught all classes to the eighth grade while older children attended the high school at Smoky Lake. Visitors, including parents, were carefully supervised. Parents were provided "Christian" tracts to take away. Reading materials supplied to the children were similarly scrutinized for "only such papers . . . as have real value in provision of good, wholesome things with a Christian point of view."[30] How these reading materials were put to use is not discussed.

As more efficient transportation linkages and public and Ukrainian parochial schools extended their reach to rural Alberta communities in the 1920s and 1930s, the WMS gradually shifted the emphasis of Kolokreeka from a school home to a "Community Centre" with Sunday schools, midweek groups including Canadian Girls in Training (CGIT) and Tuxis, a kindergarten, sewing classes for young and older women, summer camps for children, and recreation. By the mid-1930s, Mary Mansfield could report that Kolokreeka school had fulfilled "its first great need and outlived its usefulness as a school home and a change of policy is now expected." Girls' clubs continued to teach traditional skills that "help in home making—fancy work, sewing, knitting, cooking" but the mission, as with other United Church congregations, was unable to find suitable male leaders "to work with the boys and young men."[31] Kolokreeka merged with the Smoky Lake mission and women missionaries became community workers. Throughout its life, Kolokreeka staff watched over the lives of its charges, attempting to influence children with "Christian" influences. By providing Protestant religious and social services,

WMS missionaries worked to extend the mission's influence into the community.

Community mission work in Smoky Lake also emphasized religious, national, and social goals. Missionaries served settlers in many ways, by caring for the sick, treating toothaches, reading and writing letters, and holding youth club meetings. By assisting the Ukrainian settlers in whatever way they could, they attempted to demonstrate what a "Christian Canada" should be. These activities included "educational" services such as kindergartens. In 1935–36 Mary Mansfield and Eva Empey expressed joy at the apparent success of their kindergarten: "The little ones learn English and were happy to say that they make excellent progress when they start to school," coincidentally providing missionaries with access to the children's homes.[32] And they took over from the ministers' religious education classes in the rural public schools. Iva Newton and Mary Mansfield lamented that children, not parents, decided whether to attend these optional, after-school classes and, in some cases, parents opposed teaching by Protestant missionaries. Conversely, they felt that parents appreciated their initiative and, again, that it provided access to the homes of the students—by providing the missionaries with another reason to visit families in the homes. Moreover the children "enjoy[ed] the hymns and stories and often tell their parents the story when they go home from school. . . . We leave Sunday School papers in each school and the children take them home. . . ."[33]

WMS missions also extended their concern to Ukrainian "girls" and young women who migrated to Edmonton to seek employment. As with other middle-class women of the period, they worried that many young, rural, and immigrant women who sought employment in the cities might soon fall in with "bad" company, and become prostitutes.[34] In an effort to ensure that young women from the Ukrainian "colonies" of eastern Alberta did not share this fate, Margaret Sherlock Ash opened a room for "Ruthenian" girls in the Lee Building on Jasper Avenue. Volunteers operated a night school to teach English to young Ukrainian women who worked as domestics or in the restaurants in the city and provided limited shelter to them when they first arrived in the city or while temporarily unemployed. By October 1908 the work expanded to a rented building on Rice Street with two missionaries, Reta Edmonds and Jessie Munro and their housemaid, Mary Bilar, all from Wahstao.

The mission began as an experiment. After holding mothers' meetings, which were not promising, these Methodist women turned their attention to younger girls. The pattern at the Edmonton mission replicated that of the missions in eastern Alberta. "At the beginning it was simply a sewing lesson; after a short time we began the singing of hymns and an occasional Bible story, but our usual closing is with a Bible story, hymn and the Lord's Prayer." Moreover mission society members believed that it was necessary to do more for the servant girls who worked in middle-class homes.[35] Staff helped "mistresses" who had trouble with their "servant girls," responded to requests from girls who "occasionally seek . . . [spiritual] private talks,"[36] and visited "girls" when sick or in trouble. The mission became a social, educational, and religious centre, and a temporary lodging. To meet an apparent need, a second mission was opened up in Norwood in 1909 and another on the Fraser Flats. By the autumn of 1912, responding to demands on limited resources, the Woman's Missionary Society consolidated work in the "Ruthenian Home" and expanded its residential facilities.

"Ruthenian Home" clients were young women, aged from thirteen to their late twenties. Many were referred to the home through Methodist missions in Smoky Lake or Pakan. Others located the "home" by word of mouth, as an employment agency or a place to stay where "[a] girl can rent a room for the nominal fee of ten cents a night" and could have meals "at ten cents a meal. If she cannot pay she is never refused. Besides transients there is [sic] a number of young girls in residence whose support is provided by the WMS."[37] While reasons for using the home varied, all abided by the rules of the Home, which, according to Jessie Munro, were "strict, and the improvement in the conduct, of those who needed such improvement, most marked. . . ."[38] In 1912, the Edmonton "Ruthenian Home and School" had twenty-one roomers, most of whom worked in restaurants and were transient. While rescue work and care for the sick continued, providing access to education was the central activity of the Ruthenian Home.

Missionaries took pride in the success of their charges. In 1928, Miss Gray reported that of twenty-eight girls who had resided "at the Ruthenian home taking public and High School work . . . two are teaching in McDougall Sunday School, one is at Camrose Normal School, one is entering Lamont Hospital [for training as a nurse], [and] one is a worker at Kolokreeka."[39] The pattern of attendance gradually shifted from younger to older girls. In 1925, J.E. Sutherland noted the absence of primary girls and reported that "all are taking Grades XI and XII and a commercial course [and] with the exception of a very few they are attending [the United Church] Alberta College," not the public schools in the district.[40] Mrs. Sutherland praised the work resulting in two girls graduating from nursing as an example of what the church mission had accomplished. While ensuring access to schooling through the public school or Alberta College was the central function of the Edmonton mission, community or social service had been a component of the work since its opening. The goal was to make the home attractive to young Ukrainian women and to serve their needs. English language instruction and employment advice were two services attractive to Ukrainian girls and young women. Methodist and United Church women missionaries believed that among the attributes that hindered the progress of the Ukrainian woman was illiteracy, by which they meant an inability to read, write, and speak English properly. Miss Gray, in 1918, claimed that many girls "do not know English and do not see the need of learning," as the need for English in the ethnic cafés was not pressing.[41] Yet to Methodist missionaries, English was essential if these Ukrainian young women were to assimilate into Canadian society. Gray, echoing the opinion of many WMS members, urged "the Government [to] set a standard in English education before granting the franchise to these people."[42] Employment work continued throughout the existence of the mission. Although mission workers, reflecting their middle-class origins, decried the reliance of the Ukrainian women on work in cafés rather than domestic work, they understood why café work was more attractive than the drudgery and lack of privacy attendant with paid domestic work.[43] "Most girls prefer Cafe work as it is only an eight hour day. They learn to be competent in a short time doing only one thing. . . . The large wages and short hours at the Cafes appeal to the girls [yet] they seem unconscious of the dangers."[44]

However, mission workers reached out to Ukrainian domestic and café workers, providing them with club activities along CGIT lines, sewing classes, lectures on issues of personal hygiene and temperance, and religious services. These activities, along with outdoor camps, were similar to and supportive of the work of the YWCA with which it was amalgamated in 1937. By the early 1930s, the home had transferred its external religious and social services to the All People's Mission. Gradually the number of Ukrainian girls from the country who required or took advantage of the home dwindled, reflecting improved educational services in the rural region, as financial conditions tightened and as Ukrainian institutions became more widespread. By the mid-1930s the school had lost its "Ruthenian" character and was opened to any girl, "Anglo-Saxon or non-Anglo-Saxon, who cannot otherwise have an opportunity for pursuing her [high school] education . . ."[45] Mae Laycock reported that the school home could not be filled with "New Canadian girls, due to financial conditions in the rural districts." The society therefore "extended th[is] same privilege to Anglo-Saxon girls in outlying districts." Laycock claimed this new arrangement gave Anglo-Saxon girls "opportunity . . . living and working co-operatively with those of other nationalities, under Christian influence. To know and appreciate each other and build up friendships on a basis of Christian living is a great step in the unifying of Canadian life."[46]

School homes closed as public schools became more common and easily accessible. In 1937, an era ended with the closing of the Ruthenian School Home in Edmonton and the school home at Wahstao. These Alberta school homes, as Jean Gordon Forbes and Winnifred Thomas had reported in 1938, were "outpost schools,"[47] outposts of Canadian nationalism and modified Anglo-Protestant Christianity.


Conclusion


As early as 1926 the WMS recognized that overt assimilationist efforts were ineffective among the Ukrainians in western Canada. The WMS leadership believed that there was "no more effective way . . . for providing Christian leadership for non-Anglo-Saxon colonies than the School Home . . . [If] China can only be saved by the Chinese, Africa by the Africans; can we not equally realize that the great majority of the strangers within our gates can only be reached by those of their own nationality!" Hence, Ukrainian children, as "the citizens of tomorrow" who resided in WMS School Homes were thought to be "the leaders of these people within Canada." While underlining the primacy of the nation-building role of the school homes, WMS missionaries expected that as Anglo-Saxon youth gradually comprised larger proportions of the homes' clientele, "the free mingling of young people from all racial groups afford[ed] the greatest possible Canadianizing influence. The divisions of the Old World will be forgotten in the camaraderie of the New, . . . leaving behind all distinction of race."[48]

However, in their own assessment, WMS members argued that the school homes, "caring mostly for our New Canadian children," gave many young women "an opportunity of receiving an education which develops them in Christian womanhood[.]" They desired that these young women would become "ready for service, passing on to others what they have received."[49] WMS missionaries and leaders recognized that assimilation must give way to integration, that they must "bridge barriers of class and race by sincere friendship" and help "people who are in need." While they acknowledged New Canadians should "retain their love for their own cultural background" and make significant contributions to Canadian life, it was to be done within a Christian context. "The aim of all the activities," the 1935 report stated, was "to interpret the Christian way of life to those who do not know Him; to develop Christian character; and to lead boys and girls and men and women into the fellowship of the Christian Church."[50]

To achieve this goal, the WMS mission enterprise shifted from Christian evangelism to evangelical Christian community service. Being, and always remaining, staunch Canadian nationalists with a strong evangelical Protestant agenda, they argued that all immigrants needed to be remade into Canadians along the lines of the Anglo-Protestant middle class. WMS missionaries urged upon the church a more tolerant attitude toward Ukrainian Canadians. As early as 1920, Yarwood cautioned against ethnocentrism when she spoke of "the heart cry of these people against being called foreigners when they have been born in Canada and are trying to be good Canadians." Yarwood informed Alberta Branch members of the history of struggle of the Ukrainian people in Europe and, more recently, of the revival of religious enthusiasm in Canada, especially with the formation of the Ukrainian Greek Orthodox Church. "The word of God is read and talked about," and she pleaded "for the warm hand of welcome and heart to love for these people."[51] From time to time missionaries raised a warning cry that the church could undermine its initiatives by being too strident in its "Canadianism" and evangelicalism. Fifteen years later, Mrs. Thomas Powell, president of the Alberta WMS, reinforced this message and argued for "an abandonment of superior attitudes on the part of English speaking people, and . . . a finer appreciation of the fine background of character and accomplishment of the new Canadian in our land."[52]

By 1940, "the tide [of evangelical missions had] reached its peak and [was] receding."[53] The society needed new initiatives to carry on its work. It maintained school homes in Spedden, Bonnyville, and Vegreville but those were limited in scope. Medical missions (hospitals) and community missions served communities in which they were located, but as government and Ukrainian community services expanded, the need for the WMS missions decreased. As the society reflected on its years of service in Alberta, its members pointed with pride to the people whom it assisted: the children who received an education, the lonely women for whom quilting bees were important social gatherings, even if they listened patiently to evangelical talks by the "foreign" missionaries, the sick who were cared for, the children and young women for whom CGIT and other clubs permitted integration into Anglo-Canadian society, the young women for whom the "Ruthenian Home and School" in Edmonton provided cheap lodgings, education, and employment.

WMS missionaries in Alberta provided services to Ukrainian-Canadians at a time when these services were required and governments did not provide them. Missionaries counted few conversions, no doubt because they were seen by the Ukrainians as agents of the dominant society who sought to assimilate them into a narrow vision of what it meant to be Canadians. The impact of missionaries and their institutions on the lives of Ukrainian settlers was mixed, a legacy that continues to this day. There remains a need to investigate further the interactions between women church workers and immigrant women, to understand more fully the motivations and responses, as both attempted to come to terms with the agenda of the other.

*Michael Owen* is director, Research Services, at the University of Saskatchewan. His research focusses on western Canadian educational and church history with an emphasis on the relations between Canadian institutions and ethnic minorities. Michael has published articles in a range of educational studies journals and edited collections, as well as being book review editor of *Canadian and International Education* and coeditor with Denis Wall of *Distance Education and Sustainable Community Development* (Edmonton: Athabasca University and the Canadian Circumpolar Institute, 1992).

The author acknowledges the support of the Social Sciences and Humanities Research Council and Canada Multiculturalism and Citizenship, Ethnic Research Program.

Notes
1. Edith Weekes Leonard, *The Austrian People* (Edmonton: n.d.), p. 5. For other contemporary accounts of Methodist work among European immigrants to eastern Alberta, see W.H. Pike, "Ruthenian Home, Edmonton, Alberta" (Toronto: Methodist Church, Woman's Missionary Society, n.d.); Mrs. W.H. Graham, *Forty-four Years' Effort of the Woman's Missionary Society of the Methodist Church, Canada, 1881–1925* (Toronto: Methodist Church, Canada, Woman's Missionary Society, 1925); Nellie McClung, "An Insistent Call" (Toronto: Methodist Church, Canada, Woman's Missionary Society, n.d.); Will H. Pike, "Work Among the Ruthenians: Is It Worth while?" *Christian Guardian* (20 October 1915), pp. 8–9.
2. United Church of Canada (hereafter UCC) *Yearbook* (1934), p. 135. Emphasis added.
3. The activities of women as missionaries have been studied extensively over the last decade. While much of the focus of this scholarly work has been on women in the foreign mission fields, some work has focussed on women as administrators and missionaries in the home field. A small sample of the work done in Canada and the

United States includes: Ruth Compton Brouwer, *New Women for God: Canadian Presbyterian Women and India Missions, 1876–1914* (Toronto: University of Toronto Press,
1990); Robert Price Beaver, *American Protestant Women in World Mission: A History of
the First Feminist Movement in North America* (Grand Rapids: Eerdmans, 1980); Carol
Lee Bacchi, *Liberation Deferred? The Ideas of the English-Canadian Suffragists,
1877–1918* (Toronto: University of Toronto Press, 1988), pp. 59–62; Barbara Welter,
"She Hath Done What She Could: Protestant Women's Missionary Careers in Nineteenth Century America," Janet Wilson James, ed., *Women in American Religion*
(Philadelphia: University of Pennsylvania Press, 1980), pp. 112, 117–25; Wendy
Mitchinson, "Canadian Women and Church Missionary Societies: A Step Towards
Independence," *Atlantis* 2 (Spring 1977), pp. 57–75.

4. Carl Berger, *The Sense of Power: Studies in the Ideas of Canadian Imperialism, 1867–1914*
(Toronto: University of Toronto Press, 1970); R.C. Brown and R. Cook, *Canada
1896–1921: A Nation Transformed* (Toronto: McClelland and Stewart, 1974), pp.
26–82; Douglas Owram, *The Promise of Eden: The Canadian Expansionist Movement
and the Idea of the West* (Toronto: University of Toronto Press, 1980).

5. Marilyn Barber, "The Assimilation of Immigrants in the Canadian Prairie
Provinces, 1896–1918: Canadian Perception and Canadian Policies" (Ph.D. diss.,
University of London), pp. 72–120; Jaroslav Petryshyn, "Canadian Perceptions of
the North-west and the East Europeans, 1891–1914: The Case of the Ukrainians,"
*Journal of Ukrainian Studies* 6, no. 2 (Fall 1981), pp. 43–65.

6. Graham, *Forty-four Years' Effort*, p. 10.

7. Missionaries rarely remained long in their appointments. Some like Jessie Munro
left the field after one or two years because of ill-health. Others, like Edith Weekes,
married either ministers who served a charge in which the woman missionary was
stationed or a local man. Since married women with husbands were not considered
missionaries, all WMS workers who married were "lost" to the field. Those who
married ministers may have remained in the field but as unpaid and rarely
acknowledged matrons of the parsonage rather than as active missionaries. Their
stories remain untold and their work invisible.

8. W.H. Pike, "The Flame—A Story of the Church's Ukrainian Work in Alberta"
(unpublished ms., 1966), p. 8.

9. Methodist Church, Canada, Woman's Missionary Society, *Annual Report* (Toronto:
1907–08), p. lxxxvi (hereafter MCC, WMS, AR).

10. MCC, WMS, AR (Toronto: 1907–08), p. lxxxvi.

11. MCC, WMS, AR (Toronto: 1909), p. civ.

12. See M.H. Marunchak, *The Ukrainian Canadians: A History* (Winnipeg/Ottawa:
Ukrainian Academy of Arts and Sciences in Canada, 1982).

13. MCC, WMS, AR (Toronto: 1911), p. cxiii.

14. MCC, WMS, AR (Toronto: 1912–13), p. cxvi.

15. MCC, WMS, AR (Toronto: 1912–13), p. cxiii.

16. Ibid.

17. MCC, WMS, AR (Toronto: 1912–13), p. cxi.

18. UCC *Yearbook* (Toronto: 1933–34), p. 281. Also see Provincial Archives of Alberta
(hereafter PAA) 75.387/327 UC 172/3 Box UC 11, UCC, WMS, Alberta Branch
(hereafter AB), Minute Book, Seventh Annual Meeting (24–26 May 1932).

19. MCC, WMS, AR (Toronto: 1908–09), p. cii.

20. MCC, WMS, AR (Toronto: 1908–09), p. cxii.

21. For a discussion of these missions from a different perspective, see Vivian Olender,
"'Save Them for the Nation': Methodist Rural Home Missions As Agencies of
Assimilation," *Journal of Ukrainian Studies* 8, no. 2 (Winter 1983), pp. 38–51; and
Vivian Olender, "The Canadian Methodist Church and the Gospel of Assimila-
tion," *Journal of Ukrainian Studies* 7, no. 2 (Fall 1982), pp. 61–74.

22. PAA, 75.387/340 Box 12.

23. For discussion of the state of education in rural Alberta in the early twentieth century, see Paul Voisey, *Vulcan: The Making of a Prairie Community* (Toronto: University of Toronto Press, 1988), pp. 180–86; M.H. Marunchak, *The Ukrainian Canadians: A History*, pp. 441–48, 625–31.
24. MCC, WMS, AR (Toronto: 1911–12), p. cxiv.
25. Ibid.
26. MCC, WMS, AR (Toronto: 1907–08), pp. cix-cx.
27. PAA, 75.387/327 Box UC 11, WMS, AB, Annual Meeting (4–6 June 1918).
28. MCC, WMS, AR (Toronto: 1911–12), p. cxviii.
29. MCC, WMS, AR (Toronto: 1912–13), pp. cxiv-cxv.
30. UCC, WMS, AR (Toronto: 1929), p. 257.
31. PAA 75.387/327 Box UC 11, WMS, AB, Annual Meeting (1932).
32. UCC, WMS, AR (Toronto: 1935–36), p. 340.
33. UCC, WMS, AR (Toronto: 1939–40), p. 69.
34. MCC, WMS, AR (Toronto: 1909–10), p. cvi. The Canadian Protestant churches were very concerned about the extent of prostitution in Canadian cities, especially among young women who migrated to the cities from rural towns or who were recent immigrants. See Mariana Valverde, *The Age of Light, Soap, and Water: Moral Reform in English Canada, 1885–1925* (Toronto: McClelland and Stewart, 1991), pp. 77–128 and M. Owen, "'Web of the Net of Sin': Presbyterian Response to Sexual Immorality in Canada, 1905–1915," Canadian History of Education Association meetings (Toronto: 1981).
35. MCC, WMS, AR (Toronto: 1908–09), pp. lxxxviii-lxxxix.
36. MCC, WMS, AR (Toronto: 1909–10), pp. cvii-cviii.
37. W.H. Pike, *Ruthenian Home, Edmonton, Alberta* (Toronto: WMS, MCC, n.d.), pp. 2–3; MCC, WMS, AR (Toronto: 1909–10), p. cvii.
38. MCC, WMS, AR (Toronto: 1909–10), p. cviii.
39. PAA, 75.387/327 Box UC 11, MCC, WMS, AB, Annual Meeting (21–24 May 1926).
40. UCC, WMS, *Annual Report* (Toronto: 1925), p. 286.
41. PAA, 75.387, UCC, WMS, AB, Annual Meeting (4–6 June 1918).
42. Ibid.
43. For a scholarly discussion of the servant problem, see Marilyn Barber, "The Servant Problem in Manitoba, 1896–1930," Mary Kinnear, ed., *First Days, Fighting Days: Women in Manitoba History* (Regina: Canadian Plains Research Center, 1987), pp. 100–19. To witness the mixed response of middle-class women to the demands of their employees, see Glenbow Alberta Archives, M1703 Box 3 File 24(i), Local Council of Women, Calgary, Minutes 1919–1924. In these minutes, the LCW responded to the petitions of the Housekeepers' Association, an association of women workers.
44. PAA, 75.387, UCC, WMS, AB, Annual Meeting (Toronto: 4–6 June 1918).
45. UCC, WMS, AR (Toronto: 1935–36), p. 300.
46. UCC, WMS, AR (Toronto: 1933–34), p. 273.
47. *Yearbook* (1938), p. 148.
48. *Yearbook* (1926), p. 350.
49. *Yearbook* (1938), p. 147.
50. *Yearbook* (1935), p. 174.
51. PAA Accession Number 75.387, MCC, WMS, AB, Twelfth Annual Meetings (8–10 June 1920).
52. UCC, Alberta Conference, *Record of Proceedings* (1935), p. 24.
53. *Yearbook* (1940), p. 169.

CATHERINE C. COLE
ANN MILOVIC

# Education, Community Service, and Social Life

## The Alberta Women's Institutes and Rural Families, 1909–1945

A little before noon she lit the lamp. Demented wind fled keening past the house: a wail through the eaves that died every minute or two. Three days now without respite it had held. The dust was thickening to an impenetrable fog.

She lit the lamp, then for a long time stood at the window motionless. In dim, fitful outline the stable and oat granary still were visible; beyond, obscuring fields and landmarks, the lower of dust clouds made the farmyard seem an isolated acre, poised aloft above a sombre void. At each blast of wind it shook, as if to topple and spin hurtling with the dust-reel into space. . . .

Her eyes all the while were fixed and wide with a curious immobility. It was the window. Standing at it she had let her fore-head press against the pane until the eyes were strained apart and rigid. Wide like that they had looked out to the deepening ruin of the storm. Now she could not close them.

The baby started to cry. . . .

—Sinclair Ross

Sinclair Ross's poignant story of a woman losing her mind as she struggled with loneliness, poverty, and drought during the Great Depression is a powerful reminder of the obstacles people faced in the west in this period. For women, "with two rooms to live in—once a month to town and nothing to spend when they got there," the sense of isolation and futility could be overpowering.[1] From its beginnings in 1909 to the end of the Second World War, the Alberta Women's Institute (AWI) was important to rural women in several ways. It enabled them to face the loneliness of farm life in the early years by providing a social outlet, an opportunity to meet women from surrounding farms and share common concerns. Women improved their domestic skills and developed an expanded sense of home and community. The community work in which AWI branches became involved, particularly during the two world wars, was widely seen as an acceptable means to broader public participation for women.

The Women's Institutes were founded in Ontario in 1897 by Adelaide Hunter Hoodless. Hoodless was distraught when her infant son died from drinking unpasteurized milk. She felt that women needed more information about infant care and other domestic duties. Margaret Graham, a settler from Ontario, founded the first institute west of the Great Lakes in Lea Park, Alberta, on 3 February 1909. This institute encouraged the growth of other institutes around the province, and by 1915 a provincial organization was formed. About one hundred delegates, representing approximately fourteen hundred women, attended the first provincial convention later that year. In 1920, the AWI had 265 institutes with a total membership of 13,150.[2] At its peak in 1921, the United Farm Women of Alberta, a partisan organization, had 309 locals which represented only 4,536 women.[3]

The AWI was by no means the only women's voluntary association in the province around the turn of the century, although it was often the first organization established in a community. The AWI was uniquely suited to the needs of rural women. While other groups such as the Imperial Order of Daughters of the Empire, the Women's Christian Temperance Union, the Victorian Order of Nurses (VON), and the United Farm Women of Alberta (UFWA) dealt with political, social, and economic issues, the AWI was deliberately nonsectarian and nonpartisan. The membership of the AWI and other groups often overlapped, allowing alliances to be formed among individual institutes and other groups, in particular, the UFWA.

There were several distinctions between the AWI and the UFWA. The AWI was a transplanted organization which originated in Ontario, whereas the UFWA began on the prairies. Membership in the AWI was open to all women, whereas members of the UFWA had to be wives or daughters of male farmers. As well, the AWI was officially nonpartisan while the UFWA was the women's branch of United Farmers who formed the government in Alberta from 1921 to 1935. The AWI addressed issues related to its motto—"For Home and Country"; whatever touched home or country, touched AWI.

Through self-education, community, and war work, the AWI had a strong impact upon family life. However, this aspect of the AWI has received scant attention in earlier studies. The role of the AWI in providing a social outlet for prairie women was very important. In 1913, Margaret Graham recalled the early meetings of the Lea Park branch, and wrote that:

> It was common then to see a sleighload of women and children, drawn by a team of oxen, attending those first meetings. Children have always been numerous and heartily welcomed. We have had them present at two weeks old. Elderly women are less common, probably not more than one or two over fifty.[4]

The institutes had to overcome logistical details such as not being able to use the teams on summer afternoons because they were required in the fields. In some areas, summer meetings were switched to evenings and held alongside the UFA meetings so the family could attend together.[5]

In 1920, Emily Murphy looked back upon the history of the Women's Institutes and reflected that,

> The Women's Institutes arose out of the needs of lonely women on isolated farms. These women desired to meet at stated periods for the exchange of counsel and amenities, to say nothing of the opportunity of exchanging recipes, dress patterns and community news.[6]

Similarly, in a 1921 review of the history of her own institute in Daysland, provincial president Isabel Nobel said that the primary idea was a social one:

> Here too was an opportunity of getting together in pleasant social affairs throughout the years. And what can give a finer feeling of contentment and satisfaction to the mother of the family, than to fare forth to a meeting, where she is to meet others who have her problems, where she is to hear something for the betterment of the

health and education of her family, and to wit where she can wear her new dress and hat, of the latest mode, that she has learned to make at the sewing or millinery course—at minimum cost, too?[7]

For many women, the institute was a reprieve from the isolation they experienced on the farm.

Myrtle Heyer (formerly Roberts, who was provincial secretary during much of this period), wrote in a recent letter about her early experiences as a farm wife. She was active in the WI as a child because her mother had been a member in Fort MacLeod and later Drumheller. She claimed that the WI was her source of social life in the early years of her marriage.

> I fell in love with a local farmer, married him and spent my life on the farm we had bought and there raised our family.
>
> I did not know how to do anything but with the help of a very wonderful husband I did learn how to be a wife, mother, helper and also became an all around chore boy and "go for."
>
> The Institute was held at the members' homes and the husbands took their wives and also the children not attending school. Everyone stayed for the afternoon. Lunch was served to all outdoors unless the weather was bad then all found a place inside—if the home was large enough, if not in the barn or outbuilding of some kind. Unless it was very cold or the snow too deep Institute was held as scheduled.
>
> In our institute, I was the only one that ever went by horseback, but that I did, also took my two little girls with me, one in back of me the other in front. That was the way I went if the roads were too bad to go with a horse and buggy or cart.[8]

Involvement in the Alberta Women's Institutes meant different things to each woman. In an address at Queenstown, Alberta, 20 May 1914, Mrs. W. Bertrand spoke about "What club life is doing for the country woman." She suggested that

> Club life is giving us a more correct perspective of our duties. We are becoming interested in current events, reading, music and the study of domestic science.
>
> The greatest value of club life, however, lies in the social element.[9]

Many of our informants stressed the social function of the WI. Women often joined as brides, or shortly after moving to a new community, because they wanted to meet other women the same age who shared similar experiences.

A further way the AWI affected rural families was through its members, who (as wives and mothers) passed on their experiences to their families. The institute could be a supportive group emotionally. One informant told the story of a woman who had had a disagreement with her husband. Afterwards, she discussed the disagreement with her friends and realized that other women had had similar problems. By the time she returned home, both she and her husband had calmed down and placed the problem in perspective.[10] The meeting provided a way for the woman to escape the isolation and monotony of the farm and benefit from the experience of her peers.

Involvement in the AWI also affected other family members. One woman who joined a few years after her marriage, said that

> When I started, I took my two little girls. I had to because we couldn't afford babysitters for one thing, and I took my mother-in-law . . . she enjoyed it so we were off to the meetings together . . . she'd hold one of them or the other.[11]

Preschool-age children often went to meetings with their mothers. Their fathers were too busy working on the farm to look after them as meetings took place in the afternoon, the prime farming time. Much of this period was taken up by the hardships of two world wars and the Depression, when conveniences like babysitters were unavailable or unaffordable. Hence, the children often attended meetings at their mother's side. Usually there were many preschoolers at the meetings and after school they would be joined by older children who would arrive in time for the lunch. Several of the women interviewed for this study attended WI meetings with their mothers, then later joined themselves.[12] Through this family involvement, the AWI had influence within rural families.

As for husbands, if the members lived far from the meeting, "say twelve or more miles, the men would go and have their visits too, you know, they'd go off in another room and visit there."[13] The men would have their own "meeting," which was a social time, and just as much an answer to the isolation of the farm for the husbands as the AWI meetings were for the wives. Even if the husbands went home during the meeting, they would return in time to have lunch before taking their wives home.[14] Men in general were supportive of their wives' involvement in the AWI. One woman commented that the men did not dare plan anything for the second Thursday of each month because they knew that it was institute meeting and that they would have to take their wives to the meeting.[15] Another husband joked that he always knew when it was institute day because lunch was ready on time so his wife could get away early. If men were not present at the meeting, they would still learn what had transpired:

When you went home you would discuss . . . the different things that you learned. The men were very, very interested in the Women's Institute. . . . and I think women at that point were interested in all aspects of the farm life.[16]

Another vital aspect of the AWI from 1909 to 1945 emerged out of the educational aspects of the institute meetings. Many of the correspondence courses, guest lectures, and papers that members prepared described how to improve farm life and living standards. Presentations were given by local members, area residents, and, on occasion, visiting speakers. Topics addressed covered a broad spectrum, ranging from table setting and serving to the planting of trees and shrubs, contagious diseases, labour saving devices, butter making, patriotism, and canning and preserving. Information from lecturers on "poultry raising," "better nutrition for the rural family," and even "the extermination of the housefly" was applied in the home.

Short courses in domestic science were offered by the Department of Agriculture. These courses included a mixture of demonstrations and lectures about cooking, care of the sick, maternal care, first aid, child care, and sanitation. If an AWI member learned how to make cheese, her family could benefit from more and cheaper cheese in its daily diet. Where a particular institute had taught the principles of quilt making or some other handicraft, these skills could be practised in the home setting and the rural family could benefit from the knowledge gained through the AWI.

The emphasis upon domestic science remained strong, as those were the questions that "most nearly concern us." However, women were also interested in expanding their knowledge of political issues. Isabel Nobel, provincial president, demonstrated the growing politicization of the AWI members as a result of the suffrage campaign. She suggested, in 1919:

Don't you think we have, for the time at least, discussed thoroughly enough how to keep the young, the value of cheerfulness, and how to destroy the housefly—all very important we must admit, but might we not to good advantage take up this year the study of history of our Province or learn something concerning our laws and government.[17]

When women obtained the franchise in 1916–17, the AWI expanded its educational program to include more discussion of political issues. The Prairie Circle Institute commented that:

We are glad to learn that women are taking a keen interest in these questions, for now that we are to take an active part in the affairs of our province, it behooves us to really know things—especially things that so vitally concern us.[18]

Also, in the 1923 annual report, the convenor of the Legislation Committee, Adelaide Montgomery, called upon all members to

become acquainted with the legal position of the married woman, and strive to create public opinion to secure some legal recognition of the monetary value of the wife's labour in her home.[19]

Although the members were often concerned in the 1910s and 1920s with legislation that solely affected women and children, they also realized that they would be a more effective lobbying force if they looked at legislation in a wider societal context. In her 1927 report, Montgomery commented that

Our laws should be for the good of all, and if they are for the common good they will benefit any particular class of individuals if it should be benefited. Moreover, much legislation which on the surface does not appear to be concerned with the interest of women and children may in reality be of vital importance to them. . . . Let 'laws for women and children' not become a hackneyed expression.[20]

This "wider view" became apparent in subsequent reports and resolution of the Legislation Committee as the members began to look at issues such as women members of the Senate, the Old Age Pension Act, Alberta's jurisdiction over its own natural resources, and the

Bank Act. The committee finished its reports in 1943 with a discussion of the progress of the war.[21]

Other topics, such as International Relations, were likewise important to rural women. These issues were applied to farm life by placing the farm and the importance of rural communities within the world context. This way, the institute member, and in turn her family, learned what was going on in the world; she learned what events such as war, peace, and economic changes meant in relation to them.

Women faced a number of obstacles in their efforts to become self-educated. One noted that she joined the AWI because "I was interested in adult education and I thought this was a good way to further my education that I wasn't able to get otherwise."[22] Libraries were few and far between; in many cases they were later established by branches of the WI. After 1914, the Department of Agriculture would send travelling libraries, containing books about women's work, to Women's Institutes.

The Women's Institutes were engaged in a variety of community projects, some regionally specific and some more general. For example a common project in the late 1910s was the establishment of community restrooms.[23] Initially restrooms were intended to be a place for country women, a rest room and a quiet place for their young children to nap when the women came to town to run errands. Usually they had facilities to make a cup of tea and provided other comforts. In some communities the restroom incorporated a community club room, a place to hold meetings, band practices, concerts, receptions, cooperative markets, hospitals, and a reading room, which housed the village library. During the war they frequently served as the headquarters for Red Cross and Field Comforts work. By the spring of 1919, thirty-two restrooms had been established in towns throughout Alberta.[24]

Another common project at this time was the recruitment of nurses for isolated areas. In 1914, the AWI distributed a nursing bulletin offering practical suggestions for nursing the sick which was reprinted in the *Farm and Ranch Review*.[25] In some areas, the AWI worked cooperatively with the VON to provide nursing services to remote areas. For example, the Prairie Circle AWI expanded its restroom to allow for its use as a VON nursing station, and later a doctor's home and office, with the WI reserving some of the space for a meeting room and library. In October 1917, the *Farm and Ranch Review* reported that Cereal was building a home for a nurse from the Victorian Order of Nurses:

One side is to be used by the Institute and the other by the nurse. Cereal should be congratulated, as supporting a nurse for a district is one of our best lines of work.[26]

In 1917, Alberta became the second province to establish municipal hospitals. The intention was for these hospitals to be self-supporting within a community. Therefore, in the 1920s, the movement to secure community nurses developed into efforts to establish municipal hospitals. Arthur K. Whitson, secretary of the Municipal Hospitals branch of the Public Health Department considered Women's Institutes

> our greatest supporters. They are the strength of the hospital movement and the success of the organizing of municipal hospitals is due largely to the ever-zealous work of the Women's Institutes.[27]

Women were eligible to serve on hospital boards from 1920, and the town of Islay lost no time in immediately electing the first female representative.

Another aspect of AWI work was the contribution the women made to home front activity during both the first and second world wars. Initially, efforts to alleviate suffering during World War I were directed toward the home front. It was a question of women helping women:

> There are the wives and children of the men gone to the war. Some of these are on our farms and without the husband's work will surely suffer want this winter. What can we do to help them?[28]

Margaret Phillips asked this question in her "Country Women's Clubs" column in the *Farm and Ranch Review*. She appealed to women in the west to help women who were left alone, or who lived in the drought areas of the prairies, or who were in need for some other reason.

During the war, support for the war effort took many forms. For example, the Okotoks Women's Institute pledged five dollars a month toward a Canadian prisoner-of-war. Through cooperation with the Imperial Order of the Daughters of the Empire it raised funds for "patriotic purposes."[29] Through the WI, a soldiers' comforts association was established to send "care packages" to men overseas.[30] Fundraising during the war involved bazaars, dances, quilt raffles, and marketing other items made by the women, including the publication and sale of cookbooks.

Programs during the war took on a topical note as well. Papers were given on such subjects as "Why Our Boys Are Fighting," "Women's Work in War Time," "Duties of a Citizen," and "Food Conservation." The rationing of foodstuffs and materials was of concern to the AWI, and the institutes promoted recipes and techniques that could be used to economize. They considered these efforts to be an important sign of support for the men fighting at the front.

The AWI branches were often ready to help in a time of crisis. Whether it was aid for a drought-stricken region, food, clothing, and basic essentials for fire victims or nursing the ill, AWI members responded. During the influenza outbreak in the fall of 1918, some institutes discontinued meetings but they gave

> invaluable assistance in combatting the fearful Spanish influenza epidemic that so recently swept over our country. In many towns the local Institutes installed soup and diet kitchens to supply food for the sick. They also assisted in establishing temporary hospitals, and in numerous cases donated all hospital supplies required.[31]

After the influenza epidemic, the WI was preoccupied with the post-war Depression. From 1919–21, institutes were largely concerned with drought relief work. A general letter was sent to all institutes asking for help. Depots were established in Calgary, Lethbridge, and Medicine Hat to distribute aid in the form of food, clothing, and money.[32]

A wide range of community projects such as hot lunch programs for schoolchildren, beautification of cemeteries, the establishment of public libraries, town clean-up programs, well-baby clinics, fundraising for school playground equipment, making "mothers' bundles" for layettes, emergency support to fire victims, band instruments and uniforms, and clothing for needy families. A retired teacher wrote:

> Words can never express the help I got from members as a teacher! One group even renovated outdoor toilets and painted the school. Help was given with annual Christmas concerts such as music, drama, candy bags and getting the tree.[33]

Working together for various community projects helped women to improve their skills and gave them more confidence in their own abilities. As well, they benefited directly from access to services they worked for within a community. For example, the local history *Grande Prairie: Capital of the Peace*, chronicles the early achievements of the WI and emphasizes the importance of relief work during the Depression. Equally valuable was

> a program that for a number of years was to prove a God-send to many country women. From April 1934 to April 1942 the Grande Prairie W.I. operated a waiting room for expectant mothers . . . in those eight years 319 women were accommodated for periods varying from a few days to more than three weeks.[34]

The AWI also established boys' and girls' clubs on the model of the adult institutes. Boys' and girls' clubs provided children with the opportunity to work alongside their mothers. These clubs were considered an important aspect of children's development as responsible citizens:

> No line of work aside from war work can be of as much help to a community as the boy and girl club work and we hope after the war each branch institute will take up the boy and girl work with zeal; that and the baby welfare movement deserves much time and thought.[35]

Activities during the Second World War were similar to those during the Great War. A woman who had volunteered during both wars recalled the ingenuity of women trying to make the soldiers more comfortable:

> We packed parcels, wrote letters to our soldiers, *made quilts*, packed ditty bags, and hussifs [slang for housewives, or sewing kits]. When Mrs. Parker asked us to bake fruit cakes in tobacco tins I though our home made bar soaps would not hide the odor, but she was proved right. During World War I a member suggested sending eggs in tins. When the top was removed our soldiers thought they were being bombed [so strong was the smell of rotten eggs].[36]

During the three years from 1943 to 1945, the Happy Centre WI alone produced forty-nine quilts, forty-five pairs of socks, twenty-three jackets, six wristlets, nineteen helmets, twenty-one "ditty bags," and donated money to the Emergency Fund, the Cigarette Fund, and sent seeds to Britain.[37]

Through active community work the Alberta Women's Institute has shaped the face of rural Alberta in many tangible ways. Local institutes were responsible for many practical advances in community life. Members were also active in war work during both world wars. In addition to its impact upon rural family life, the AWI offered educational programs for its members which improved their ability to cope with life on the farm. Through regular attendance at institute meetings members developed critical social links with their neighbours and an expanded social and political life. Individual members acquired knowledge and skills which allowed them to improve their home situation, build their local communities, and contribute broadly to the public sphere.

*Catherine C. Cole* is the former curator of Western Canadian History at the Provincial Museum of Alberta. She is currently pursuing a Ph.D. at the University of Leicester and working as Cultural Affairs Advisor for the Western Province of the Soloman Islands.

*Ann Milovic* received her M.A. in History from the University of Alberta and is a Ph.D. student at Corpus Christi College, Cambridge.

The authors would like to acknowledge the support of the Provincial Museum of Alberta which enabled Catherine Cole to hire Ann Milovic as a research assistant during the summer of 1989; we would also like to thank Sylvia McInley, executive director of the AWI, for introducing us to many members of the organization, and to the members of the AWI who willingly shared their memories, time, and tea.

Notes

1. Sinclair Ross, "The Lamp at Noon," *The Lamp at Noon and Other Stories* (Toronto: McClelland and Stewart, 1968), pp. 13–23.
2. Records of the Sixth Annual Convention of the AWI, Baptist Church, Edmonton, 16 March 1920, Provincial Archives of Alberta (henceforth PAA), 75.58 5 (3); The AWI was at its peak around 1920. Figures are not available for all years but membership declined in the late 1920s and early 1930s. At the end of World War I memberships expanded to include cities, and the Farm Women Institutes of Canada was formed. Membership grew from eight thousand in 1918 to ninety-five hundred in 1919 (Records of the Fifth Annual convention of the Alberta Women's Institutes, Central Methodist Church, Calgary, 11 March 1919); In 1935, only 184 Institutes reported with a total membership of 3,532; however, information is contradictory in various annual reports. There may in fact have been 264 institutes at the time, some of them not reporting. Report of the Twentieth Provincial Convention of the Alberta Women's Institutes, 24–28 May 1937, p. 21, PAA 74.1, 229, Box 9.
3. R.W. Barritt, History of the United Farm Women December 1934, p. 7, PAA 69, 193/2a.
4. *Farm and Ranch Review* (henceforth *FRR*) (20 October 1913).
5. Ibid.
6. *FRR*, 5 October 1920.
7. *FRR*, 15 November 1920.
8. Personal correspondence, Myrtle Heyer to Catherine Cole, 12 September 1989.
9. *FRR*, 20 May 1914.
10. Personal conversation, Marie Plaizier to Ann Milovic, 5 June 1989.
11. Personal interview, Nellie Whitson to Catherine Cole and Ann Milovic 21 July 1989.

12. Personal interviews, Roma Simonson to Catherine Cole, 1 December 1989; Ruth Corlett to Catherine Cole, 8 December 1989.
13. Personal interview, Nellie Whitson to Catherine Cole and Ann Milovic 21 July 1989.
14. Personal interview, Roma Simonson to Catherine Cole, 1 December 1989.
15. Ibid.
16. Personal interview, Nellie Whitson to Catherine Cole and Ann Milovic, 21 July 1989.
17. *FRR*, 5 April 1919.
18. *FRR*, 5 November 1917.
19. Report of the Annual Convention of Alberta Women's Institutes and Women's Institutes Girls' Clubs held in Convocation Hall, University of Alberta, Edmonton, 25, 26, 29, 30, 31 1923, p. 30, PAA 74.1, 228, Box 9.
20. Report of the Annual Convention of Alberta Women's Institutes held at the University of Alberta, Edmonton, 24–27 May 1927, p. 36, PAA 74.1, 228, Box 9.
21. See various reports of the Legislation Committee from 1927 to 1943, PAA 74.1, 228, 229, Box 9.
22. Private interview, Nellie Whitson to Catherine Cole and Ann Milovic, 21 July 1989.
23. Personal interviews, Roma Simonson to Catherine Cole, 1 December 1989; Ruth Corlett to Catherine Cole, 12 December 1989 and 7 February 1990.
24. *FRR*, 20 March 1919.
25. *FRR*, 5 September 1914.
26. *FRR*, 5 October 1917; in later years, the Chinook WI supported a doctor at the Cereal hospital, Minutes of Chinook WI, 6 September 1933, PAA 69.167, Box 1, 5.
27. *FRR*, 20 August 1920; see also Records of the Fourth Annual Convention of AWI, Hotel MacDonald, Edmonton, 9–11 March 1918, PAA 75.58.3 for reference to providing headquarters for district nurses, supporting municipal hospitals, securing doctors, and ensuring medical inspections of schools; see also Minutes of Northern Division of AWI, 14 November 1917, PAA 75.58.3, when delegates decided that "Save the Babies" would be the focus of AWI in 1918.
28. *FRR*, 21 September 1914.
29. *FRR*, 5 July 1917.
30. Ibid.
31. Ibid.
32. Advisory Board Meeting, 10 November 1919, PAA 75, 58, Box 1, 5.3; see also Report of Relief Work, 1919–20, PAA 75.58, Box 1, 5.3
33. Personal correspondence, Dorothy Hosegood, née Sissons, to Catherine Cole, 18 November 1989.
34. Isabel M. Campbell, *Grande Prairie: Capital of the Peace*, (n.p., 1968), p. 119.
35. *FRR*, 20 July 1918.
36. Personal correspondence, Dorothy Hosegood, née Sissons, to Catherine Cole, 18 November 1989; see Reports of Annual Conventions, PAA 74.1, Box 9, for an indication of the full range of activities the AWI was involved in; see also local histories for accounts in specific school districts.
37. Personal correspondence, Nellie Cotter to Catherine Cole, 8 November 1989.

BARBARA EVANS

# "We Just Lived It As It Came Along"

## Stories from Jessie's Albums

I had the privilege of meeting Jessie Umscheid and discovering her albums, filled with photographic treasures of the past, when I was researching *Prairie Women*, a film about farm women and the agrarian movement on the Canadian prairies in the early part of the century.[1] In the course of making the film, I had interviewed a number of women who had been actively involved in the struggle to bring about social and political change. As they looked back on their lives on the farm, they recalled not only the frequently gruelling work and the disappointments of crop failure and economic decline, but also the excitement they had felt at being part of the agricultural process and sharing the challenge to produce, with its myriad joys and heartaches. Through their words, they drew a collective picture of lives filled with resolution, vigour and passion, dedicated to overcoming the injustices which farm women faced. For the film, I needed photographs to represent these women, both as inspiring individuals in their own right, and as representatives of a movement in which hundreds of farm women had participated, working to transform society and women's role in it.

   Photographs of the period were all too rare and those taken from a woman's perspective almost nonexistent. As I travelled from house to house, archives to archives, asking hopefully if there might be any pictures of women's work on the farm in the early years of settlement,

Jessie Umscheid, née Burk, self-portrait, 1918

I would almost invariably be disappointed. The occasional constrained shots I was able to find gave an overall impression of listlessness and despondency, corresponding to the commonly held stereotype of the farm woman as long-suffering and overburdened. These photographs, while no doubt accurate reflections of many farm women's lives, were in no way representative of the energy and commitment to bring about change I had found in both the women I had interviewed and the many personal letters, diaries, and farm journals I had read.

But the photographs in Jessie's albums were different. Her pictures, many of which she had taken herself with her own camera, were lively depictions of farm life and women's work on the farm. As a result, I used many of her photographs in the film and was so impressed with both them and the woman from whose albums they came that I subsequently returned to make another film, *Jessie's Albums*, which deals exclusively with Jessie's life story as she tells it through photographs and interviews.[2]

Jessie's love of life and her matter-of-fact attitude toward its exigencies are reflected in the directness and unposed naturalness we see in her photographs, so unlike most of the pictures I had found up till then. In this short space, through her pictures and words, I hope to show not only that the depiction of any historical period depends on who has control of the means of representation but also that the popular portrayal of the farm woman of the time as downtrodden, anxious, and unhappy with her lot is by no means universally appropriate.

Jessie Burk, as she then was, had been born in Baker City, Oregon in 1900, which makes her, in her words, "as old as the century." In 1907, in common with many other Americans of the period, her family migrated to southern Alberta, settling near what was to become the town of Milo, approximately half-way between Calgary and Lethbridge, the area where Jessie still lives. The potential for wheat growing was believed to be limitless; the population was sparse and scattered.

Jessie's life on the farm was not a particularly unusual one, but for one important factor: with her camera she had the means of recording it. She had been given the camera in 1915, as a gift for her fifteenth birthday, and had almost immediately set about taking pictures of the everyday activities of farm life. Not surprisingly, these were the jobs done mainly by women, with which she was most familiar. It was unusual for a woman of that time to own a camera, particularly a

Picking berries, ca. 1918

young girl in a remote rural area, and Jessie's albums provide the closest thing to a pictorial essay of a pioneer farm woman's life that I have yet encountered. Remarkably, although she was completely untrained in photography, her work was of a consistently high quality, displaying an extraordinary sense of composition and ability to catch the transient moment.[3]

The striking absence of dynamic photographic portraits of pioneer women in general can be attributed to a variety of factors. In the early part of the century, photography was largely a white, middle-class male preserve. Most frequently, photographs of the time showed women dressed in their bonneted, beribboned Sunday best, decked out for special occasions often associated with church-going, such as weddings or christenings, or an "official" event, such as a meeting or convention. Studio portraiture showed women surrounded by children, maternal centres of their family universe. Exotic backdrops such as Oriental rugs, plants, and expensive furniture supplied by the studio bore little resemblance to the domestic environment in which the subjects actually lived. Posed, static, frozen moments, these photographs were generally without personality or purpose other than to preserve for posterity, to mark and demarcate the family's and the woman's place in the patriarchal sphere.

If out of the studio, the action almost invariably belonged to the men; the women appeared passive, as if having nothing better to do than stand or sit demurely, waiting to be photographed, or downcast, subjected to the tyranny of the lens and the person who operated it. "Stand still! Don't move!" These were—and often still are—the imprecations of the photographer to the subject. The subject's most usual response was, not surprisingly, to strike a "suitable," emblematic pose. For men, this was often one of proud, statuesque virility; for women, passive acceptance, in accordance with the popular sexual iconography of the time as portrayed not only in photography, but in painting and literature as well. Very few photographs showed the activities of women, or showed them dressed in everyday clothes, in everyday surroundings.[4] This is hardly surprising, since the purpose of the family photograph was not to provide a social document, but to preserve the family's image and relationships for future generations. Susan Sontag, writing on the photography of the period, points out:

> As that claustrophobic unit, the nuclear family, was being carved out of a much larger family aggregate, photography came along to memorialize, to restate symbolically, the imperiled continuity and vanishing extendedness of family life. Those ghostly traces, photographs, supply the token presence of the dispersed relatives. A family's photograph album is generally about the extended family—and, often, is all that remains of it.[5]

What is surprising about Jessie's photographs, then, is that they offer much more than a memorial to the past. Since she owned the means of photographic reproduction, she was able to choose the images she wished to preserve. Atypically, her photographs show women as subjects and range from thoughtful psychological studies to robust, vital, and joyful depictions of farm life. Her photographic work was doubly unusual in that it came not from the point of view of a privileged woman of means, but from the grassroots perspective of a relatively uneducated, frequently impoverished, but invariably hardworking young farm woman.

Jessie's father and uncle had already established a homestead before the seven-year-old Jessie and her mother came to join them. Mother and daughter arrived in Alberta by train in "a howling old blizzard" in the middle of May. After staying with relatives for several weeks, they optimistically set out for the homestead with horses and wagons filled with settlers' effects. As Jessie recalls:

> *We got across the hill where we could see the homestead and, of course, a prairie fire had gone over and everything was black as could be. Boy, mom was sure homesick that time. But the shack was still there, because some-*

Jessie's mother and sister Helen digging potatoes,
ca. 1916

*body had fireguarded it, where they plough a little bit or spade it out and
then burn the grass on each side of it so that it protects it from burning in.
The fire had jumped the fireguard, but they put it out and we had the
shack, anyhow.[6]*

Undaunted, the family proceeded to settle into their new home.
Never one to dwell upon difficulties, Jessie recounts the events in her
life with the same lack of pretentiousness we find in her photographs:

*Well, you just built your shack and just lived. We lived off the land as
much as we could. We picked wild berries, saskatoons and strawberries,
and my dad had already put out some plants, fruit bushes and things.
And we had antelope meat and prairie chickens and what not.*

*I slept on a big packing box and we put up a tent. We lived in that
until the winter drove us in the house, and then somehow or other we
stacked up in this two-roomed shack.*

Although this was no life of privilege, the overall impression Jessie
gives us is not one of self-pity; obstacles were regarded as challenges,
merely things to get over or around. Despite hardships, life could be

The two-roomed shack where Jessie spent much of her life

Jessie's mother, Nellie Burk, and Jessie's sister, Helen, feeding pigs, ca. 1915

full of fun and excitement if you let it be. Jessie's photographs reflect her adventurous attitude toward life, while never losing their connection to the daily realities farm women faced.

*That's my mom feeding the pigs. And Helen was with her, my sister. I bought the pigs to start out with, and they all helped me raise them (see photograph above).*

Jessie's sister, Helen,
and Jimmy, Jessie's son,
ca. 1923

## WHAT KIND OF PERSON WAS YOUR MOTHER?

*Oh, she was a very likeable and friendly person. Everybody that came along was her friend. Nobody left without a meal if she could help it. Of course, she would have liked to have been able to get out more.*

## DID SHE EVER FEEL LONELY, DO YOU THINK?

*Yes, I think she did, at times. But she always sent me out to help dad and*

The Burk family at harvest time, ca. 1923

*to do things outside, because there wasn't too much room in the shack,*
*and she liked to have the room more than she did me. (LAUGHS)*
*    She sewed and made all my clothes. And mom used to bake bread for*
*the bachelors and wash for them and one thing and another, so we had*
*quite a bit of bachelor company coming in.*[7]

The invention of modern photography is dated as early as 1826,
with the shadowy but temporary images of Joseph Nicéphore Niépce.
The daguerreotype and other more permanent processes followed,
but cameras were still the instruments of a well-to-do few. It wasn't
until the introduction in the late nineteenth century of the inexpensive
Kodak camera and roll film that photography was freed from the
exclusive domain of the wealthy and made available to people of
more modest means. These advances provided, for the first time in
history, the opportunity to record the daily lives of ordinary people
which would otherwise have been unknown to those who came after.
A busy farm woman like Jessie had no time to paint or draw; if she
wished to document the details of everyday life, the camera was the
ideal tool. Of course, handicrafts such as embroidery, needlework,
and quilting were practised by farm women, but these tended to be
personal and decorative, as opposed to illustrative of the wider
panorama of farm life.

A number of the photographs in Jessie's albums are self-portraits.
For these, she used a home-made remote control device consisting of
a string attached to a shutter release which she would pull after she

Jessie and her uncle, Bob Burk, on the Burk farm, Milo,
ca. 1917 (sister Helen on left)

had scrambled into the frame. In the many pictures taken of Jessie by others, she was obviously comfortable in front of the camera, unlike many women of her time. Her familiarity with the photographic medium gave her an unusual consciousness and control of the image she wished to be recorded. These pictures show a strong, confident woman in a wide variety of moods ranging from quietly thoughtful to joyously extroverted, unabashed by the camera lens.

For some time after she received her camera, Jessie was sought out by members of the district to record important occasions. Because she was photographing from her own life experience, recording the people and activities which surrounded her daily, her pictures lack the voyeuristic qualities of many professional photographs of farm life. Abigail Solomon-Godeau describes the work of photographers such as Walker Evans, Dorothea Lange and Ben Shahn, members of the Farm Security Administration's celebrated photographic project in the United States in the 1930s:

> When subjects smiled into the camera, they were stage-managed into more sombre poses; sharecroppers who wore their best clothes to be photographed were told to change into their ragged everyday wear, persuaded not to wash begrimed hands and faces for the camera.[8]

The Howell Family listening to the gramophone, ca. 1915

For Jessie, her subjects were not exotic beings to be conformed to an external point of view, they were part of her community.

*They'd ask me to come and take some pictures for people, if they were having a family gathering or something, so I used to go to their place whenever they would ask me, and take some.*

DID THEY PAY YOU?

*They paid me for the pictures I took for them, yes.*

SO YOU WERE SORT OF THE LOCAL PHOTOGRAPHER, THEN?

*Well, I don't know whether I was good enough or not, but I answered the purpose for awhile.*

Photographs taken by professionals, like those of the Farm Security Administration, were meant for public consumption. For better or worse, it is these images which most frequently shape our perceptions of the past. Photographs taken by those who actually lived the recorded experiences are more elusive.

*That's one of the Howell family. They didn't have room in the house for us, so they gave us dinner on the installment plan and we'd all take out chairs and go out on the hillside and listen to the gramophone . . . I thought it would make a nice picture of everybody enjoying the outdoors, so I just backed off and took the picture (see photograph above).*

Jessie's sister playing with cats, Milo, ca. 1917

## DID YOU TAKE YOUR CAMERA WITH YOU OFTEN?

*Yes. So many people asked me to take pictures for them, I usually had it with me.*

Through Jessie's photographs and recollections, we are given not only insights into the details of daily farm life, but a perspective on the wider rural society as well.

Education was often erratic in rural areas. Since there had to be a minimum number of pupils in a district to start a school, its fate could depend on the arrival or departure of one or two families. Jessie herself did not start school until she was nine years old because, prior to that, there had been no school. She describes the excitement felt by the community when the school opened:

*We were all quite thrilled. There were people going to school from beginners of seven years old up to sixteen who hadn't been to school before. And when they got too much for the teacher she'd send some of the smarter ones and the better educated ones to help the little ones. But we had lots of fun at school. There were always games and exercise and what not.*

*I did the janitor work one year, and I carried the drinking water about a quarter of a mile from the neighbour's well. A fresh pail of water each morning, and sometimes at noon.*

Pioneer School with teacherage and car, ca. 1915


*YOU WERE ALWAYS WORKING AT SOMETHING. YOU HAD A LOT OF RESPONSIBILITY.*

*(LAUGHS) Yes, it just worked into my life, I guess . . .*

In all my discussions with Jessie, the only note of bitterness I ever heard her express was when she talked about the disappointment she felt at being unable to finish school:

*I didn't get a very good education. Of course in those days, they didn't think that women needed an education, you know. They were just house-wives. We were not very important people.*

*I finished my grade eight. I was fifteen, sixteen, somewhere in there. But it was a lot of hit and miss, not really getting it thoroughly. I would have liked to have been a nurse, but it took too much education.*

Over the years, Jessie's camera captured many aspects of women's work which usually went unrecorded. While the activities of men and threshing machines at harvest time were well-documented, women's less visually dramatic part in the harvesting process was generally overlooked.

From an early age, Jessie worked with her mother during the busy harvest season cooking for the threshing crews which travelled from farm to farm.

Group of men and women at threshing time, Milo area, ca. 1916

Nellie Burk, Jessie's mother, Jessie Burk and Jessie's sister, Helen, working on cook car, ca. 1916

The influenza epidemic of
1918–19

*That's one of the cook cars that my mom and I cooked on. We had a bed in the corner that we slept on, the both of us together. It was just a single cot. And in the daytime we put a plastic cover on it and used it for a table. And then there was a stove across the end there that we cooked on. We'd have breakfast at five o'clock, and another one at seven. And it just kept you busy. You see, you'd have from twelve to sixteen men, usually, in a threshing outfit. We took lunch out in the afternoon. I had my pony on the buggy and I'd go and take the lunches out to the field and that sort of thing. It paid us five dollars a day, and boy, that was good wages at that time. It would go on maybe for several months. If there was a break you'd lose a lot of time, and be feeding the men for nothing. I missed quite a bit of school on account of it (see photograph bottom left).*

In 1918 and 1919, a deadly influenza epidemic swept over the prairies. In Canada, fifty thousand people died from it, worldwide over twenty-one million.

Jessie with baby Jim on "Old Prince," 1921

Babies having dinner in field during harvesting, ca. 1923

*Well everybody it just seemed like was stricken all of a sudden. Whole families came down with it at once and there was nobody to do chores or anything. Somebody'd go out to milk the cows and catch a chill or pneumonia and that was it. It just seemed to take them off like flies.*

*The United Farmers of Alberta had just built a hall in Milo and they turned it into a hospital. Everybody lent their sheets, and they cut the hall in three sections. The women were on one side and the men on the other*

Clarence and baby Jim with team of horses, 1922

*and the children in the middle. Anybody that had a cot or a bed of any kind that they could use took it down. The schools were all closed, and the teachers nursed in the hospital. I used to go around the district and gather up food for the patients that were in there. One time we had thirty people in the hall. I helped to nurse people and was in among it a lot, and it never touched me until it was all over, and then I got it. I really had a dose of it.*

In 1920, Jessie married Clarence Umscheid, who had come from Oregon to the Milo area to do seasonal work as a farmhand. By that time, Jessie's parents had moved into a larger house on the farm property and, to save money, the newly-wed couple moved into the two-roomed shack in which Jessie herself had been raised. Over the next few years, five children were born into its confines.

At the outset of the marriage, Jessie made sketches of the house she dreamed of building when the young family's finances improved. But, as the Depression of the 1930s loomed closer and economic conditions grew worse, the family was forced to remain in the shack for the next twenty years.

*When Clarence and I were married in 1920, we borrowed $3,000 to get horses and things to farm with. We never got that paid off until 1950. (LAUGHS)*

Jessie with children Bob
and Jim on packing crate,
ca. 1923

*YOU MUST HAVE THOUGHT YOU WOULD NEVER GET IT
PAID OFF.*

*Well, we were all in the same boat, you know. People seemed to get along
without very much complaining. Just lucky to have what we did have,
you know.*

For much of the 1920s, Jessie's camera was largely devoted to docu-
menting her growing family.

The energy Jessie put into farm work extended to work in the community and, despite her demanding work on the farm, she somehow
found time to attend meetings of local groups. Like a great many
other women in the district, Jessie and her mother were actively
involved in the United Farmers of Alberta (UFA) and its counterpart

Jessie's mother-in-law and mother with Jessie's sons Bob and Jimmy, Milo, ca. 1923

Women riding to town in grain box pulled by horses, ca. 1918

women's organization, the United Farm Women of Alberta (UFWA), committed to improving conditions in the rural community and particularly the position of women.

*We were all interested in what was going on. . . . When we came to this country, everything was down in Ontario, you know. Everything was for Ottawa, and we were all interested in becoming a part of Canada. I went*

The Milo United Farm Women of Alberta go to Arrow-
wood, ca. 1925

*to several of the conventions in Edmonton, and one in Calgary. We had
cots, you know, a bunch of us in one room. It was cheaper living that way.
So we got to go to those things. We were always working and building up
our UFA to have some say in the government and the like.*

The Depression arrived with full force in 1929. The droughts and
duststorms which accompanied the collapse of wheat prices wrought
havoc and misery all across the prairies, bringing ruin to countless
farms. Yet, although she and her family were severely affected,
Jessie's memories of the late 1920s and 1930s are remarkable for their
lack of rancour. Her memories centre on how people coped, rather
than on the deprivation they experienced:

*Well, the Depression was just something that happened, and you just took
it as it came. We just lived it as it came along, the same as any other thing
that happens that way.*

*We had a beef ring. We'd each supply a beef every so often and we'd
divide it up amongst twelve of us. And we had chickens and eggs so we
didn't fare too badly. We didn't have any orange trees, but then you don't
have to have.*

*One year, there was no crop. Insects had moved in, and the dust and
everything, and we didn't have any crop. We sold our cattle because we*

*didn't have feed for them. And you know the funny part of it was that nobody was complaining too much. Everybody seemed to keep on the cheery side. You just kind of made do with what you had.*

The Depression provided previously undreamt-of photo opportunities for outside observers. Professional photographers, both in Canada and the United States, travelled to the most seriously depressed areas during the 1930s, recording the suffering they encountered there. Often, as Susan Sontag points out, they took dozens of photographs to capture "the precise expression on the subject's face that supported their own notion about poverty, light, dignity, texture, exploitation, and geometry."

But for Jessie, the Depression destroyed her delight in photography. Unlike the professionals, she had neither the money to take pictures nor the desire to record the devastations of duststorms and crop failures:

*We didn't want pictures of it. We didn't want to spend the money on it, for one thing. We didn't use money for anything that we didn't have to, because it just kept you going to keep going.*

WERE THERE THINGS THAT YOU WANTED TO TAKE PICTURES OF?

*I don't think so. It didn't seem there was any point in taking pictures of a duststorm, nor the army worms and that sort of thing.[9] We didn't think it was anything too nice to take pictures of. (LAUGHS)*

THAT MUST HAVE BEEN A PRETTY BLEAK TIME.

*Yes, it was, but then that's the way life goes.*

LIFE JUST SEEMED TOO MISERABLE, I GUESS.

*I don't know if it was so miserable, we just didn't have the wherewithal to take them.*

Throughout our discussions, both in recorded interviews and later, over the years, Jessie was consistently wary of any interpretation she feared might trap her into what she viewed as a falsely sentimental portrayal of the past. This refusal to dramatize her experiences of farm life was paralleled in the unsentimental immediacy of her approach to photography. For Jessie, it was not a question of a look, or a geometry. In representing her own life, she did not wish to be immortalized as the downtrodden, powerless woman of popular stereotype, the victim of circumstance, that outsiders, whether photographers, historians, filmmakers, or writers, have all too often presented.

This is not to diminish the hardships that farm women encountered—and still encounter to this day—but rather to say that there can be no monolithic view of women's history. Instead, we must listen to the multiplicity of voices and experiences which make up that history in order to understand it. In Jessie's case we are fortunate to have not only her words, but also the images she created to help us uncover a part of the complex, multilayered narrative of women's lives.

*Barbara Evans,* an award-winning filmmaker, is a graduate of the University of British Columbia and the British National Film and Television School. She has worked as a director, producer, writer, researcher, and editor of film and television. Her work dealing with farm women and prairie politics includes the films *Prairie Women,* a film on the history of organized farm women on the Canadian prairies, *In Her Chosen Field,* a documentary on issues facing contemporary farm women, *Jessie's Albums,* the story of a farm woman who documented her life through photographs in the early years of the century, and a video, *Now That We Are Persons,* which celebrates the sixtieth anniversary of the Persons Case. She is currently working on a feature-length documentary film which chronicles the early years of the Co-operative Commonwealth Federation. Since 1990, she has taught film and video production at York University.

Notes

1. The film *Prairie Women* is distributed by the National Film Board of Canada.
2. *Jessie's Albums* is available from Filmwest Associates, 2399 Hayman Road, P.O. Box 1437, Kelowna, BC, V1Y 7V8.
3. All photographs included in this article have been deposited with the Glenbow Archives in Calgary and copies may be ordered from there.
4. Unless they belonged to a culture other than the predominant Anglo-Saxon one, in which case their "difference" might be emphasized by showing them in "foreign" dress, burdened by hard labour.
5. Susan Sontag, *On Photography* (New York: Delta, 1977), p. 9.
6. The quotations throughout this chapter are edited excerpts from interviews with Jessie Umscheid by the author on 4 August 1986 and 1 and 2 September 1987.
7. In order to provide extra income for the household, it was a common practice among farm women to bake and do laundry for bachelors.
8. Abigail Solomon-Godeau, *Photography at the Dock: Essays on Photographic History, Institutions and Practices* (Minneapolis, University of Minnesota Press, 1991), p.179.
9. Throughout the Depression, southern Alberta was plagued by crop-destroying infestations of grasshoppers and "armies" of caterpillars.

COLLETTE LASSITER
JILL OAKES

# Ranchwomen, Rodeo Queens, and Nightclub Cowgirls

## The Evolution of Cowgirl Dress

The history of the west has been dominated by images of the male figure. In American and Canadian western annals particularly those concerning the development of the cattle frontier, the cowboy has become an enduring mythological figure. The purpose of this paper is to examine the evolution of the female counterpart to the cowboy—the "cowgirl"—by looking at the evolution of the cowgirl style of dress.

This study briefly traces the origins of the "real" cowboy, how he dressed, the functional nature of his attire, and how his image came into public favour. Over the years the cowboy/cowgirl look has diverged, with cowgirl dress becoming a less clearly defined fashion style. How the frontier woman dressed in actuality is briefly discussed in order to temper the romanticized vision history and popular culture have of the early cowgirl. That vision has changed and evolved throughout the twentieth century. From the "Wild West" shows of the turn of the century to the Hollywood Western, and the styles rodeo women have adopted throughout the decades, our culture appears to continuously recreate its version of the cowgirl.

Early Dress in Cowboy Country

The long standing love affair with the cowboy or cowgirl image in North America is perhaps as durable as the clothes the first cowhands wore.

55

*Funk & Wagnall's New Encyclopedia* defines the cowboy as

the name given to the mounted herdsmen hired by cattle owners in the United States to look after their stock. Cowboys keep the cattle together, guide them to pasture, prevent their being mixed with other droves, protect them from rustlers, brand them at the proper season, and drive them to the shipping point.[1]

This source adds that cowboys figure most significantly in American history from the 1850s to 1890s, "when transportation facilities were scanty in the western and southwestern sections of the U.S. and cattle had to be driven to shipping points over long distances."[2] Performing such tasks on a daily basis undoubtedly called for endurance and good horsemanship; the man's clothes would have to be functional and able to withstand inclement environments.

The working cowboy of the nineteenth century dressed appropriately for his work. His attire, it is said, was not fickle to the whims of fashion, "In cowboy country the fashions of apparel do not change"[3]; "it [cowboy dress] knew nothing of variable fashion and suffered from no change in style."[4] From his hat to his boots the cowboy's attire is functional.

Of the infamous western hat or "genuine Stetson," Hough says the following:

There has been no head covering devised so suitable as this for the uses of the plains. The heavy boardlike felt is practically indestructible . . . the heavy felt repels the blazing rays of the sun better than any helmet . . . the cowboy can depend upon his hat at all seasons. In the rain it is an umbrella. In the sun it is a shade and a safeguard . . . in the winter he can tie it down about his ears with his handkerchief.[5]

Shirts were made from wool or cotton and were usually pullovers although a few used buttons. Shirts were usually checked, striped, or one solid colour,[6] but were rarely red because "the latter tone was reputed to go badly among the cattle."[7]

Denim was popularized by the working cowboy due to its inherent durability and comfort. "According to the Levi Strauss Company, the levis that appeared in Texas in the 1850s—certainly by the 1860s, were originally brown or natural canvas color; later they became blue.

Copper-riveted levis were introduced in 1872–1873, but cowboys considered them a low-caste innovation and did not adopt them until the '90s."[8] Boots invariably had two-inch high heels.[9] One source describes them as

> vertical at the front, and were in length and breadth much smaller at the bottom than at top. The tall heel, highly arching the wearer's instep, insured, as did the elimination of all projections, outstanding nails, and square corners from the sole, against the wearer's foot slipping through the stirrup or being entangled in it . . . the sole usually quite thick, this to grant to the wearer a semiprehensile "feel of the stirrup."[10]

These items of cowboy attire, along with gloves, chaps, and a kerchief, were chosen for the tasks at hand and to suit varying environmental conditions. Vanity may also have played a role. From the styles of dress portrayed in archival photographs, it is evident that many cowboys ". . . took pride in their appearance."[11] The cowboy and the west have often symbolized the common man and his struggles. Wilson indicates that "because cowboy dress was such an evident characteristic of the cowboy image, dressing the part elevated an individual into the heroic replica. . . ."[12]

The image of a tight-jeaned and booted cowboy, sporting a Stetson and a long-sleeved shirt, has varied little for more than a century. Working cowboys of the nineteenth century and the contemporary image are somewhat similar, with the exception of the Hollywood dandy-style cowboys of the 1940s and 1950s. In contrast, cowgirl dress styles, particularly the image of the woman on horseback in popular culture, has been far more dynamic. "The female garb seems to have changed primarily to reflect contemporary fashion rather than to recreate authentic Western fashion."[13]

Early Frontier Women

Women preparing for the journey west were advised to take no fine clothing, only "things suitable for everyday wear," such as a "calico frock, plainly made, no hoops, and a sun-bonnet." Some women invented garments to suit their new western chores. A few, annoyed by long skirts that forced them to ride sidesaddle while they tended cattle, dared to create outfits that permitted them to ride comfortably astride: shorter skirts with blue denim knickers to wear underneath.[14]

Thus, the "cowgirl" was created. The image of the spirited heroine on horseback in the frontier was, at least in the early days of western expansion, quite a rarity. She existed in dime novels to a greater degree than she did in reality. As Calder has indicated, "women were not a plentiful commodity in most parts of the frontier. It was often easier to import pianos and champagne than to bring out suitable mates for the frontiersman."[15] The west was dirty, rugged, often lawless; it offered few opportunities for "respectable" single women. Of the first women who did come one has only to look at their stern, wrinkled young faces, their plainly made cotton dresses, a succession of young children and perhaps a look of sombre determination. These were the first women of the west and they were not cowgirls. Of such women, Isabella Bird, a traveller and writer in nineteenth-century America states:

> She looks like one of the English poor women of our childhood—lean, clean, toothless, and speaks like one of them, in a piping, discontented voice, which seems to convey a personal reproach. All her waking hours are spent in a sun-bonnet. She is never idle for one minute, is severe and hard, and despises everything but work.[16]

Calder emphasizes that few people would recognize the above image as reflective of the life and appearance of many frontier women (Photo. 1.).

Popular culture has romanticized the female settler as the serene beautiful wife, the adventuress, or more commonly as the rancher's pretty young daughter. Female settlers were not romanticized as range wranglers, accountants, cooks, or ranch owners. However, women eventually did come west, often as daughters, wives, and nieces,[17] who worked alongside men:

> Although cattle ranching is usually portrayed in movies and television as a completely male world dominated by gun-slinging cowboys and outlaws, the cattle culture had its share of women. A number of women were wives of ranchers and worked side by side with them in keeping books, and managing the feeding of cowboy

Photo. 1. Few earlier frontier women could be
called "cowgirls" as we
have come to know them.
(D. Gray, "Women on the
Cattle Frontier," *Women of
the West*.)

employees and caring for stock. A number of women actually
owned cattle ranches themselves.[18]

## Changing Dress Standards for Early Cowgirls

The life history of Agnes Morely illustrates the need for change in "traditional" female dress in cattle country. As a teenager in 1886, Agnes
Morely went to a New Mexico cattle ranch along with her mother, sister, brother, and a step-father who soon after deserted the family.
Agnes and her mother ran the cattle ranch themselves in order to save
the family's only fortune.[19] Liberating herself from restrictive feminine
clothing Agnes recounted the following:

> First, I discarded, or rather refused to adopt, the sun-bonnet, con-
> ventional headgear of my female neighbors. When I went
> unashamedly about under a five-gallon (not ten-gallon) Stetson,
> many an eyebrow was raised; then followed a double-breasted blue
> flannel shirt, with white pearl buttons, frankly unfeminine. In time

came blue denim knickers worn under a short blue denim skirt. Slow evolution (or was it decadence?) toward a costume suited for immediate needs. Decadence having set in, the descent from the existing standards of female modesty to purely human comfort and convenience was swift. A man's saddle and a divided skirt (awful monstrosity that it was) were inevitable. This was in the middle nineties.[20]

Inevitably, more women became involved in cattle ranching. Some learned how to ride, rope, and shoot exceptionally well. During pre-rodeo days, cowboys or cattlehands showed off their skills to each other on early cattle round-ups. In 1847, Captain Mayne Reid, author of *The Rifle Rangers*, recorded:

This round-up is a great time for the cowhands, a Donnybrook fair it is indeed. They contest with each other for the best roping and throwing, and there are horse races and whiskey and wines.[21]

Cowboys and a few cowgirls joined Buffalo Bill's "Wild West" show, thereby demonstrating their skills to a wider public. As a result, cowgirl dress received broad exposure. As Swallow-Reiter points out, "Rodeo cowgirls, most of whom first learned their skills in real ranch work, encouraged public acceptance of women riding astride as well as popularizing such practical equestrian fashions as divided skirts"[22] (Photo. 2.).

Androgynous Yet Fancy Styles for North America's Rodeo Sweethearts

Annie Oakley became the "greatest personality developed by the 'Wild West' shows."[23] The western frontier was fast disappearing by the turn of the century and the public adored the acts of this flamboyant show.[24] Rodeos soon gained popularity and one of the most famous rodeos, The Calgary Stampede, began in 1912. Female rodeo participants wore a loose long sleeved shirt, long divided skirt, (Photo. 3.), flat boots and a large light coloured Stetson. An example of these cowgirl fashions is worn by "Flores La Due, wife of the Stampede's founder, Guy Weadick, who won the Cowgirls' Trick Roping prize. . . . "[25] Flores La Due was originally from Oklahoma and a veteran of the Wild West Shows.[26] Dress styles of the early

Photo. 2. Cowgirl
(1904–1908) (Vancouver
Museum, *Panache*
(1990–91), p. 27.)

fancy riders such as La Due at the Calgary Stampede in 1912 and "Buffalo Bill's" beloved early show cowgirls were often identical.

By the 1920s, rodeo cowgirls wore simple blouses, "high-waisted, loose-fitting slacks (riding breeches), tight at the ankles and usually worn tucked into high-topped boots."[27] As Fenin and Everson point out, the Hollywood cowgirl of this era was also "dressed in practical blouses, and skirts were shorter. There was no longer quite the same hesitation about showing something of a well-shaped female leg, in western or other films, but fashions were still modest."[28] Martin terms the 1920s as a "kind of golden age of the show cowgirl, an innocent time" for the country's rodeo sweethearts.[29] Changes in styles of riding garments made riding astride acceptable for women.

Photo. 3. Flores La Due . . . simple blouse and trousers.
(Courtesy Glenbow Archives, NA 628–2 to 4)

North America's affection for country music began in the 1930s, "when cowboys and cowgirls began popping up on radio shows that had once hollered convincingly about their hillbilly allegiances."[30] The most memorable singing cowgirl of the era was Patsy Montana who is said to have had: "campfire-by-night eyes, and the full regalia of boots, buckskin, bandanna, and Stetson . . . off came the ginghams, bonnets, and down-home long dresses; out came the wardrobe of Annie Oakley."[31]

Rodeo cowgirls reflected the flamboyance of the singing cowgirls. Consider for example, Margaret (née Brazeau) Fry's outfit which included a skirt, vest, gauntlets, boots, and even spurs. The elaborate leather fringe work, glass and steel beading, and silk lining leave one wondering if this rosebud-embellished cowgirl's dress was even fancier than anything worn by emerging Hollywood or Nashville cowgirls. This ensemble was beaded by Margaret's mother Louise Belcourt (1861–1926), a woman of French and Cree ancestry. The dress is a unique and beautiful merging of native and western ideals in dress; a sure cowgirl prize winner (Photo. 4.).

Photo. 4. Brazeau's
Decorative Work . . . now
a cowgirl museum trea-
sure. (Courtesy Glenbow
Archives, C 13282 A-D)

## Hollywood Cowgirls

By the 1940s a more glamorous cowgirl look emerges. The inspiration
for the new image coincides with the popularity of Roy Rogers and
Dale Evans and her "cover-girl costumes in dozens of tumble-weed
musicals."[32] Cowgirls at the Burns's Chuckwagon Radio Program in
Calgary, 1940, wear smaller hats than previously seen (Photo. 5.).
Arched eyebrows, red lipstick, and permanent waves are "de rigueur"
for these ladies of the rodeo, who were even pictured smoking and
drinking. Their white outfits and costumelike hats no longer suggest
any inspiration from the working ranchwoman, but rather that of starlets. Other cowgirls at the Calgary Stampede are pictured in similar
costume; however, an even more refined white hat and a tailored satin
cowgirl blouse seemed more popular overall. A similar ensemble is
worn by the candidate poster for a 1952 rodeo queen which reads:
"Doreen Wynee—Candidate for Calgary Stampede Queen, Sponsored
by the Motion Picture Industry." The cowgirl had gone Hollywood.
    The cowgirl image of the 1950s continued with the trend for glam-
our and femininity. Fringed skirts were worn up until about 1959.
Fenin and Everson state that "short skirts and ankle boots came into

Photo. 5. Burns's Chuckwagon Radio Program—
Cowgirl Performers Lipstick, nailpolish and "dandy
style" cowgirl outfits for the rodeo girl of the 1940s.
(Courtesy Provincial Archives of Alberta, Harry Pollard
Collection, P 3929)

vogue by the 1950s.[33] This was the era of Patsy Cline: "the Virginian
who took country torch songs to the pop charts, might belt out tales of
urban despair, but she'd do so wearing outfits that glittered with cowgirl glamour."[34]

New Trends for the 1960s and 1970s

By 1963, rodeo queens were pictured for the first time in contour-fit-
ting jumpsuits (Photo. 6.). Rodeo cowgirls and queens have predominantly worn pants even though earlier pant styles were made to look
like skirts. It is uncertain whether this is a reflection of real change in
views of women's roles or as a result of more emphasis being placed
on horsemanship, which required the use of pants. As in the 1950s,
the cowgirl look mirrored Hollywood's ideal of the cowgirl. As one
source notes:

Women have changed externally in Western films during the last
eight decades, with the trend always in the direction of revealing

Photo. 6. Canadian Finals Rodeo Queens (1976). Stretch
polyester (?) jumpsuits on the cowgirl of the 1970s.
(Courtesy Provincial Archives of Alberta, Edmonton
Journal Collection, J 2851/1)

more and more of their bodies . . . heroines in pants and blouses
calling attention to their figures.[35]

In the early 1970s man-style suit jackets and tight pants with bell-
bottom legs were adapted for rodeo queens. These fashions were worn
up to about 1983, long after the style became unfashionable elsewhere.
Printed fabrics and stretch polyester were used instead of leather
fringe, denim, and satin. As Martin points out "no rodeo worthy of the
name is complete without a rodeo queen and her attendants—each
decked out in matching aqua or lavender or gold polyester pants, jack-
et, and hats."[36] Miss Universe-like sashes appeared on rodeo queens of
the 1970s and 1980s. Hair was generally worn long and straight and
makeup was minimal, perhaps to reflect a clean, fresh-scrubbed country girl ideal.

## Urban Cowgirls

During the 1970s, the cowgirl image in popular culture became less
popular as, "many country singers . . . abandoned cowgirl duds for

approximations of folk music fashions."[37] Although rodeo queens were crowned with white Stetsons, the look was unpopular among movie stars and country singers. By the end of the decade a dramatic turnaround occurred. Tom Robbins's novel, *Even Cowgirls Get the Blues*, revived the cowgirl image.[38] By the late 1970s, journalist Aaron Latham, working for *Esquire* magazine, wrote an article entitled, "The Ballad of the Urban Cowboy: America's Search for True Grit."

Latham had travelled to Houston, America's newest boomtown, in search of modern-day cowboys. What he found were dead-end blue-collar workers, who lacking . . . any sort of romance or success in their own lives, spend their nights in a honky-tonk called Gilley's—which bills itself as the world's biggest saloon—acting out their cowboy fantasies—hardhats, bread-truck drivers, accountants—they pull on their Tony Lama cowboy boots, square a Stetson on their heads, and for the next few hours rope and ride and drink like the long-gone real McCoys. At least that's how Latham saw it.[39]

Paramount Pictures was equally intrigued with using the cowboy fantasy as the basis for a movie. Eventually a script was written for *Urban Cowboy*, which went on to become a North American box office hit. The country was once again in love with the cowboy mythology:

By the summer of 1978, Texas fever had struck every town in America. Anything and everything that was fringed, tooled, Stetsoned, denimed or otherwise smacked of Texas cowboy gear was the fashion rage.[40]

Even *Newsweek* published a piece on the "Nightclub Cowboy" before the movie opened across the country.

The capital of urban cowboyland attracts a remarkedly diverse clientele . . . but their mainstays are young men who work in nearby refineries, shipyards and grain elevators, and women who toil as waitresses . . . women who sport ultra-tight jeans, abundant make-up and Farrah Fawcett hairdos.[41]

In the same movie Debra Winger wore straight-legged jeans and tight tank tops for her role as Sissy, a nightclub cowgirl. Critics and audiences adored and copied this new definition of cowgirl sexiness. Critic Pauline Kael wrote, "that she looked like she wore her clothes over damp skin."[42] Advertisers of women's wear took advantage of this new-found cowgirl look. Country nightclubs across the country thrived, as "wanna be" cowboys and cowgirls came wearing designer blue jeans and increasingly fancy boots and belt buckles. During Stampede week in Calgary, people from a wide variety of occupations were willing to stand in line for hours to enter western inspired nightclubs and bars. The same people were captivated by one of North America's boldest myths. As children, many grew up in the 1950s and 1960s watching television or movies that depicted beloved cowboy figures such as the freckled, bandanna-sporting puppet "Howdy Doody." As adults, this generation remembered an era in the 1950s when young boys and girls dressed up as cowboys and cowgirls for birthday parties and ventured to local fairs or rodeos. Fabrics depicting the cowboy theme were not uncommon during the 1950s. They were used for children's bedspreads or curtains. The cowboy and cowgirl ideology endures to the present day as another generation redefines an interest in the image.

## Nashville to Alberta Ranch Women

Cowgirl fashions reflect contemporary fashion and a more explicit sexuality. With the current popularity of country music at the outset of the 1990s, the cowgirl look is unashamedly "traditional" or at least traditional in the sense that the look is overtly western. "The new traditionalists of country music, such as performers Reba McEntire, Holly Dunn, and Kathy Mattea, are not at all averse to sporting Stetsons and other western gear for their outing in front of the public."[43] High fashion has embraced the cowgirl-look, creating combinations never worn by ranchwomen.

Rodeo cowgirls, such as barrel racers, are perhaps less likely to succumb to the whims of fashion than are rodeo queens or entertainers. Today the "modern cowgirl (rodeo competitor) wears a colourful variation of the basic western wardrobe of hats, boots, long-sleeved shirts, and close-fitting trousers."[44] Gloves that protect the cowgirl's hands from rope burns and chaps to prevent abrading her legs against bushes are worn. As for her male counterpart, the Canadian Professional Rodeo Association Rules require such attire as hats and long-sleeve shirts.[45] Ranchwomen of Alberta continue to wear clothes reflecting practicality and harmony with the environment.

## Conclusion

In popular culture the dress of the cowgirl constantly changed with current ideals of fashion and morality. Styles have been more practical and stable for contemporary female rodeo competitors and working ranchwomen. However, North American culture views the cowboy/ cowgirl look as representative of a sort of freedom and adventure, and entailing perhaps a sense of "country" purity and tradition.

The dress of the rodeo queen, the entertainer, or the working ranchwoman may vary, but her image is as much a part of western ideology as the cowboy. As Roach proclaims in her book, *The Cowgirls*, "I am inclined to attach some importance to a theory . . . that the emancipation of women may have begun when they mounted a good cow horse and realized how different and fine the view was."[46] The west is said to have a history of its own. The evolution of cowgirl dress reflects the double duty for women to be "feminine" and to get the job done.

*Collette Lassiter* has a long term interest in cowgirl dress. She is a graduate of the Department of Clothing and Textiles, University of Alberta (1991).

*Jill Oakes* (B.H.Ec., MSc., Ph.D., University of Manitoba) studies the meaning and evolution of clothing styles within a cultural and historical perspective. She is a professor in the Department of Human Ecology, University of Alberta.

### Notes

1. *Funk and Wagnall's New Encyclopedia 7*, s.v. "cowboy," p. 112.
2. Ibid.
3. E. Hough, "The Cowboy's Outfit," *The Story of the Cowboy* (Upper Saddle River, NJ: Literature House/Gregg Press, 1970), p. 50.
4. P. Rollins, "What the Cowboy Wore," *The Cowboy: An Unconventional History of Civilization on the Old-time Cattle Range* (New York: Charles Scribner and Sons, 1936), p. 103.
5. Hough, "The Cowboy's Outfit," p. 54.
6. Rollins, "What the Cowboy Wore"; D. Gorsline, "The Cowboy," *What People Wore: A Visual History of Dress from Ancient Times to Twentieth-Century America* (New York: The Viking Press, 1952), pp. 229–30; Hough, "The Cowboy's Outfit."
7. Rollins, "What the Cowboy Wore," p. 108.
8. Gorsline, "The Cowboy," p. 229.
9. Rollins, "What the Cowboy Wore"; Gorsline, "The Cowboy"; Hough, "The Cowboy's Outfit."
10. Rollins, "What the Cowboy Wore," p. 114.
11. L. Wilson, "I Was a Pretty Proud Kid" (an interpretation of differences in posed and unposed photographs of Montana cowboys), *Clothing and Textiles Research Journal 9*, no. 13 (Spring 1991), p. 51.
12. Ibid., p. 57.
13. Fenin and Everson, "The Western Costume," *The Western: From Silents to the Seventies* (New York: Grossman Publishers, 1973), p. 109.
14. J. Swallow-Reiter, "A Burst of Free Spirits," *The Old West: The Women* (Alexandria, VA: Time-Life Books, 1978), p. 28.

15. J. Calder, "Women in the West," *There Must be a Lone Ranger* (London: Hamish Hamilton, 1974), p. 158.
16. Ibid., p. 157.
17. Ibid.; D. Gray, "Women on the Cattle Frontier," *Women of the West* (Millbrae, CA: Les Femmes, 1976), pp. 109–19.
18. Gray, "Women on the Cattle Frontier," p. 109.
19. Ibid.
20. Gray, "No Life for a Lady," *Women of the West*, p. 109.
21. D. Russell, "A Dazzling Prelude to a Mighty Spectacle," *The Wild West* (Fort Worth: Amon Carter Museum of Western Art, 1970), p. 2.
22. Swallow-Reiter, "A Burst of Free Spirits," p. 189.
23. Russell, "A Dazzling Prelude," p. 21.
24. E. Lawrence, *Rodeo: An Anthropologist Looks at the Wild and the Tame* (Knoxville: University of Tennessee Press, 1982), p. 45.
25. C. Eamer and T. Jones, *The Canadian Rodeo Book* (Saskatoon: Western Producer Prairie Books, 1982), p. 9.
26. R. Martin, "Cowgirl Country," *Cowboy: The Enduring Myth of the Wild West* (New York: Stewart, Tabori and Chang, 1983), pp. 320–51.
27. Eamer and Jones, *The Canadian Rodeo Book*, p. 82.
28. Fenin and Everson, "The Western Costume," p. 190.
29. Martin, "Cowgirl Country," p. 335.
30. S. O'Shea, "Cowgirl Cults," *Elle* 6, no. 6 (September 1990) p. 219.
31. O'Shea, "Cowgirl Cults," p. 222.
32. Ibid.
33. Fenin and Everson, "The Western Costume," p. 190.
34. O'Shea, "Cowgirl Cults," p. 222.
35. J. Tuska, "Women," *The American West in Film: Critical Approaches to the Western* (Westport: Greenwood Press, 1985), pp. 224–28.
36. Martin, "Cowgirl Country," p. 350.
37. O'Shea, "Cowgirl Cults," p. 222.
38. Ibid.
39. M. Cahill, "Proving Everybody Wrong," *Debra Winger: Hollywood's Wild Child* (New York: St. Martin's Press, 1984), p. 22.
40. Ibid., p. 23.
41. D. Shah and R. Henkoff, "Nightclub Cowboys," *Newsweek* 94 (9 July 1979), p. 81.
42. Cahill, "Proving Everybody Wrong," p. 23.
43. O'Shea, "Cowgirl Cults," p. 222.
44. Eamer and Jones, *The Canadian Rodeo Book*, p. 82.
45. Ibid.
46. Martin, "Cowgirl Country," p. 329.

NANCI LANGFORD

# "All That Glitters"

## The Political Apprenticeship of Alberta Women, 1916–1930

Having secured the vote, we sat down satisfied without grasp-
ing that the work had only begun. In other words, we had
obtained the tools, but it remained to use them. . . . We, ourselves, were more or less dazzled when we secured the franchise; things seemed to be coming our way so easily. It has taken
a few years for us to bite the coin and to learn once more, that all
that glitters is not gold.[1]

One of the missing pieces in scholarly work on Alberta is an examination of women's political activism right after receiving the vote. Limited analysis of the postsuffrage period characterizes it as one in
which women activists retreated from political action, suggesting a
decade or more of inactivity in both political lobbying and electoral
politics. Compared to the success of the "votes for women" movement, which unified women's organized reform activities and groups
into a strong political caucus, the fifteen years following the passage
of suffrage legislation were ones of confusion and adversity. Veronica
Strong-Boag claims that feminism—particularly as an organized
movement—was unable "to mount a sustained attack on male prerogatives in the public sphere after the suffrage campaign."[2]

Legal reform campaigns of the early twentieth century, to secure prohibition legislation, dower laws, and female suffrage, were the first public political debates in which Alberta women participated with great energy and skill. These campaigns provided a focus for women to come together to influence electoral politics through effective political lobbying activities. They can be seen as the beginning of Alberta women's political apprenticeship. The period 1916–30 was a time of regrouping, experimentation, and coming to terms with new political realities, particularly the inability to meet many of the reform goals espoused during the suffrage campaign. Women's new equality in electoral politics also brought a new diversity of goals and concerns to women's political activities, both within and outside the political parties. More significantly, women learned that their new legal equality did not automatically bring inclusion, as equals, in political processes and organizations.

There is no doubt that Alberta women who had been active in securing the vote expected great changes to occur when women gained access to the ballot box. Despite the fact that many of these expectations were never met, Alberta women activists demonstrated a new sense of purpose and determination to use their new political rights effectively. They continued to organize to influence the political process; they launched an impressive education initiative to reach the new woman voter; and beginning almost immediately with the provincial election campaign of 1917, they participated in all facets of political campaigns in ways they never had before. In 1917 they elected the first women legislators ever to sit in any elected house in the British Empire. The immediate postsuffrage years, 1916–30, proved to be a difficult but productive period of political apprenticeship for Alberta women.

Alberta Women Organize to Influence Electoral Politics

Some of Alberta's prominent women responded immediately to the opportunity to work together as a coalition of people with common interests and concerns to use their new rights most effectively. In the week following the passage of the suffrage bill, a meeting was called at Nellie McClung's Edmonton home, "for the purpose of considering the best method of forming a committee to consider the bills desirable for the women of the province of Alberta."[3]

The women who assembled at McClung's home had a broader vision of their political role. They stated their goals in terms that reflected both their newly granted political equality, and their desire to move beyond gender politics to focus on society as a whole:

It shall be our aim and constant endeavour to make such use of these privileges as shall best forward and conserve the interests of the public as a whole, rather than those which pertain either to party or sex.[4]

At this historic meeting the women formed a Provincial Laws Committee under the auspices of the provincial organization of the National Council of Women. Irene Parlby, a prominent spokeswoman for rural women, was unable to attend the meeting. Had she been present, one of the divisions that occurred between urban and rural women may have been prevented. Farm and country women viewed the local Councils of Women as urban based and often upper class organizations, not representative of rural needs and interests. Although not intended to divide women into interest groups with different political agendas, the strategy to organize the Laws Committee under the council did exactly that. It was formulated in an environment of a growing class consciousness of farm women. Their new motivation for political action was stimulated by the franchise victory as well as the growing political influence and concerns of the United Farmers of Alberta.

Other new political organizations were formed in the decade following enfranchisement. Despite the urging of many women to their sisters to retain "independence of thought" and nonpartisanship, the majority of these were party-allied organizations. Women who had worked together for common political goals now found themselves working against each other by affiliating with political parties. In the process, the party agenda took precedence over women's political reform goals. Women's Liberal Clubs were established in both Edmonton and Calgary. Calgary women created the Women's Labour League. Women's sections were created within the Dominion Labour Party's provincial organization and the Conservative Party. Nonpartisan groups were also formed for the purpose of political education and activity of their members. For example, branches of the Women's International League for Peace and Freedom were formed in both urban centres in the decade following the first World War, as was the Calgary Women's Political League.

The Political Education of Alberta Women

Some women activists were also acutely aware of the need to educate the new woman voter about her new responsibility as well as the issues of the day. In the years following the granting of suffrage, prominent women such as Emily Murphy, Cornelia Wood, Nellie McClung, and Irene Parlby, as well as journalists such as Francis Beynon, Miriam Allen de Ford, Eleanor Mack, and Margaret Donelly turned their attention to the political education of Alberta women. Speaking in 1916 to the opening of the Liberal Club in Edmonton South, Nellie McClung more clearly defined how women would use their votes, suggesting that they stay with the strategies and methods they had used as clubwomen and suffragists, influencing the political system from the outside:

> The great field for the new woman voter is not that of practical politics though nor does it concern the machinery of government. It is easy to get legislation when public sentiment is sufficiently strong, and it is in the education of public sentiment that the woman voter will be most in evidence I hope. . . . I can see that the great, independent unfettered body of women voters carefully studying the questions of human and social welfare, without bias, not looking for favours, or jobs, or preference, might become a factor in shaping the policies of governments, or in forming the platforms of oppositions.[5]

Miriam Allen de Ford appealed to young women voters in her column in the *Alberta Labour News*, urging them to interest themselves in legislation that had their welfare in view, and "to use their brains when they vote."[6] Francis Marion Beynon offered this practical instruction to women who read her page in the popular *Grain Grower's Guide:*

> the first obligation of the new citizen is to refuse to be swept off her feet by any of the silly shibboleths of party politicians. Since there are no really independent newspapers she ought at election time to read at least two and try to assess as accurately as possible as to the truth concerning the questions up for discussion. This is the ABC of good citizenship.[7]

Not all women were enthusiastic about the franchise, but they nevertheless received a political education through local newspapers and their participation in a variety of women's organizations. Emily Murphy, Nellie McClung, and Roberta MacAdams all addressed the Women's Canadian Club in Edmonton in the early 1920s urging them to take an interest in laws being passed, to read newspapers, and to keep abreast of current affairs, so that they may use their franchise intelligently.[8] Emily Murphy wrote an article for the Imperial Order of the Daughters of the Empire's (IODE) 1916 Yearbook entitled "The Use of the Franchise."[9] Reverend S.W. Fallis, in an address to the women at the annual meeting of the Calgary Young Women's Christian Association (YWCA) warned women against the dangers of party politics, and urged women "to make a study of conditions for themselves that they might vote as intelligent citizens."[10] Speaking to the newly formed Calgary Women's Political League in October 1921, Irene Parlby, newly elected member of the United Farmers of Alberta (UFA) government, suggested that "If we can give up looking at politics through the prejudiced eyes of old party politics, then you will have no trouble in getting women interested in the formation of a good government."[11]

Both the Alberta Women's Institutes and the Local Councils of Women set up active committees within their organizations to study and recommend legislation to address the social reforms needed, particularly those dealing with the concerns of women and children. One organization that appeared most earnest about the political education of its members was the United Farm Women of Alberta (UFWA). The success of organized women in urban centres in influencing the political system did not go unnoticed by farm women. Irene Parlby, in her report as president, spoke in 1916 to the UFWA:

> The passing of the Equal Franchise Bill, early in this year, along with other things, showed the necessity of mobilizing the forces of farm women. The women in towns were well organized in different societies, and keeping a keen and watchful eye on passing events and legislation. It is also just and right that farm women should also be organized as a class, that they may have the opportunity of expressing their views in regard to the legislation which may vitally affect their interests; also that by their united effort they may take their share in the building up of this new country. [12]

The UFWA not only encouraged women to develop knowledge and skills for participation in public affairs, they also gave their members opportunities to do so. The UFWA, through their locals and their annual conventions, disseminated knowledge of public institutions and services, provided training in parliamentary procedure and the conduct of meetings, and helped women to develop public speaking skills. In her president's report at the 1919 annual convention, Irene Parlby defined the organization's mission. "That most of us need a great deal of education along political lines is undoubted, and as we are likely to have both a provincial and federal election on our hands within the next year or two, this should probably be our chief line of work for the immediate future."[13] The political education focus of farm women was partly motivated by the political aspirations of the United Farmers of Alberta. By 1919 the UFA decided to enter electoral politics with a farmers' policy platform, both federally and in Alberta. The report of the Committee on Legislative Investigation, delivered by Mrs. O.S. Welch to the annual convention in 1920, reveals the expectations farm women held for themselves as political participants:

A great many women have declared themselves thoroughly disgusted with politics or not interested in politics and no time to bother with it. They are still thinking of politics in the worst old-time sense, bargaining politics. But they must have a cleaner and a higher meaning to us. We must realize what we can do in politics and begin at the right end. Politics should be met at our doorstep, in our own yard. . . . We must realize our individual responsibility and accept that responsibility. We must thoroughly understand every question that comes before us, and with this understanding only, can we give our assistance in improving conditions. With the right of franchise it is our duty to use our vote intelligently at every opportunity.[14]

The UFWA did not retreat from their political education program when the United Farmers of Alberta formed the government in 1921. S.E. Kiser, Chair of the Legislative Investigation Committee in that year, identified a "concern to build up a class of intelligent and enlightened workers from our own ranks and when a change in present laws or a new law is needed, we would feel satisfied that as an organization we were making no mistake in asking for same."[15]

The concern for the political education of the new woman voter generated an astonishing demonstration of interest and rhetoric by women across the province. Punctuated by idealism and good intentions, these new understandings would prove difficult to apply in the established system of party politics and government bureaucracy dominated by powerful men.

## Alberta Women Enter Political Campaigns

With the calling of the 1917 provincial election in Alberta, women seized the opportunity to participate in political meetings and campaigns as they never had before. Rallies and all candidates forums at which women were the majority of the audience were common. Women often spoke on behalf of candidates, as well as about issues and the women's vote. At a Conservative meeting in Edmonton during the 1917 campaign, Mrs. Macdonald declared "that women were anxious for the franchise . . . because it was hoped that women's influence would help to bring about better and more humane legislation, and that it would mean greater, cleaner and more economic administration."[16]

Cornelia Wood, speaking on the platform on behalf of a Liberal candidate, wound up a passionate plea to women voters with this statement:

Or shall we by the right of our common womanhood wake sufficiently from our indolence as to public affairs to say that our influence is going to be used at the polls to right many wrongs, to better many conditions, to give justice and ambition for one's country before personal greed and power.[17]

And Nellie McClung, who claimed nonpartisanship by speaking for all "good" candidates, but advocated a return of the Liberal party because of their record of legislation that improved women's status, made an appeal to women voters at a Liberal candidate's meeting in Calgary. The *Calgary Herald* reported: "Mrs McClung said she would not be disappointed in the spirit of helpfulness, good fellowship and orderliness which the women would bring into political life."[18] One of the real ironies of this period of political apprenticeship is that often women who were, by personal example, pioneering new political roles and new attitudes towards women's place in party politics were also those individuals, like Nellie McClung and Cornelia Wood, who asked women to remain impartial and fair-minded, and not fall prey to party politics. McClung's support of the Liberals while asking women to be nonpartisan did not go unnoticed. She was singled out for criticism, but she was not the only woman who advocated this precarious political stance. During the 1917 campaign, Alberta newspapers published letters from women who wondered how they were to carry out the contradictory message of "remaining independent" and at the same time being asked to support a particular party.

Nellie McClung was one of the most prominent female participants on political stages in the 1917 provincial campaign. She was also elected to the legislature, along with Irene Parlby, former president of the UFWA, in the 1921 campaign. The active role played by women in the 1917 election was of great concern to some women who believed that this activity was not in keeping with the ideal of womanhood. Eleanor Mack, writing in her columns in the *Calgary Herald*, was most critical:

> Party politics is a condition of affairs which the women have abhorred for many years. It is little wonder that everyone is amazed to find a few of the prominent women of the province sticking their fingers in the political pie for the present election. . . . Let the women stand afar off on the hills of independence and keep cool until the political fray has passed.[19]

The most apparent result of the first postsuffrage election campaign was the election of Louise McKinney and Roberta McAdams to the provincial legislature. Newspaper stories about the election noted the importance of this milestone to women in other countries. Its significance as a beacon of change of women's position in society was recognized by suffrage campaigners throughout the British Empire. For Alberta women, who had petitioned for suffrage since 1905 and played significant roles in building new communities throughout the province, the election of women to the legislature was an endorsement of their demonstrated abilities in public affairs. In some respects, the successful candidacies of McKinney and McAdams were predictable developments, given Alberta society's emerging attitudes toward women.

More telling, however, are the reasons for which both women won their electoral campaigns. Roberta McAdams seems at first an unlikely political candidate, and certainly seeking a seat in the legislature was not her idea. Her candidacy and campaign were engineered by another Alberta woman, Beatrice Naismith, who was employed at the time by the Alberta government in its London, England, office.

McAdams was stationed in England as a nursing sister, with the rank of lieutenant, and eligible to be elected to the legislature as one of the two representatives of Albertans serving overseas in the First World War. She typified the "New Woman" of the period: single, independent, and accomplished. In 1915 she left her career as a teacher of home economics in Edmonton to serve in the war effort as a hospital dietician. Her campaign platform was two-fold: to represent the families of war veterans and returning soldiers, for whom she felt she could speak; and to represent the "other voice," the voice of women in politics. The campaign slogan, created by Naismith, was "after you have voted for the man of your choice, give your other vote to the sister." Naismith's understanding of gender politics paid off, but equally important was the recognition by soldiers and other nurses that McAdams was a capable individual because of the abilities and sense of duty she had demonstrated in her war work.

If McAdams symbolized what was new about women and their place in society, the success of Louise McKinney's candidacy can be seen as symbolizing what was expected of a mature woman entering politics in 1917: she ran as an "independent" for the Non-Partisan League; she was a long time campaigner for suffrage, prohibition, and property rights for married women; and she was a living example of gracious Christian womanhood. In short, she was as an individual a true expression of the values and ideas of her time. She particularly represented the mood of the area in which she lived. Southern Alberta was the breeding ground for a new approach to politics, as farmers and ranchers there, many with American roots, were disaffected by the tactics and policies of the Liberal and Conservative parties. Both their experiences with other political alternatives and ideas in the United States, such as agrarian radicalism and the Non-Partisan League, and, in some cases, their lack of loyalty to Canadian political traditions, contributed to this region's political atmosphere. McKinney believed strongly, as did many suffragists, that in bringing their own point of view to the legislature, women would have a reforming influence on society and on politics. She was widely viewed as a person who stood for a set of principles at a time when the population was hungry for a more principled approach to politics.

The demands for women's political "purifying" role as well as for their abstention from partisan political activity were not just rhetoric of the suffrage campaign, but a reflection of society's views about women, their attributes, and their roles. It was a view slow to change, as appeals to women on election campaign platforms throughout the

1920s in Alberta demonstrate. Not all Alberta women then "seemed to stand more squarely on their feet than in the pedestal days" and "to have a new sense of responsibility of opportunities," as Mrs. F.F. McWilliams reported to the annual meeting of the National Council of Women of Canada in 1917.[20] But the belief about the impact of women's votes on the political system and the social order persisted, partly because it was supported by real evidence of women's increasing involvement in federal and provincial election campaigns. As Marion Sears, president of the UFWA, declared after the campaigns of 1921:

> I was wonderfully pleased with the intense and active interest that our women took everywhere in our provincial and federal campaigns. They showed a desire to cast an intelligent vote. . . . with the majority of women taking part, the type of candidate we often have will disappear, and in future our representatives will be chosen for their greater integrity, honesty and morality, as well as their ability. Women's house-cleaning propensities are going to be carried out in public life.[21]

The Political Apprenticeship of Alberta Women

Several features of the postsuffrage campaign period, 1916–30, are striking. One is the degree to which the old ways of influencing political decision-making were still viewed as the most appropriate. For Alberta women, this meant trying to maintain a united bloc vote as women, organizing it through their clubs and organizations, bringing pressure to bear on both government and opposition parties to achieve specific goals. The enduring belief in this strategy is found in the continued appeals to women to join together to influence the political system. Mrs. Sears (UFWA) urged city and country women to unite their strength on common ground:

> The aim of women's organizations of today should be to strengthen their forces so that they will have an influence on the legislation of the country. . . . Now that the women are enfranchised let them get busy and do what they can to make that enfranchisement of real value and something that will be of real service to our country and the good of humanity.[22]

Another reality was that women's clubs and organizations were not representative of the majority of Alberta women. Despite unprecedented growth in both the number and membership of women's organizations, they were still largely composed of well educated middle- and upper-class women. And although there was significant cross-fertilization and cooperation among many groups, the organizations were still characterized by class and special interest differences. Most difficult to overcome were the tensions between urban and farm women, based on the fundamental differences in their lifestyles. The ability to unite to win causes such as suffrage and prohibition obscured temporarily the divisions and differences within the women's community. New issues would make these divisions more apparent.

Women who chose to educate themselves politically by joining the traditional political parties were seen by some as betraying the interests of women and succumbing to the evils of corrupt party politics. There seemed to be a greater tolerance for women's involvement in the Non-Partisan League and the Labour Party, as both presented "nonpartisan" philosophies, despite their identification with class interests. Louise McKinney's election to the legislature in 1917 as a Non-Partisan member, for example, was seen as consistent with her personal "good" values and her public roles in temperance and suffrage campaigns. Roberta McAdams's candidacy appealed to the armed forces voters on the grounds that she was an "independent," that she was one of them, and she represented a special constituency rather than an established political party.

The idea of political neutrality was in direct conflict with other political realities. The party system, dominated by men, was alive and healthy in Alberta. Despite the significant role played by the Non-Partisan League in Alberta politics at the time, the choice for voters in 1917 was in most cases restricted to two parties: the Liberals and the Conservatives. The parties and the men who organized and represented them were essentially the same as they were before women achieved suffrage. Women's influence as voters was, with few exceptions, limited by the necessity to choose between two alternatives which some women found equally unacceptable. The entry of the United Farmers of Alberta into federal politics in 1919 and provincial politics in 1921 offered a fresh provincewide alternative. Built on the success of its forerunner, the Non-Partisan League, which elected two members from southern Alberta to the legislature in 1917, the UFA was an alternative that appeared to many to be politically independent. However, "nonpartisan" tended to mean "not Conservative or Liberal." Both the Non-Partisan League and the United Farmers of Alberta had definite platforms that favoured the farmer and supported a number of contentious issues such as the nationalization of banking and credit systems, abolition of the Canadian Senate and a compulsory national insurance scheme covering accident, illness, old age, and death. Non-Partisan candidates and UFA candidates did present themselves as "Independents," a label which had significant appeal to voters disenchanted with the established parties, which were identified with big business Eastern Canadian interests. Political "independence" came to be interpreted as freedom from both Eastern influence and from corrupt political practices. In the absence of voter statistics we can only speculate to what extent the votes of women who believed in political "independence" may have been responsible for the overwhelming success of the UFA in being elected to form its group government in 1921.

Despite the significant changes that had occurred in women's lives and outlooks as a result of their involvement in the prohibition and suffrage campaigns, in women's organizations, and in the war effort, the Victorian ideal of womanhood persisted. Women were already public persons, taking on new social and professional roles even before the Equal Suffrage Bill granted them equal political status with men. Francis Marion Beynon suggested that the standards expected of women voters, to be knowledgeable, pure, independent, and fair, were standards that many men had never been able to meet. In question was women's "special" role in politics. The Victorian notion of women's moral superiority and accompanying social responsibilities would gradually erode, as would women's belief in men's superior knowledge about political life.

For conscientious women activists, who fought long and hard for the right to participate as equals in the political system, the postsuffrage years were a painful period of transition. They had to confront the realities of a confused, uninformed, and often indifferent female electorate, the potency of the male dominated party structures, and the gradual realization that the old ways of organizing and lobbying might no longer be possible or effective. Nellie McClung recognized the difficulties of this transition during the 1921 provincial election campaign:

> The game of politics is new to women. We know what we want, but this method of achieving it is not so simple, nor so clear to us.

We are endeavouring to find the way. There are two ways before us:—One is to take things as we find them—and try to make them better, working with the tools already here, improving them as we can, never losing sight of the ideal, but using every means, imperfect though they may be. The other is to stand aloof from the real business of life, and cry out for what we want, howling and protesting against every evil, but refusing to take part in politics until everything has become ideal.[23]

Despite women's past political successes in organizing for prohibition and suffrage campaigns, the mystique of male politics remained intact. As Irene Parlby discovered in her campaign for political office in 1921, old prejudices about women's abilities survived. It was a difficult, personal campaign, with her opponents declaring that as she was a woman and inexperienced in politics, she was unfit to legislate.[24]

Even in this political climate, significant gains were made in women's access to political office and in their ability to influence legislators. Cornelia Wood, campaigning for the Liberals in 1926, assessed women's progress this way:

During the past nine years since equal franchise was granted, women have not been idle and much progress has been made. The study of political events and the entrance of women into Public Offices from Alderman, School Trustee up to M.P. has made a great many women capable of marking an intelligent ballot as the majority of men are capable of doing.[25]

Several writers of the period commented that the Alberta experience with the new female electorate was less of a failure than that experienced in other provinces. In her critical review article "Is Women's Suffrage a Fizzle?" Anne Anderson Perry wrote in 1928: "In Alberta ... much social legislation has been definitely furthered because of the urge of the women's vote."[26] Alberta women's new political activism was not as evident as some would have liked or anticipated it to be. In a biting article aimed at women voters in the 1930 election, Margaret Donelly commented:

In the present election campaign the ladies are conspicuous by their absence. It seems that the securing of the vote did not give women the proper place in society, and we are forgetting that the vote was not an end in itself, but only a means to an end, namely the bringing about of a new type of legislation. . . . Well, when the women want a bill, we turn it over to the men and they fix it up for men![27]

It is significant that women of this period did not measure the success of their political activities by how many women held office at each level of government. They recognized from experience that political influence could be organized and exerted in a variety of ways, and the success of their committees and clubs in political education, lobbying, and effecting real political change in Alberta should not be underestimated. As a result, after gaining the vote, Alberta women did not restrict themselves to the traditional party system. Perhaps this reflects women's orientation to politics as a means to accomplish specific goals, rather than as an end in itself. The potency of the disappointing lessons learned by women in party politics immediately after the vote was won may also be responsible. Women found themselves outsiders in the mainstream parties, not welcomed as equals, and relegated to performing secondary roles.

The new awareness women gained of the real limitations of any advance in formal equality is a bitter but significant accomplishment of Alberta women's political apprenticeship. Recognition that legal reform is a gain, but a limited one, full of contradictions which remain to be addressed, was a powerful and important lesson for women to learn. The wiser, more reflective and analytical viewpoints expressed in the late 1920s and into the 1930s by women prominent in the suffrage campaign reflect these difficult lessons. Mary Ellen Smith described it aptly in 1928: "so far we women have been pretty well chloroformed in politics but we ought now to refuse all anaesthetics."[28] And in 1936, Nellie McClung admitted, "I blush when I think of all the things we were going to do when we got the vote."[29] Despite the fact that they did not meet the idealistic expectations of the suffrage promoters, women of Alberta did not fail in their assertion of their new political rights. The political education and apprenticeship of Alberta women, however painful and disillusioning, was a tangible and significant outcome of the fourteen years following the achievement of female suffrage in Alberta.

*Nanci Langford* is a doctoral candidate in the Department of Sociology at the University of Alberta. Her research interests include the experiences of homesteading women on the prairies, the life and work of Louise McKinney, and theoretical approaches to analyses based on gender. She is currently writing a book on organized farm women in Alberta, entitled *Politics, Pitchforks and Pickle Jars*.

The author gratefully acknowledges the financial support of the Social Sciences and Humanities Research Council in preparing this article.

Notes
1. Helen Gregory MacGill, "Are Women Wanted in Public Life?" *Chatelaine* (September 1928), p. 50.
2. Veronica Strong-Boag, "'Ever a Crusader': Nellie McClung, First Wave Feminist," *Rethinking Canada: The Promise of Women's History* (Toronto: Copp Clark Pitman, 1986), p. 188.
3. *Edmonton Journal*, 19 March 1916.
4. Ibid.
5. *Edmonton Journal*, 31 March 1916.
6. Miriam Allen de Ford, "When a Girl Is Young," *Alberta Labour News* (Edmonton: 18 September 1920).
7. Francis Marion Beynon, "Wanted: A Sense of Responsibility," *Grain Growers Guide* (Winnipeg: 23 April 1917).
8. Elise Corbet, "Woman's Canadian Club of Calgary," *Alberta History* 25, no. 33, 1977.
9. Emily Murphy Papers, City of Edmonton Archives.
10. *Calgary Daily Herald*, 22 May 1917.
11. *Alberta Labour News* (Edmonton: 5 October 1921).
12. Irene Parlby, "Report of the President," *UFA Annual Report, 1916*, p. 23.
13. Irene Parlby, "Report of the President," *UFA Annual Report, 1919*, p. 81.
14. O. S. Welch, *UFA Annual Report 1920*, p. 109.
15. S. E. Kiser, *UFA Annual Report 1921*, p. 97.
16. *Edmonton Journal*, 29 May 1917.
17. Campaign speech on behalf of Frank Oliver, 1917 Provincial Election Campaign, Cornelia Wood's papers, Provincial Archives of Alberta.
18. *Calgary Daily Herald*, 4 June 1917.
19. Eleanor Mack, "A Word to Women Voters," *Calgary Daily Herald*, 23 May 1917.
20. *National Council of Women of Canada: The Year Book 1917–1918* (Toronto: National Council of Women of Canada, 1918), p. 13.
21. Marion L. Sears, "The Place of Women in Public Life," *UFA Annual Report 1921*, p. 111.
22. *Alberta Labour News* (Edmonton: 11 June 1921).
23. *Alberta Labour News* (Edmonton: 4 June 1921).
24. Una MacLean, "The Honourable Irene Parlby," *Alberta Historical Review* 7, no. 4 (1959).
25. Campaign speech, 1926, Cornelia Wood papers, Provincial Archives of Alberta.
26. Anne Anderson Perry, "Is Woman's Suffrage a Fizzle?" *Maclean's* (1 February 1928), pp. 59, 63.
27. Margaret Donelly, "What's the Matter with the Ladies?" *Alberta Labour News* (Edmonton: 14 June 1930).
28. Anne Anderson Perry, "Women Begin to Speak Their Minds," *Chatelaine* (September 1928), p. 50.
29. *Globe and Mail*, 13 November 1937.

LINDA TRIMBLE

# A Few Good Women

## Female Legislators in Alberta, 1972–1991

Do women make a difference in political office beyond fostering the democratic principle of self-governance? Studies have found that the sexual division of labour shapes women's values, perspectives, and patterns of social and political interaction.[1] Differences in life experience may also be manifested in the attitudes and rhetoric of political elites;[2] research conducted in the United States, Norway, and Canada indicates that female legislators are more likely to support the women's movement than their male counterparts and tend to have different policy preferences. Yet in all three countries female legislators are at times unwilling or unable to translate these preferences into action because their choices are inhibited by ideological and institutional factors such as party positions on gender equality goals, support for (or antipathy toward) women in the institutional environment, and the mechanics of the legislative process itself.

This article briefly reviews the relevant literature on the impact of women in legislative office. I argue that while female politicians in the United States have a certain amount of legislative freedom, their female counterparts in other countries often do not. In particular, institutional factors such as party discipline and parliamentary procedure act as significant impediments to women's representation in the Canadian case, as is illustrated by the province of Alberta. The statements and actions of female elected representatives in the Alberta

Legislative Assembly between 1972 and 1991 illustrate that a "critical mass" of female legislators is a necessary but not sufficient prerequisite for the development of a policy-making process which effectively takes gender into account and promotes the status of women. In the Canadian parliamentary system, the institutional constraints and opportunities confronting legislative women can be as important as the attitudes and motivations these women bring to public office. On the other hand, the Alberta case shows that "a few good women" can begin to challenge long-standing institutional norms, values, and practices.


Making a Difference?


Legislative women who support the goals of feminism can voice, and act on, these principles in three (overlapping) ways. First, they can articulate women's lived experience, by, for example, drawing attention to problems or concerns traditionally considered women's responsibility because of the sexual division of labour, such as child care and care of the elderly, or by raising examples of the double discrimination faced by disabled, visible minority, native, or lesbian women. Second, female legislators can take gender into account when commenting on legislation, from labour policy to fiscal and tax policy. The impact of policy choices on women and men can be analyzed at all stages of policy formation and legislative debate. Third, women in political office can demand or formulate public policies which will ameliorate sex-based discrimination and promote the social and economic status of women.

   Studies of women in legislative office in the United States and western European countries conducted in the 1970s found that women elected to political office tended not to make a difference beyond advancing the democratic principle of representation.[3] While female legislators were inclined to be sympathetic to feminism and the goals of the women's movement, women in political office seemed reluctant to act on these principles.[4] Such findings led sociologists and political scientists to introduce the concept of the "critical mass."[5] Rosabeth Moss Kanter discovered that when small numbers of women entered male-dominated fields they were treated as tokens; this finding led political scientists to conclude that women must comprise a significant proportion of legislators to be effective at the elite level.[6] Bystydzienski, based on the Norwegian experience, argues that "when female representation reaches at least fifteen percent it begins to make a difference."[7]

The "critical mass" hypothesis has been supported by recent studies in the United States and in Scandinavian countries. In legislatures where women comprise more than ten to fifteen percent of the total legislators they tend to stimulate discussion of issues related to the socioeconomic status of women; identify women's issues as legislative priorities; propose more legislation in women's interest areas than their male counterparts; and argue in support of feminist principles and objectives.[8] But a critical mass of women, even one which includes those committed to the goals of the women's movement, is not in and of itself a sufficient condition for feminist dialogue in legislative institutions. Skjeie's work on female legislators in Norway illustrates that gender differences in attitudes and preferences do not always manifest themselves in voting and other forms of parliamentary conduct.[9] As Skjeie states:

> While most women politicians want to make a difference, they do not want to act too differently. They use power strategies that create limited issue-specific alliances. But they avoid confrontations with male colleagues. Many seek to influence party viewpoints, but most do not challenge party priorities. . . . It is indeed difficult to maintain difference among peers.[10]

In other words, female politicians may sympathize with and support the women's movement. They are less likely to speak for women in the formal institutions of political power. And *acting for* women is quite another matter.

This conclusion is borne out in the Canadian case. In Canada, female delegates to party leadership conventions tend to be more sympathetic to feminism and its goals than male delegates.[11] But partisanship strongly affects the attitudes and behaviour of female political elites. For instance, Tremblay's survey of candidates for the 1988 provincial election in Québec found party affiliation to be as important as gender in shaping attitudes about the women's movement and the representative role of women.[12] Party was a better predictor of approval for the women's movement among Québec candidates, for instance.[13]

Even if female partisans support the women's movement, this is no guarantee that they will articulate, or act on, such views. For this reason we must ask what female legislators actually say and do in their legislative roles. Do they raise different issues from their male counterparts? Do they discuss generic issues in a woman-sensitive manner? There is little Canadian research which examines the actions and statements of women in the legislative arena, although the existing evidence supports the argument that female politicians tend to speak on behalf of women's equality. For example, Manon Tremblay found many female politicians in Québec express egalitarian and feminist ideas in their speeches before the National Assembly.[14]

Do female politicians also act for women? Tremblay and Boivin's study of House of Commons debates on abortion in July 1988 discovered female MPs were more likely to take a feminist position (pro-choice) than their male counterparts, but the gender differences were attenuated by party affiliation.[15] Parliamentarians in this case were allowed to speak and vote according to conscience rather than according to the party line. But free votes are few and far between in Canadian legislatures, and there are infrequent opportunities for legislators to act outside the purview of party discipline. Carroll reports that female legislators in the United States have the following strategies at their disposal: voting, developing legislation, influencing colleagues, and building coalitions.[16] Parliamentary behaviour in Canada is structured by parties and thus the approaches outlined by Carroll are unavailable to individual legislators. As well, because of the structure of parliamentary government, the opportunities open to governing party women will differ from those open to opposition party women.

In the parliament and legislatures of Canada, power is concentrated in the political executive—the prime minister or premier and his or her cabinet. In theory, the executive branch is responsible to the elected representatives of the people and must resign *en masse* if defeated on an important bill or on a motion of nonconfidence.[17] In practice, if the governing party enjoys a majority in the House or Assembly it has virtual *carte blanche* when it comes to introducing policy initiatives, and can easily resist attempts by the opposition parties to amend or block legislation. Because every motion is treated as a confidence matter, tight party discipline is exercised. The practice of voting along party lines is rarely violated, thus encouraging a highly organized and scripted contest between governing and opposition parties which is dominated by the party in power.[18] Party whips, in consultation with party leaders, determine who is allowed to speak during debates and Question Period, and assign committee roles and other parliamentary tasks. MPs and MLAs, therefore, do not act as "free agents" and the ability of political representatives to raise women's concerns is therefore largely determined by the willingness of the party to encourage this kind of discourse. If a party is unsympathetic to feminist demands its female members will have little recourse.[19]

What women say and do in the legislature will depend on where they sit. Women elected to serve with the governing party may be chosen as cabinet ministers, in which case they will have the opportunity to develop gender equality policies and influence their cabinet colleagues. Once policy decisions are reached in cabinet, the principle of cabinet solidarity holds; all cabinet ministers (indeed, all party members) must support the policy in public and in the legislature. Backbench women (members of the governing party who are not appointed to cabinet) can raise gender-related issues in caucus meetings but must toe the party line in the legislature by speaking on behalf of, and voting for, government bills and motions.

Party discipline is not quite as confining for opposition members because their parties are not defending specific policy programs; the task of the opposition is to criticize the government's policies. As a result opposition parties tend to exhibit more in-fighting and may even air fundamental differences of opinion. Opposition party women have more freedom to articulate feminist positions, as opposition parties generally eschew tight party platforms in favour of flexible responses to government actions. Opposition women can use debates and daily Question Period to attack the government on its program for women or to criticize legislation which is insensitive to gender differences. Daily Question Period is the most effective forum, but it is only forty-five minutes long; the lack of sufficient time for opposition to present its views means that many issues are either overlooked altogether or are not discussed thoroughly.[20] Opposition members can also introduce private member's bills, though these rarely if ever come to a vote. In sum, while opposition women have little chance to directly influence policy, they have more institutional "room," if their party is sympathetic, to raise gender equality issues in the legislature.

Legislative women of all partisan stripes can make a difference by redefining the role of the legislator. In other words, they may have an impact on process as well as on rhetoric. Rhetoric, or speech, refers to the *content* of legislative discourse. Process refers to the *style* of political action, the manner in which issues are raised and discussed, and conflicts settled. Since one of the goals of feminism is to challenge patriarchal structures and processes, the impact of women on the style of legislative debate is of vital importance.

Methodology

To determine whether a critical mass of women can make a difference within the parliamentary system, and to assess the extent to which factors such as institutional norms, party discipline, and legislative procedure provide opportunities or barriers, the Alberta legislative debates between 1972 and 1991 regarding women, gender equality issues, and policy issues of particular concern to women were examined. Both the quantity of legislative debates on status of women issues and the nature and direction of the debates were analyzed. Alberta Hansard entries on women and gender equality issues were tabulated from 1972 (the year Hansard was introduced) to 1991. Each reference by an MLA to an issue such as abortion, day care, midwifery, or immigrant women, was counted as one entry. (See Appendix for a full list of topics.) The data were analyzed by gender, party, and role in the party. As well, the debates themselves were read to determine whether or not the female MLAs employed a different analysis of women's issues and gender equality issues, and whether or not they adopted a different style of legislative debate.

The role and impact of women in the Alberta legislature between 1972 and 1991 are examined for two reasons. First, this time period spans years of low representation of women (less than five percent) as well as more recent sessions in which between twelve and sixteen percent of the MLAs were women (see Table 1). An analysis of women's legislative role over these two decades indicates whether the entry of significant numbers of women into elected office can change legislative debate. Secondly, the Alberta case study isolates two other important variables; party and role in the legislature. The Alberta legislature was dominated by one political party, the Progressive Conservative party (PCs or Tories), between 1971 and 1986. Opposition members only comprised eight percent of the MLAs in 1975, and the numbers dropped slightly as a result of the elections in 1979 (six percent) and 1982 (five percent). During this time period, all female legislators were members of the governing party, all refused to identify with the feminist movement, and few were in cabinet.

A new cohort of women was elected in 1986 and reelected in 1989. This contemporary group was dominated by government members but was distinguished by the introduction of several opposition women. After the 1986 election there were four opposition women and six governing party women; the 1989 election brought five opposition and eight governing party women into the legislature. The 1986 and 1989 elections also yielded sizable (for Alberta) legislative oppo-

*Table 1* Women MLAs in Alberta, 1917–89

| ELECTION YEAR | TOTAL SEATS | SEATS WON BY WOMEN | % WOMEN MLAs |
|---|---|---|---|
| 1917 | 58 | 2 | 3.4% |
| 1921 | 61 | 2 | 3.3% |
| 1926 | 61 | 1 | 1.6% |
| 1930 | 63 | 1 | 1.6% |
| 1935 | 63 | 2 | 3.2% |
| 1940 | 57 | 1 | 1.7% |
| 1944 | 57 | 3 | 5.3% |
| 1948 | 57 | 2 | 3.5% |
| 1952 | 60 | 2 | 3.3% |
| 1955 | 61 | 2 | 3.2% |
| 1959 | 65 | 4 | 6.2% |
| 1963 | 63 | 2 | 3.2% |
| 1967 | 65 | 1 | 1.5% |
| 1971 | 75 | 2 | 2.6% |
| 1975 | 75 | 2 | 2.6% |
| 1979 | 79 | 6 | 7.6% |
| 1982 | 79 | 6 | 7.6% |
| 1986 | 83 | 10 | 12.0% |
| 1989 | 83 | 13 | 15.7% |

Complied from Michael Palamarek, *Alberta Women in Politics: A History of Women and Politics in Alberta* (Report for Senator Martha Bielish, December 1989), Appendix C, and *Report of the Chief Electoral Officer on Alberta Elections 1905–1982.*

sitions; twenty-two opposition members in 1986 (26.5%) and twenty-four in 1989 (29%). Several of the new female MLAs are self-identified feminists and these women have introduced new ideas, and a new style, to the Alberta legislature.

## Women in the Alberta Legislature, 1971–85

Only two women were elected in 1971 and 1975, but both the 1979 and 1982 elections ushered six female MLAs into the legislature (see Table 2). These women were representatives of the governing party and did not identify with the women's movement; in a 1982 interview for *Chatelaine* all six Tory women serving in the Alberta legislature at the time stated that they did not consider themselves feminists.[21] As well, most were confined to the backbench, as Table 2 indicates.

## Table 2 Women Elected to the Alberta Legislature, 1971–86

| NAME | DATE ELECTED | ROLE IN THE LEGISLATURE |
|---|---|---|
| Hunley, Helen | 1971 | Minister Without Portfolio (1971–73) Solicitor General (1973–75) |
| | 1975 | Minister of Social Services and Community Health (1975–79) |
| Chichak, Catherine | 1971 1975 1979 | Backbencher (1971–86) |
| Le Messurier, Mary | 1979 1982 | Minister of Culture (1979–86) |
| Osterman, Connie | 1979 1982 | Backbencher (1979–82) Minister of Consumer and Corporate Affairs (1982–86) |
| Embury, Sheila | 1979 1982 | Backbencher (1979–86) |
| Cripps, Shirley | 1979 1982 | Backbencher (1979–86) |
| Fyfe, Myrna | 1979 1982 | Backbencher (1979–86) |
| Koper, Janet | 1982 | Backbencher (1979–86) |

Compiled from Michael Palamarek, *Alberta Women in Politics: A History of Women and Politics in Alberta* (Report for Senator Martha Bielish, December 1989), pp. 170–73.

Issues of concern to women were merely touched upon in legislative debate between 1972 and 1978, when only two members of the Assembly were women. As Table 3 indicates, women and women's issues were barely mentioned in 1974—there were sixteen entries in the Hansard index—while in 1972, 1973, 1975, and 1976, thirty or so entries was the norm. Given that there are thousands of entries in the index for any given legislative session, and hundreds for most topics, the amount of attention given to women's concerns was indeed tiny. In 1978, the Matrimonial Property Act was passed, thereby accounting for the increased attention to gender-related issues in that session, which featured ninety-eight entries. Table 3 also shows that women's concerns and gender equality issues between 1972 and 1978 were not, for the most part, raised or discussed by women. Female MLAs were responsible for, on average, fourteen percent of the entries during this period.

The 1979 election brought four more women into the Legislative Assembly, and discussion of women's issues increased, but the two facts are seemingly unrelated, as Table 3 shows. While the number of

*Table 3* Alberta Hansard Entries on Women and Gender Equality
Issues per Year and by Sex, 1972–85

| YEAR (*= ELECTION) | % WOMEN MLAs | TOTAL ENTRIES | ENTRIES BY SEX Female (%) | Male (%) |
|---|---|---|---|---|
| 1972 | 2.6% | 32 | 2 (7%) | 30 (94%) |
| 1973 | 2.6% | 32 | 8 (25%) | 24 (75%) |
| 1974 | 2.6% | 16 | Data Not Available** | |
| 1975* | 2.6% | 37 | 6 (16%) | 31 (84%) |
| 1976 | 2.6% | 36 | 4 (21%) | 32 (79%) |
| 1977 | 2.6% | 63 | 8 (13%) | 55 (87%) |
| 1978 | 2.6% | 98 | 12 (12%) | 86 (88%) |
| 1979* | 7.6% | 63 | 9 (14%) | 54 (86%) |
| 1980/81 | 7.6% | 122 | 23 (20%) | 99 (81%) |
| 1981/82* | 7.6% | 76 | 14 (18%) | 62 (82%) |
| 1983 | 7.6% | 138 | 27 (20%) | 111 (80%) |
| 1984 | 7.6% | 196 | 32 (16%) | 164 (84%) |
| 1985 | 7.6% | 141 | 21 (15%) | 120 (85%) |

** Names were not provided in the 1974 index.

entries on women and gender equality issues increased after 1978 (ranging from 63 entries in 1979 to 196 in 1984) the percentage of entries attributed to female MLAs remained about the same— between fourteen percent and twenty percent, with an average of seventeen percent. In 1984, Tory backbencher Eric Musgreave tabled a series of motions regarding the creation of an advisory council on women's issues. These motions largely account for the higher number of Hansard entries in 1984 (196), as in the ensuing debate a wide variety of gender-related issues were raised.

## Who Was Speaking about Women's Issues in the Legislature?

As Tables 4 and 5 indicate, discussion of issues like equal pay, maternity leave, and abortion was dominated by male members of the opposition parties and the governing party. Governing party men accounted for forty-seven percent of the entries in 1972 and well over fifty percent of the entries in subsequent years; on average, men in the Conservative party uttered sixty-seven percent of the comments made about women and gender equality issues in the legislature. Table 5

*Table 4* Alberta Hansard Entries on Women and Gender Equality
        Issues by Party, 1972–85

| YEAR | TOTAL ENTRIES | GOVERNING PARTY PC (%) | OPPOSITION PARTIES | | | |
|---|---|---|---|---|---|---|
| | | | Social Credit (%) | New Democratic (%) | Independent/ Representative (%) | Liberal (%) |
| 1972 | 32 | 15 (47%) | 16 (50%) | 1 (3%) | 0 (0%) | 0 (0%) |
| 1973 | 32 | 22 (69%) | 10 (31%) | 0 (0%) | 0 (0%) | 0 (0%) |
| 1974 | 16 | | Data Not Available* | | | |
| 1975 | 37 | 20 (54%) | 8 (22%) | 5 (14%) | 4 (11%) | 0 (0%) |
| 1976 | 36 | 19 (53%) | 11 (30%) | 2 (6%) | 4 (11%) | 0 (0%) |
| 1977 | 63 | 39 (62%) | 21 (33%) | 2 (3%) | 1 (2%) | 0 (0%) |
| 1978 | 98 | 70 (71%) | 20 (20%) | 5 (5%) | 3 (3%) | 0 (0%) |
| 1979 | 63 | 47 (75%) | 9 (14%) | 7 (11%) | 0 (0%) | 0 (0%) |
| 1980/81 | 122 | 94 (77%) | 16 (13%) | 11 (9%) | 1 (8%) | 0 (0%) |
| 1981/82 | 76 | 54 (70%) | 9 (12%) | 9 (12%) | 4 (5%) | 0 (0%) |
| 1983 | 138 | 107 (78%) | 2 (1%) | 24 (17%) | 5 (4%) | 0 (0%) |
| 1984 | 196 | 145 (74%) | 0 (0%) | 38 (19%) | 13 (7%) | 0 (0%) |
| 1985 | 141 | 102 (72%) | 0 (0%) | 33 (23%) | 6 (4%) | 0 (0%) |

* Names were not provided in the 1974 index.

indicates that, with the exception of the 1983 and 1984 sessions, male cabinet ministers were more vocal than male backbenchers. Opposition MLAs were collectively responsible for more entries than were the female MLAs; between 1972 and 1985 they accounted for an average of thirty-one percent of the statements while female MLAs accounted for an average of sixteen percent of the statements.

Clearly, female MLAs did not often raise issues of concern to women in the legislature. Male members of the opposition occasionally asked the government questions about its response to the 1970 *Report of the Royal Commission on the Status of Women* and issues like employment equity and wife battering.[22] The Tory women were not outspoken on these matters, and confined their remarks, for the most part, to statements of support for their party's policies. An analysis of the debates themselves shows that the Conservative women only spoke about gender equality in response to motions or questions from the opposition or government backbenchers.[23]

The fact that the female MLAs were all on the government side of the chamber limited their ability to represent women's concerns, how-

*Table 5* Alberta Hansard Entries Per Year on Women and Gender Equality Issues by Role in Governing Party and Sex, 1972–85

| YEAR | PC TOTAL ENTRIES | TOTAL FEMALE (%) | ROLE IN GOVERNING PARTY | | | | |
|---|---|---|---|---|---|---|---|
| | | | Backbenchers | | Cabinet Members | | Premier |
| | | | Male (%) | Female (%) | Male (%) | Female (%) | (Male) (%) |
| 1972 | 15 | 2 (13%) | 4 (26.5%) | 1 (6.5%) | 8 (53%) | 1 (6.5%) | 1 (6.5%) |
| 1973 | 22 | 8 (36%) | 2 (9%) | 3 (13.5%) | 12 (54.5%) | 5 (23%) | 0 (0%) |
| 1974 | | | Data Not Available* | | | | |
| 1975 | 20 | 6 (30%) | 8 (40%) | 0 (0%) | 6 (30%) | 6 (30%) | 0 (0%) |
| 1976 | 19 | 4 (21%) | 3 (16%) | 0 (0%) | 11 (58%) | 4 (21%) | 1 (5%) |
| 1977 | 39 | 8 (20.5%) | 8 (20.5%) | 1 (2.5%) | 31 (56.5%) | 7 (18%) | 1 (2.5%) |
| 1978 | 70 | 12 (17%) | 23 (33%) | 8 (11.5%) | 34 (48.5%) | 4 (6%) | 1 (1%) |
| 1979 | 47 | 9 (19%) | 12 (26%) | 7 (15%) | 23 (49%) | 2 (4%) | 3 (6%) |
| 1980/81 | 94 | 23 (24%) | 31 (33%) | 23 (24.5%) | 39 (41.5%) | 0 (0%) | 1 (1%) |
| 1981/82 | 54 | 14 (26%) | 16 (29.5%) | 13 (24%) | 24 (44.5%) | 1 (2%) | 0 (0%) |
| 1983 | 107 | 27 (25%) | 43 (40%) | 24 (22.5%) | 35 (32.5%) | 3 (3%) | 2 (2%) |
| 1984 | 145 | 32 (22%) | 59 (41%) | 32 (22%) | 54 (37%) | 0 (0%) | 0 (0%) |
| 1985 | 102 | 21 (20%) | 34 (33%) | 19 (19%) | 47 (46%) | 2 (2%) | 0 (2%) |

* Names were not provided in the 1974 index.

ever tentatively. The powerbrokers in the ruling Conservative party refused to recognize all but the most egregious examples of gender-based discrimination. In the period between 1971 and 1986, the Conservatives created few policies designed to help women: 1977 labour regulations offering eighteen week unpaid maternity leave after one year in the job; the Matrimonial Property Act of 1979 which provided a more equitable distribution of marital assets after divorce; and the 1983 Widow's Pension Act. The Individual Rights Protection Act, passed in 1973, provided little help to women; for instance, it did not protect pregnant working women, who could be fired without recourse.[24]

Gender equality issues were unimportant to the government of the day for two reasons: first, they were tangential to the Conservatives' main purpose, which was supporting the oil and gas industry and defending provincial jurisdiction over resource pricing and sales; secondly, the political executive believed equality was achieved by guaranteeing formal, legal equality in the Bill of Rights.[25] Hugh Horner, the deputy premier, stated in a 1976 speech to a women's group, "We have equality in Alberta." He went on to say that women did not need or want "special protection" and could "take care of themselves."[26]

The legislative debates reveal that the Tory women distanced themselves from the feminist movement while cautiously supporting some of its goals. Helen Hunley's 1972 statement to the legislature regarding feminism provides a perfect example:

> I'm not exactly a Women's Lib type myself. I haven't burned anything but the garbage for years, but I am concerned about the role of women in today's society. . . . Most of us do not expect special consideration. We only wish to get full marks for talents, ideas and capabilities that we have. And we insist we have a right to contribute according to those capabilities. It is my firm intention to aid, abet and encourage other women to take their rightful place in society.[27]

When given an opportunity to speak about gender equality without challenging party policy, some of the Conservative women did point out problems faced by women in the labour force as well as in the household. This is illustrated by the lengthy debate about the establishment of an provincial advisory council on the status of women. Some Alberta women began lobbying for a council in the early 1970s, but through the 1970s and early 1980s the government's position was a firm "no." Helen Hunley, the only woman in the cabinet from 1971 to 1979, was the government spokesperson on this issue and delivered the negative response.[28] In 1981 a very persistent lobbying effort by women's groups in the province began, supported by Eric Musgreave, a Tory backbencher who, in 1984, tabled several motions urging the creation of a council. Two of the six female MLAs, Sheila Embury and Shirley Cripps, refused to support the motion, as they felt women already had access to all government departments and agencies and were well served by the Women's Bureau and its successor, the Women's Secretariat.[29] Yet in her comments, Shirley Cripps discussed the role of women on the farm and the need for pension plan reform,[30] and Sheila Embury raised the issue of shelters for battered women.[31] Janet Koper and Myrna Fyfe spoke in favour of the motion to create a council. Fyfe said this:

> To comment on the views of the Member for Calgary Mountain View and his concern about the extreme views of feminists, I would like to suggest that although I'm not going to agree with the

### Table 6 Women Opposition MLAs in Alberta, 1986–93,* by Party and Term in Office

| NAME | PARTY | TERM |
|---|---|---|
| Barrett, Pam | ND | 1986–93 |
| Laing, Marie | ND | 1986–93 |
| Mjolsness, Christie | ND | 1986–93 |
| Hewes, Bettie | Liberal | 1986–93 |
| Gagnon, Yolande | Liberal | 1989–93 |

Compiled from Michael Palamarek, *Alberta Women in Politics: A History of Women and Politics in Alberta* (Report for Senator Martha Bielish, December 1989), pp. 170–73.
* The government of Alberta called an election in 1993.

views of many feminists, I respect the fact that feminists who have taken some extreme positions also deserve credit because of what they bring forward in the thought process. . . . As a consequence, attitudes have changed. . . . I think this motion is certainly worthy of support.[32]

Janet Koper took the opportunity to discuss the thirty-two cent wage gap between men and women and the concentration of women in temporary, part-time, and dead-end jobs.[33]

Given the opportunity—the "safe" context of legislative debate of a motion which had no chance of being brought to a vote—Conservative women in the backbenches did speak to women's concerns while distancing themselves from feminism and the women's movement. It was opposition party *men* who queried the government about such issues as day care, abortion services, emergency shelters, and maternity leave and governing party *men* who dominated the debate about these issues.

### Women in the Alberta Legislature, 1986–91

The 1986 and 1989 Alberta elections significantly increased the representation of women, and opposition parties, in the legislature. Ten women were elected to the eighty-three-member legislature in 1986 (three ND, one Liberal, six PC) and thirteen won seats in 1989 (three ND, two Liberal, eight PC). By 1989 all but one of the female MLAs was new to the legislature; only Connie Osterman remained. (See Tables 6 and 7).

## Table 7 Women Governing Party MLAs by Role and Term in Office, 1986–93

| NAME | ROLE IN THE LEGISLATURE | TERM |
|---|---|---|
| Betkowski, Nancy | Minister of Education | 1986–89 |
| | Minister of Health | 1989–92 |
| | Backbencher[+] | 1992–93 |
| McCoy, Elaine | Minister of Consumer and Corporate Affairs | 1986–89 |
| | Minister Responsible for Women's Issues | 1987–92 |
| | Minister of Labour | 1989–92 |
| | Backbencher[+] | 1992–93 |
| Osterman, Connie | Minister of Social Services | 1986–89 |
| | Minister of Career Development and Employment | 1989–92 |
| McClellan, Shirley | Backbencher | 1987–89* |
| | Associate Minister of Agriculture | 1989–92 |
| | Minister of Health | 1992–93 |
| Mirosh, Diane | Backbencher | 1986–92 |
| | Minister of Community Development | 1992–93 |
| | Minister Responsible for Women's Issues[++] | 1992–93 |
| Black, Pat | Backbencher | 1986–92 |
| | Minister of Energy | 1992–93 |
| Calahasen, Pearl | Backbencher | 1986–93 |
| Cripps, Shirley | Associate Minister of Agriculture | 1986–89 |
| Koper, Janet | Backbencher | 1982–88** |
| Laing, Bonnie | Backbencher | 1986–93 |

Compiled from Michael Palamarek, *Alberta Women in Politics: A History of Women and Politics in Alberta* (Report for Senator Martha Bielish, December 1989), pp. 170–73 and *The Edmonton Journal*, 1992–93.

[+] Premier Don Getty resigned in 1992 and Ralph Klein was elected party leader and premier in December 1992. Nancy Betkowski and Elaine McCoy, who also ran for the leadership, were not chosen by the new premier to sit in cabinet.

* Shirley McClellan was elected in a 1987 by-election.

[++] Diane Mirosh is also Minister Responsible for Culture and Multiculturalism, the Citizenship and Heritage Secretariat, Seniors, and Recreation.

** Janet Koper passed away in 1988.

*Table 8* Alberta Hansard Entries on Women and Gender Equality
  Issues per Year and by Sex, 1986–91

| YEAR (*= ELECTION) | % WOMEN MLAs | TOTAL ENTRIES | ENTRIES BY SEX | |
|---|---|---|---|---|
| | | | Female (%) | Male (%) |
| 1986* | 12% | 368 | 185 (50%) | 183 (50%) |
| 1987 | 12% | 313 | 155 (50%) | 158 (50%) |
| 1988 | 12% | 549 | 270 (49%) | 279 (51%) |
| 1989* | 15.7% | 250 | 152 (61%) | 98 (39%) |
| 1990 | 15.7% | 331 | 188 (57%) | 143 (43%) |
| 1991 | 15.7% | 237 | 137 (58%) | 100 (42%) |

*Table 9* Alberta Hansard Entries on Women and Gender Equality
  Issues by Party, 1986–91

| YEAR | TOTAL ENTRIES | GOVERNING PARTY PC (%) | OPPOSITION PARTIES | | | |
|---|---|---|---|---|---|---|
| | | | Social Credit (%) | New Democratic (%) | Independent/ Representative (%) | Liberal (%) |
| 1986 | 368 | 174 (47%) | 0 (0%) | 136 (37%) | 1 (.3%) | 57 (16%) |
| 1987 | 313 | 154 (49%) | 0 (0%) | 84 (27%) | 8 (3%) | 67 (21%) |
| 1988 | 549 | 243 (44%) | 0 (0%) | 204 (37%) | 2 (.4%) | 100 (18%) |
| 1989 | 250 | 132 (53%) | 0 (0%) | 97 (39%) | 0 (0%) | 20 (8%) |
| 1990 | 331 | 172 (52%) | 0 (0%) | 120 (36%) | 0 (0%) | 39 (12%) |
| 1991 | 237 | 113 (48%) | 0 (0%) | 80 (34%) | 0 (0%) | 44 (19%) |

As we can see from Tables 8 and 9, the appearance of a legislative opposition and the addition of several women to the Legislative Assembly are associated with the increased number of Hansard entries on gender equality and women's issues. There were more than double the number of entries in 1986 (368) than in 1985 (141), and in 1988 a record 549 entries were counted. As well, fifty percent or more of the entries are attributed to women, as compared with an average of sixteen percent between 1972 and 1985. And whereas discussion of gender equality issues was previously dominated by the governing party (on average, sixty-seven percent of entries were attributed to the PCs), after 1986 the Conservatives were responsible for forty-four percent to fifty-two percent of the entries. This is not surprising given the appearance, in 1986, of a good-sized opposition. The Liberals and

*Table 10* Alberta Hansard Entries Per Year on Women and Gender
Equality Issues by Role in Governing Party and Sex, 1986–91

| YEAR | PC TOTAL ENTRIES | TOTAL FEMALE (%) | ROLE IN GOVERNING PARTY | | | | Premier (Male) (%) |
|---|---|---|---|---|---|---|---|
| | | | Backbenchers | | Cabinet Members | | |
| | | | Male (%) | Female (%) | Male (%) | Female (%) | |
| 1986 | 174 | 59 (34%) | 29 (17%) | 25 (14%) | 85 (49%) | 34 (19.5%) | 1 (.5%) |
| 1987 | 154 | 62 (40%) | 19 (12%) | 8 (5%) | 70 (46%) | 54 (35%) | 3 (2%) |
| 1988 | 243 | 91 (37%) | 44 (18%) | 5 (2%) | 77 (32%) | 86 (36%) | 30 (12%) |
| 1989 | 132 | 59 (45%) | 15 (11%) | 10 (8%) | 51 (39%) | 49 (37%) | 7 (5%) |
| 1990 | 172 | 60 (35%) | 18 (10%) | 3 (2%) | 89 (52%) | 57 (33%) | 5 (3%) |
| 1991 | 113 | 37 (33%) | 8 (7%) | 2 (2%) | 63 (56%) | 35 (31%) | 5 (4%) |

New Democrats (NDs) have had equal billing with the Conservatives
since 1986, with the New Democrats responsible for thirty percent to
thirty-nine percent of the entries and the Liberals accountable for
eight percent to twenty percent.

Tables 10, 11 and 12 indicate a significant gender difference between
the governing and opposition parties. Female MLAs accounted for
slightly over a third of the Conservative entries, with the exception of
1989, when the percentage was forty-five percent. Well over half of
the opposition party entries are attributed to women (fifty-five percent to eighty-two percent for New Democrat women and fifty-eight
percent to seventy-seven percent for Liberal women). Between 1986
and 1991 opposition women clearly took a leading role in their parties
with respect to gender equality issues.

Conservative women from 1986 to 1991 were more vocal than their
predecessors (prior to 1986) but there were only four women in cabinet during this time period, and cabinet ministers dominate legislative discussion. Indeed, female cabinet ministers uttered the majority
of the statements by Conservative women on status of women issues.
Between 1987 and 1991, they were responsible for eighty-seven percent to ninety-five percent of the entries by PC women. Table 10
shows the minor role played by backbench women in the Conservative party, who account for between two percent and eight percent of
PC entries between 1987 and 1991. The exception was 1986, when
backbenchers were responsible for forty-two percent of entries by PC
women, largely due to the efforts of Janet Koper, who was quite vocal
on a number of issues and introduced a motion to encourage workplace day care.

*Table 11* Alberta Hansard Entries per Year on Women and Gender
Equality Issues by Opposition ND Party and Sex, 1986–91

| YEAR | ND TOTAL ENTRIES | FEMALE MLAs (%) | MALE | |
|---|---|---|---|---|
| | | | MLAs (%) | Leader* (%) |
| 1986 | 136 | 89 (65%) | 42 (31%) | 5 (4%) |
| 1987 | 84 | 49 (58%) | 25 (30%) | 10 (12%) |
| 1988 | 204 | 112 (55%) | 81 (40%) | 11 (5%) |
| 1989 | 97 | 79 (81.5%) | 17 (17.5%) | 1 (1%) |
| 1990 | 120 | 98 (82%) | 13 (11%) | 9 (7%) |
| 1991 | 80 | 65 (81%) | 9 (11%) | 6 (8%) |

* Grant Notley led the New Democrats until his death in a plane crash in 1984. Ray
Martin succeeded Notley.

*Table 12* Alberta Hansard Entries per Year on Women and Gender
Equality Issues by Opposition Liberal Party and Sex, 1986–91

| YEAR | LIB. TOTAL ENTRIES | FEMALE MLAs (%) | MALE | |
|---|---|---|---|---|
| | | | MLAs (%) | Leader* (%) |
| 1986 | 57 | 33 (58%) | 18 (32%) | 6 (10%) |
| 1987 | 67 | 42 (63%) | 14 (21%) | 11 (16%) |
| 1988 | 100 | 62 (62%) | 24 (24%) | 14 (14%) |
| 1989 | 20 | 14 (70%) | 5 (25%) | 1 (5%) |
| 1990 | 39 | 27 (69%) | 8 (21%) | 4 (10%) |
| 1991 | 44 | 34 (77%) | 7 (16%) | 3 (7%) |

* Nick Taylor led the Liberals until 1986 (including the 1986 legislative session), when
Laurence Decore won the party's leadership contest in October.

To summarize, the data show that between 1986 and 1991 the interests and concerns of women were raised more frequently in the legislature than in the previous period (1972–85); women's issues were
discussed *by women,* who were responsible for over half of the entries;
opposition women were much more vocal than governing party
women; opposition party women were much more likely to speak to
women's concerns than their male counterparts; and women on the
Conservative backbench were virtually silent about gender equality.

Increased discussion of women's concerns in the legislature is partially attributable to the changed climate for female politicians, as
contemporary female MLAs enjoy widespread public acceptance of
women's role in the political arena. A 1991 survey of Albertans found

85% of respondents strongly agreed with the statement "It makes no difference to me whether a candidate for public office is male or female."[34] As well, there is broad public support for the women's movement; for example, 1984 survey data showed that eighty-five percent of women and eighty percent of men agreed that more should be done for women's rights in Canada.[35] The changed climate makes it easier for female political elites to advocate gender equality. While female legislators in the 1970s and early 1980s eschewed any association with feminism and the women's movement, a few contemporary female MLAs did not hesitate to identify themselves as feminists. Both Marie Laing and Pam Barrett of the New Democrats saw "themselves as feminists and campaigned vigorously on the women's issues platform."[36] The third ND MLA, Christie Mjolsness, did not receive as much press coverage as her colleagues, but her statements in the legislature illustrated a feminist approach and a strong interest in high quality child care.[37] The ND women were joined by Liberal MLA Bettie Hewes, who was vocal about a wide range of gender equality issues, including after school child care, employment equity, women's health, women in the public service, and pay equity.

The Conservative women were notably more cautious about being associated with feminism. As we will see, some backbench Tory women are more aptly labeled antifeminists. Female cabinet ministers with high-profile portfolios, Elaine McCoy and Nancy Betkowski, were more progressive in their views,[38] but did not identify strongly with the women's movement and its goals. While she was a cabinet minister, Elaine McCoy refused to be termed a feminist when queried by the press, but called herself an "advocate for women."[39] Nancy Betkowski told a reporter, rather ambiguously, that she considered herself to be a feminist "in the sense that women have choices."[40] Yet she told the legislature in 1986: "I am a very active advocate for women's issues and women's rights."[41]

The entry of a few feminist women into the legislature in 1986 had a significant impact on the content and style of legislative debate. Opposition women between 1986 and 1991 were willing to speak and act for women in three ways: by articulating women's unique experiences; by taking gender into account when discussing public policy of all types; and by demanding policies designed to eliminate sex-based discrimination and promote the status of women. Governing party backbenchers tended to say very little, and when they did speak they often promoted patriarchal ideas and structures (such as the traditional family). Cabinet women discussed gender issues in response to queries from the opposition.

An analysis of the content of the debates shows that, in general, opposition party women, supported by their male colleagues, used Question Period and debates to quiz the government about a variety of issues, especially day care standards, pay equity, and government support for battered women's shelters. Opposition party members formed a united front against the government, taking very close positions on issues and offering similar criticisms of government actions and legislation. The opposition parties saw the Tories as vulnerable on women's issues and sought to score political points by pointing out government inaction. For example, in the debate about the spring 1988 budget estimates, the opposition led their attack with a critique of government funding for the Women's Secretariat, the Advisory Council on Women's Issues, and battered women's shelters.[42] Both opposition parties were critical of the government's negative stance on pay equity and its rather vague commitment to protect and enhance "the family unit."

The debates also show that opposition party women took a leadership role on gender equality issues by speaking first on these issues during debates and querying cabinet ministers about them during Question Period. As well, opposition women introduced feminist analysis of broader issues, such as labour legislation and health care policy. For example, in an 1988 debate regarding changes to labour legislation, New Democrat Marie Laing and Liberal Bettie Hewes led the debate by criticizing the bill for failing to take women's differential participation in the paid work force into account.[43] Other members of the opposition, including ND leader Ray Martin, followed suit, echoing the points made by Laing and Hewes.

Marie Laing, in particular, challenged traditional assumptions about gender roles and spoke eloquently about the plight of women, especially those abused by their partners. In her comments about the 1986 Speech from the Throne, which stressed the importance of family values and spoke of the family unit as the cornerstone of society, Laing said:

> When I hear about the value placed on the family, I reflect upon the fact that the most dangerous place in this society for women and children is the family. One in ten wives is battered. Where else can a woman be that the odds for assault are so high?[44]

Laing's statements were not accepted calmly by government members. In 1988, for example, Tory backbencher Stockwell Day deemed Laing's remarks about women in the work force and child care "irresponsible" and accused Laing of "browbeating" members of the Assembly.[45] On another occasion, Laing reminded the legislature that when she spoke about rape a government member laughed; "Other times members have talked . . . and joked around when I have spoken, as if in shutting out the information I talk about, they can deny it."[46]

Indeed, the clearly feminist stance taken by Laing, Barrett, Mjolsness, and Hewes, and supported by some of their male colleagues, represented a radical departure from the traditional view of women and the family held by many government members of the legislature, including the premier at the time, Don Getty.[47] Discussions about pay equity reveal this disjunction. The Conservatives supported equal pay for the same work but argued that equal pay for work of equal value is too costly and difficult to implement.[48] More importantly, the Tories asserted that because women make different educational and career choices, pay equity policy is misguided. For example, a Tory backbencher said that equal pay "might very well destroy women's initiative" by encouraging women "to remain in traditionally female jobs and not [to] try to compete for equal status in the workforce."[49] Opposition members, on the other hand, saw the wage gap as evidence of systemic discrimination and viewed pay equity policy as an important step toward addressing women's poverty.[50] The Liberals and NDs introduced pay equity bills in the legislature,[51] and during her presentation of such a bill in 1987, Marie Laing stated:

> To argue, as some do, that we cannot afford the cost of equal pay is to imply that women have a duty to be less well paid until other financial priorities are accommodated. This is absolutely unacceptable in a society committed to equity, fairness and justice. The gender-based wage gap is nothing more than discrimination on the basis of sex and is fundamentally wrong.[52]

Many members of the governing Conservative party supported the 1950s-style nuclear family, complete with stay-at-home mom, and resisted measures designed to promote women's equitable labour force participation.[53] Mr. Getty described his government's "family initiative" this way in 1988: "Our initiative is to strengthen the family, to provide reasons why the family is stronger, why mothers will stay in the house, in the family, while not having care outside the house."[54] The next day, when questioned by ND leader Ray Martin about his stance on the family, Getty clarified: "When I talk about a mother being one who cares for the home, I want to make it very clear that I believe that a home is hardly a home without a mother. You cannot replace a mother in a home."[55] Two female backbenchers shared Mr. Getty's view. Diane Mirosh stated in the legislature, " . . . Ninety percent of women still enjoy being at home, raising a family. . . . They do want to go back to the home and promote the family unit."[56] Shirley McClellan blamed feminism for denigrating homemakers: "What's evident now is that feminism overlooked the contributions of parents who chose to stay home and raise their children."[57] There was an outspoken antifeminist contingent in the governing Progressive Conservative party which included female members of the caucus.[58]

The Tories were not united in this view, however; in fact, the Alberta government was quite divided on women's issues between 1986 and 1991. While many members of the government asserted the primacy of traditional families, some Tories, including cabinet ministers Nancy Betkowski and Elaine McCoy, saw a need for policies designed to promote the full participation of women in the paid labour force.[59] In theory, the governing party should stand as an indivisible team, protecting itself from an "organized, institutionalized opposition bent on demonstrating the inappropriateness and inefficiencies of government policy."[60] While it is not entirely unusual for party members to disagree, it is rare for disagreements to occur among cabinet members, as has been the case in Alberta. There were well-publicized cabinet disputes about abortion and the mandate of the Alberta Advisory Council on Women's Issues, and not-so-public debates about pay equity, homemaker's pensions, and day care subsidies.[61] Female cabinet ministers Elaine McCoy and Nancy Betkowski tested the principle of cabinet solidarity by supporting the women's movement on some of these issues.

Any cracks in the government armour were easily exploited by opposition members. For example, in 1986 PC backbencher Janet Koper tabled a motion to urge government support of workplace child care facilities and the ensuing debate revealed considerable disagreement among Tory backbenchers. Koper noted women's increasing labour force participation and their need for high-quality day care.[62] But Shirley Cripps said it was wrong for government to "encourage" women to put their children in day care rather than caring for them at home.[63] Male backbenchers were on the whole opposed to the motion, with one MLA asserting that it was inconsistent with the party's objective of less government involvement in peoples lives[64] and another questioning the need for day care altogether.[65] Female opposition members expressed approval for the principle of the motion and commended Koper for her concern, while criticizing the government's policy of funding for-profit child care centres.[66] However, male opposition MLAs took the opportunity to point out divisions in the Tory ranks, as indicated by the following statement by an ND MLA:

> Mr. Speaker, I'm enjoying these debates on these motions, not only for the content that they have in them, but also for the growing cracks that we on this side see in the government members and their caucus. Can they ever get it together or are they always speaking in this kind of double speak and double talk?[67]

C.E.S. Franks argues that parliament exhibits two modes of operation—adversarial and consensual. However, he observes the adversarial tendencies in debate and Question Period and finds the consensual approach only in committees, where parties must work together.[68] But the Alberta debates show that the sexes tend to exhibit different approaches to legislative debate (at least on women's issues). Male MLAs are much more likely to take an adversarial "team" approach by attacking the other side on ideological or partisan grounds whereas female MLAs tend to focus on the issue at hand and adopt a cooperative style of debate which can, at times, transcend party boundaries. The former more closely fits the style of parliamentary debate described in political science textbooks, while the latter is atypical.

Examples of traditional adversarial politics include the following statements by male members of the governing party: [opposition criticisms of day care standards are] "knee-jerk and regrettably predictable";[69] "I think the New Democrats are really showing their socialist tendencies on this one . . . ;[70] and "Mr. Speaker, I hesitate to get into this debate, because I've heard so many half-statements, half-truths, and generalizations that I must confess I could not retain my temper. . . ."[71] Opposition men are not immune to this style of discourse, as we saw above, and both sides occasionally indulge in personal accusations; for example, when ND Leader Ray Martin charged Premier Getty with using "recycled Vander Zalm rhetoric" Getty countered by saying, "If you had checked with Hansard, you could have found that all the things you just said were completely false."[72]

The approach of female MLAs to Question Period and debate indicated a desire to exchange information about particular issues and to achieve policy goals. Opposition women complimented government members about responses to questions or aspects of policy. For instance, in response to Janet Koper's motion on workplace child care, Bettie Hewes said, "I'm always pleased to see the initiatives of members of this House to promote improved child care in Alberta."[73] During a Question Period exchange about child care, Christie Mjolsness responded to one of Connie Osterman's replies by saying "That's good to hear."[74] And while Marie Laing criticized 1988 labour legislation for failing to take gender into account, she also had this to say: "I must applaud the minister; this Bill does go beyond maintaining maternity leave benefits and includes benefits for a parent of an adoptive child."[75]

Female cabinet ministers also complimented women in the opposition parties. Two examples illustrate this tendency. During an exchange between Bettie Hewes and Connie Osterman during Question Period, Osterman commented, "Mr. Speaker, the honourable member makes an excellent point."[76] Elaine McCoy praised Marie Laing: " . . . I know that the honourable member opposite is very supportive of some of the things we are doing, and I also know that she is a wonderful advocate for women."[77]

In general, post-1986 legislative debates show that, on many occasions, exchanges between women in the legislature were cordial and more focussed on the *issue* at hand than on the *adversarial process* of legislative debate. While an issue-based approach would seem, to the casual observer, intrinsic to the legislative process this is not what parliamentary politics are typically all about. As Franks states:

> The division into government and opposition is a great simplifier. There are only two sides to every issue. A member is either for a motion or against. All different shades of opinion are forced into these two aggregations. *There is no room for single-issue politics in the parliamentary system.*[78] [emphasis added]

While this may be the case, it is not the whole picture. An analysis of the gender of the legislative actor clearly reveals that there is more to parliamentary politics than is generally assumed. For instance, the Alberta debates indicate that female MLAs sought to overcome party boundaries. Opposition women took a "tag team" approach to Question Period by following up on each other's questions. Each MLA recognized by the Speaker during Question Period is allowed one question and a supplementary question on the same topic, a restriction which female opposition MLAs overcame by teaming up to pursue a line of inquiry. Liberal Bettie Hewes often continued the questioning begun by ND MLAs Laing, Mjolsness, and Barrett, and vice versa.[79] In other words, the opposition women supported each other across party lines. Occasionally opposition women pursued a woman-related topic raised by one of their male colleagues or a male MLA from the opposition party, but I did not find an instance where a male opposition member did the same.

Conclusion

In a 1991 speech at the University of Alberta, then Labour Minister and Minister responsible for Women's Issues Elaine McCoy said that while she used to resent the question "Do women politicians make a difference?" she had changed her view:

> Women politicians do make a difference. . . . And that's why I believe our agenda for the 1990s—the agenda of women and women's organizations—must be to encourage and help more women get into politics [because]. . . . if more of us take seats in the legislature, at the cabinet table and in the top ranks of the public service, then gradually issues of concern to half the human race will no longer be ghettoized as "women's issues". . . . If more of us sit at the table, we will transform the table.[80]

The evidence gathered from Alberta legislative debates supports McCoy's belief that "women make a difference to process."[81] The amount of attention given to women and issues of particular concern to women increased dramatically after entry of opposition women in 1986, and the debates reveal that discussion of women included analysis of systemic discrimination. The evidence also shows that legislative role conditions the impact of female MLAs. Before 1986, six governing party women had little effect, while opposition men (and one Tory backbencher) occasionally raised gender equality issues. The 1986 election brought four opposition women to the legislature, and these women had a significant effect on the tone and direction of debate. They introduced feminist analysis of a wide range of issues, analysis which was adopted by their male colleagues in the opposition ranks.

More surprisingly, the debates themselves indicate that women in the legislature by-passed some of the institutional constraints on effective representation of women's interests. Female MLAs, from all three parties, but particularly the two opposition parties, illustrated a willingness to cooperate across party lines. Moreover, their approach to debate and Question Period challenged long-standing institutional norms. By avoiding the adversarial process in favour of a more consensual, issue-oriented discourse, legislative women may be nudging legislative politics in a new direction. In short, the evidence shows that women politicians have the capacity to "transform the table."

*Linda Trimble* received her Ph.D. from Queen's University and has been an assistant professor in the Department of Political Science at the University of Alberta since 1989. Her research and writing is in the area of women and politics in Canada, especially representation and public policy. She has published articles on the CRTC policy on sex-role stereotyping, women and politics in Alberta, and the constitution; these have appeared in *Canadian Public Policy* and various books. Her present research examines the impact of female legislators on political life and public policy.

Notes

1. See, for instance, S.J. Carroll, "Women State Legislators, Women's Organizations, and the Representation of Women's Culture in the United States," *Women Transforming Politics*, Jill Bystydzienski, ed. (Bloomington and Indianapolis: Indiana University Press, 1992), pp. 24–40.
2. S.J. Carroll, "Women Candidates and Support for Feminist Concerns: The Closet Feminist Syndrome," *Western Political Quarterly* 37, no. 2 (1984), pp. 307–23; and H. Skjeie, "The Rhetoric of Difference: On Women's Inclusion into Political Elites," Politics and Society 19, no. 2 (1991), pp. 209–32.
3. Vicky Randall, *Women and Politics: An International Perspective*, 2nd ed. (Chicago: University of Chicago Press, 1987), pp. 151–56; Joni Lovenduski, *Women and European Politics* (Amherst: University of Massachusetts Press, 1986), pp. 243–44.
4. F. Gehlen, "Women Members of Congress: A Distinctive Role," *A Portrait of Marginality*, Marianne Githens and Jewel Prestage, eds. (New York: David McKay, 1977); S.J. Carroll, "Women Candidates and Support for Feminist Concerns"; S.G. Leader, "The Policy Impact of Elected Women Officials," *The Impact of the Electoral Process*, Louis Maisel and Joseph Cooper, eds. (Beverley Hills: Sage, 1977), pp. 265–84; J. Kirkpatrick, Political Women (New York: Basic Books, 1974); and E. Vallance, Women in the House (London: Althone Press, 1979).
5. Lovenduski, *Women and European Politics*, p. 243.
6. R. M. Kanter, "Women Effects of Proportions on Group Life: Skewed Sex Ratios and Responses to Token Women," *American Journal of Sociology* 82, no. 5 (1977), pp. 965–90.
7. Bystydzienski, "Influence of Women's Culture on Public Politics in Norway," p. 15.
8. See, for instance, Carroll, "Women State Legislators"; J. Bystydzienski, "Influence of Women's Culture on Public Politics in Norway," *Women Transforming Politics*, J. Bystydzienski, ed. (1992), pp. 11–23; M. Saint-Germain, "Does Their Difference Make a Difference? The Impact of Women on Public Policy in the Arizona Legislature," *Social Science Quarterly* 70, no. 4 (1989), pp. 956–68; S. Thomas and S. Welch, "The Impact of Gender on Activities and Priorities of State Legislators," *The Western Political Quarterly* 44, no. 2 (1991), pp. 445–56; M.M. Tremblay et G. Boivin, "La question de l'avortement au Parlement canadien: de l'importance du genre dans l'orientation des débats," *Revue juridique la femme et le droit* 4 (1990–91), pp. 459–76;

S. Sinkkonen and E. Haavio-Mannila, "The Impact of the Women's Movement and Legislative Activity of Women MPs on Social Development," *Women, Power and Political Systems*, Margherita Rendel, ed. (London: Croom Helm, 1981), pp. 195–215.

9. Skjeie, "The Rhetoric of Difference"; also see S. Thomas, "Voting Patterns in the California Assembly: The Role of Gender," *Women and Politics* 9, no. 4 (1989), pp. 43–56.

10. Skjeie, "The Rhetoric of Difference," p. 235.

11. See J. Brodie, "The Gender Factor and National Leadership Conventions in Canada," *Party Democracy in Canada*, G. Perlin, ed. (Scarborough: Prentice-Hall, 1988), pp. 172–87, and S. Bashevkin, "Political Participation, Ambition and Feminism: Women in the Ontario Party Elites," *American Review of Canadian Studies* 15, no. 4 (1985), pp. 405–19.

12. M. Tremblay, "Quand les femmes se distinguent: féminisme et représentation politique au Québec," *Revue canadienne de science politique* 25, no. (1992), pp. 55–68.

13. Ibid., pp. 62–63.

14. See C. Maillé, *Primed for Power* (Ottawa: Canadian Advisory Council on the Status of Women, 1990), p. 31.

15. Tremblay et Boivin, "Le question de l'avortement au Parlement canadien."

16. Carroll, "Women Candidates and Support for Feminist Concern," p. 308.

17. For a discussion of responsible government, see P. Hogg, "Responsible Government," *The Canadian Political Tradition*, R.S. Blair and J.T. McLeod, eds. (Scarborough: Nelson, 1989), pp. 17–41.

18. See C.E.S. Franks, *The Parliament of Canada* (Toronto: University of Toronto Press, 1987), especially Chapter 7.

19. See Charlotte Gray, "The New 'F' Word," *Saturday Night* (April 1989).

20. Franks, *The Parliament of Canada*, p. 153.

21. Suzanne Zwarun, "Women in Provincial Politics: Alberta," *Chatelaine* 64 (April 1982), p. 190.

22. See Alberta Legislative Assembly *Debates*, 22 March 1983, pp. 215–24 (hereafter referred to as *Debates*) for the debate on a motion regarding wife battering. Male members of the opposition quizzed the government on this issue: see *Debates*, 17 May 1983, pp. 1007–08; 18 May 1983, pp. 1056–57; 2 November 1983, p. 1585; and 30 April 1984, p. 574.

23. Between 1971 and 1985, female members of the legislature rarely spoke to gender issues, and only did so in response to motions or questions from the opposition. See, for instance, in *Debates*, responses to the 22 March 1983 motion regarding wife battering and a similar motion on 28 May 1985. As well, see the discussions on the advisory council: 17 April 1984 and 1 November 1984.

24. See Suzanne Zwarun, "*Chatelaine* Grades the Provinces on Women's Issues," *Chatelaine* (April 1985), pp. 70–74.

25. Linda Trimble, "The Politics of Gender in Modern Alberta," *Government and Politics in Alberta*, Allan Tupper and Roger Gibbins, eds. (Edmonton: The University of Alberta Press, 1992).

26. Ibid.; Hugh Horner, "Comments on Joint Initiatives" (Address to the Alberta Status of Women Action Committee, 29 October 1976), p. 2.

27. *Debates*, 23 March 1972, p. 71.

28. See *Debates*, 9 June 1975, p. 533 and Suzanne Zwarun, "Women's Bureau had inauspicious start," *Calgary Herald* 29 April 1983.

29. *Debates*, 14 April 1983, p. 554 and 17 April 1984, p. 528.

30. *Debates*, 17 April 1984, pp. 528–29.

31. *Debates*, 1 November 1984, p. 1325.

32. *Debates*, 1 November 1984, p. 1330.

33. *Debates*, 1 November 1984, p. 1331.

34. Survey conducted by the University of Alberta Population Research Laboratory, Spring 1991.
35. Brodie, "The Gender Factor," p. 182.
36. *The Newsmagazine* (July/August 1986), p. 25.
37. *Debates*, 30 July 1987, pp. 874–75; 31 July 1987, p. 924; 1 August 1986, pp. 934–35; 2 June 1987, p. 1572; 11 August 1988, p. 1021.
38. See Trimble, "The Politics of Gender in Modern Alberta," pp. 235–36.
39. *The Newsmagazine* (January/February 1988), p. 19.
40. C. Owen, "Nancy Betkowski: 'Because She Cares,'" *The Trustee* (Fall 1986).
41. *Debates*, 3 September 1986, p. 1430. Such advocacy was not apparent during Betkowski's bid for the Tory leadership in 1992, however. She avoided discussion of so-called "women's issues."
42. *Debates*, 17 April 1988, pp. 694–98.
43. *Debates*, 6 June 1988, pp. 1506–13.
44. *Debates*, 23 June 1986, p. 184.
45. *Debates* 3 May 1988, p. 784.
46. *Debates*, 20 March 1987, p. 239.
47. Getty was replaced by Ralph Klein in December 1992.
48. See comments by various ministers; *Debates*, 28 July 1986, p. 814 and 11 May 1987, p. 1149. Also, see Don Braid, "Brontosaurus chorus is pleased when McCoy is under fire," *Calgary Herald* (28 January 1989).
49. *Debates*, 21 May 1987, p. 1330.
50. See statement by Laing, *Debates*, 21 May 1987, pp. 1327–30.
51. This is a futile endeavour, especially in Alberta. As Fred Engelmann notes, after first reading such bills are "dropped to the bottom of the list of private member's bills and must work their way up to second reading. . . . In the order of business, they rank lowest. . . ." Frederick Engelmann, "The Legislature," in *Government and Politics of Alberta*, Allan Tupper and Roger Gibbins, eds. (Edmonton: The University of Alberta Press, 1992), p. 149.
52. Ibid., p. 133.
53. See *Debates*, 25 June 1986, p. 224.
54. *Debates*, 8 June 1988, p. 1577.
55. *Debates*, 9 June 1988, p. 1606.
56. *Debates*, 3 September 1986, pp. 1429–30.
57. *Debates*, 3 May 1988, p. 784.
58. Astute readers will notice that Mirosh and McClellan are part of the new cabinet, chosen in 1992 by Premier Klein.
59. "The New Wave Pounds Feminism," *Alberta Report* (13 November 1989), p. 36, and Braid, "Brontosaurus chorus. . . ."
60. Michael M. Atkinson, "Parliamentary Government in Canada," *Canadian Politics in the 1990s*, 3rd edition, Michael Whittington and Glen Williams, eds. (Scarborough: Nelson, 1990), p. 343.
61. Braid, "Brontosaurus chorus"; George Koch, "The Cabinet Erupts in Schisms," *Alberta Report* (7 March 1988), p. 5.
62. *Debates*, 17 June 1986, p. 70.
63. Ibid., pp. 200–01 and pp. 206–07.
64. Ibid., p. 199.
65. Ibid., p. 202.
66. *Debates*, 24 June 1986, p. 203.
67. Ibid.
68. Franks, *The Parliament of Canada*, p. 6.
69. *Debates*, 24 June 1986, p. 196.
70. *Debates*, 21 May 1987, p. 1330.

71. *Debates*, 24 June 1986, p. 199.
72. *Debates*, 9 June 1988, p. 1599.
73. *Debates*, 24 June 1986, p. 197.
74. *Debates*, 30 July 1986, p. 874.
75. *Debates*, 6 June 1988, p. 1507.
76. *Debates*, 16 June 1987, p. 1934.
77. *Debates*, 22 June 1988, p. 1946.
78. Franks, *The Parliament of Canada*, pp. 144–45.
79. See, for example, *Debates* 19 March 1987, pp. 209; 19 May 1987, pp. 1251–52; 29 March 1988, pp. 188–89; 30 March 1988, pp. 230–31.
80. Elaine McCoy, "Winning More Seats at the Table: The Challenge for Women in the 1990s" (speech given at the University of Alberta, 4 March 1991).
81. Ibid.

# APPENDIX

# Alberta Hansard Index Topics Counted as Women's Issues or Gender Equality Issues

(in alphabetical order)

Abortion(s)
Ad Hoc Committee of Canadian
  Women
Access Orders Information Act
Affirmative action programs
Alberta Action Council of the Status
  of Women Act
Alberta Advisory Council on the Sta-
  tus of Women
Alberta Advisory Council on
  Women's Issues
Alberta Advisory Council on
  Women's Issues Act
Alberta Association of Child Care
  Centres
Alberta Association of Midwives
Alberta Automobile Insurance
  Board, sex discrimination
Alberta Council of Women's Shelters
Alberta Dialogue on Economic
  Equality for Women
Alberta employees—career develop-
  ment programs for women
Alberta employees—female
Alberta employees—female/male
  wage differential
Alberta employees—women in man-
  agerial positions

Alberta employees—women in
  senior management
Alberta Federation of Women United
  for the Family
Alberta Health Care, coverage of
  counseling for family violence
  abusers and victims
Alberta Housing Corporation,
  approval of mortgages to women
Alberta Human Rights Commission,
  consultant's report on male-
  female wage disparities
Alberta Human Rights Commission,
  employment equity resolution
Alberta Human Rights Commission,
  sex discrimination investigation
Alberta Human Rights Commission,
  study of women's salaries in the
  public service
Alberta Native Women's Association
Alberta Plan of Action for Women
Alberta's Special Report on Family
  Violence
Alberta Status of Women report,
  response to
Alberta Status of Women Action
  Committee
Alberta Widow's Pension Program

Tax incentives—child care tax credits
Teenage pregnancy
Tribute to women awards
United Nations Decade for Women
Unmarried mothers
Unmarried mothers—public assistance
Visible Minority Women
Vocational Guidance for Women
Wages—day care employees
Wages—equal pay for equal work
Wages—public service, women
Wages—women
Widows—government assistance
Widows—pensions
Widow's Pension Act
Widow's Pension Act, and act to amend
WIN House, Edmonton
Women
Women—Advisory Committee
Women—Alberta
Women—artists
Women—education
Women—emergency shelters
Women—employment
Women—employment, Alberta government
Women—employment discrimination
Women—government hiring policy
Women—government programs
Women—health services
Women—housing, emergency shelters

Women—legal status
Women—Metis and Native
Women—pensions
Women—"Person's Case" commemoration
Women—poor
Women—proposed council of
Women—rights of
Women—scientists
Women—social conditions
Women—suffrage
Women Associates Consulting study of women's salaries in the public service
Women in agriculture
Women in business
Women in politics
Women in public service
Women in war/military
Women medical students
Women scientists
Women's Affairs, Minister responsible (Québec)
Women's Bureau Act, repeal of
Women's Career Resource Centre
Women's issues
Women's issues: status of women council proposal
Women's rights
Women's rights—history
Women's Secretariat
Women's Secretariat Act
Women's shelters

ELAINE H. CHALUS

# From Friedan to Feminism

## Gender and Change at the University of Alberta, 1960–1970

Change in women's roles entered Canadian society from the youth culture of the 1960s, and more specifically from the university culture. Female university students were the catalysts for change. They formed a relatively homogeneous group. Not only were they united by age, class, and the idealism of youth, but they also shared a common college setting where they were unhampered by traditional obligations to husband or family. According to Jonah Churgin, "middle-class college women who initially sought to transform society, transformed themselves in the process...."[1] This was certainly true at the University of Alberta. The student newspaper, *The Gateway*, notes that the membership of the first feminist group, the Student Committee on the Status of Women, had approximately the same female membership as the New Democratic Youth, Student Power, Students for a Democratic University (SDU), and the University of Alberta Vietnam Action Committee (UAVAC).[2]

For undergraduate students at the University of Alberta, the 1960s were a period of transition, a gradual movement away from the "feminine mystique" toward feminism. Enrolment statistics and primary sources such as those supplied by *The Gateway* and the Wauneita Society (an all-women's organization) show that gender roles did not change quickly or easily; in fact, changing gender beliefs attracted strong opposition, sometimes from women but more often from men.

The old perceptions of gender remained to challenge the new. For organizations, the result was often schizophrenic, as they attempted to incorporate the new beliefs into an old structure. At the beginning of the decade, the writers for *The Gateway* decried university women's acceptance of the feminine mystique with its sex-determined emphasis on *Kinder, Küche, Kirche*[3] (children, kitchen, church), yet, as the women's movement began to take shape in the latter half of the decade, the newspaper became increasingly antifeminist, objectifying women and largely denigrating their concerns. By 1970 university students reading the newspaper received two very polarized views: on the one hand, the paper's advertising and photo strategy pointedly presented women as sex objects or supports for male egos; on the other hand, it carried a growing number of articles informing the public of women's oppression and the need for women's "liberation."[4] The Wauneita Society echoed this polarity. In the early 1960s, the society was a robust women's social and service club, emphasizing charm, etiquette, social graces, and womanly (that is, domestic) skills. By the end of the decade the group was desperately struggling to remain alive, interspersing talks on table-setting and advice on purchasing linens with the more timely issues of birth control, drugs, and women's rights.[5]

Before moving on to an examination of the sources, it is necessary to acknowledge the limitations of this research. This paper has been confined to an analysis of the effects of changing gender beliefs on full-time female undergraduate students at the University of Alberta between 1960 and 1970. This concentration does not imply that part-time female undergraduate students or female graduate students were unimportant; rather, it acknowledges that many of the trends affecting female undergraduates would have also affected these other groups. In addition, the primary source material provided by *The Gateway* and the Wauneita Society were created with an undergraduate audience in mind.

I

The University of Alberta was a reasonably representative Canadian university in the 1960s. In spite of some students' attempts to promote radical action, it had the reputation of being a moderate, or even conservative institution.[6] Still, trends which affected the Alberta student body were broadly similar to those affecting students across the country. Although the University of Alberta was already one of the country's larger universities at the start of the decade, it grew rapidly and

*Table 1* Full-time winter session undergraduate registration (degrees only) at the University of Alberta, 1960–70[7]

| YEAR | MALE | FEMALE | TOTAL | MALE (%) | FEMALE (%) |
|------|------|--------|-------|----------|------------|
| 1960/61 | 4333 | 2102 | 6435 | 67.3% | 32.7% |
| 1961/62 | 4940 | 2476 | 7416 | 66.6% | 33.4% |
| 1962/63 | 5426 | 2834 | 8260 | 65.7% | 34.3% |
| 1963/64 | 6008 | 3280 | 9288 | 64.7% | 35.3% |
| 1964/65 | – | – | – | – | – |
| 1965/66 | 5703 | 3421 | 9124 | 62.5% | 37.5% |
| 1966/67 | 6290 | 3923 | 10213 | 61.6% | 38.4% |
| 1967/68 | 6928 | 4494 | 11422 | 60.7% | 39.3% |
| 1968/69 | 7802 | 5383 | 13185 | 59.2% | 40.8% |
| 1969/70 | 8848 | 6057 | 14905 | 59.4% | 40.6% |

was subject to many of the same growing pains felt by other post-secondary institutions. The undergraduate student population in Canada rose from 105,911 students in 1960–61 to 235,629 in 1969–70, an increase of 122.5%.[8] At the University of Alberta the undergraduate population rose by 131.6%, going from 6,435 in 1960–61 to 14,905 in 1969–70.[9] During the decade, the number of men attending university consistently outnumbered the number of women; however, women formed a gradually increasing proportion of the Canadian university population. In 1960–61, women formed 32.2% of the total Canadian university enrolment[10] and 32.7% of the total undergraduate enrolment at the University of Alberta.[11] In 1962–3 women formed 10.1% of the University of Alberta's total graduate enrolment.[12] Whereas men still dominated the Alberta campus in 1970, 40.6%[13] of the undergraduate students and 19.3%[14] of the graduate students were female. These demographic shifts highlight not only the growing demands on physical plant that rapidly increasing university populations placed on Canadian institutions, but also intimate that significant changes were occurring in the social climate within the institutions themselves.

As a newpaper written by students for students, *The Gateway* provides not only a massive body of material extending in an unbroken series over the space of the decade, but also a comprehensive overview of the period from a source which integrates local and national news, contemporary issues and opinions, and corporate image management

*Table 2* Percentage of change in female undergraduate population at
the University of Alberta as compared to total undergraduate
population, 1960–70

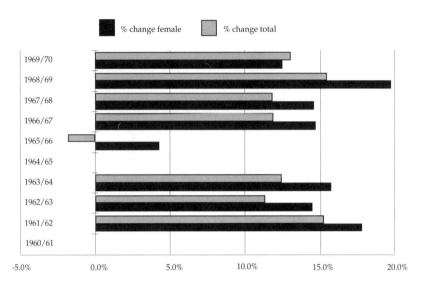

via the medium of advertising.[15] It is doubly useful, for it was primarily created by males for a male audience and provides samples of
contemporary male reactions to women's issues.[16]

The Wauneitas' agendas and minute books provide a counter-
weight to the newpaper, as they reflect a uniquely female view of the
university during the period and exemplify the growing conflict in
women's roles. The Wauneita Society arose from the Society of Independent Spinsters in 1911 and became a sorority in 1928. All women
who attended the university became automatic members. The society
was a social and service club whose object was "to promote a spirit of
mutual helpfulness among the women of the University."[17] Members
could gather at meetings or in the exclusively female Wauneita
lounge in the Students' Union Building. The society provided female
students with an introduction to women's clubs through its structure
and range of traditional female social activities—teas, coffee parties,
bazaars, formals, and lectures by experts on women's subjects. As a
service organization, its members put on teas, or served coffee and
sweets for activities sponsored by other university organizations.
Wauneitas also acted as hostesses or "usherettes" for conferences that
were being held on campus. All women's clubs performed some kind

of charity work: as a group, the Wauneitas supported the Salvation Army with yearly donations; as individuals, the members were expected to contribute gifts for needy children to the club's White Gift Party every Christmas.

By 1960, the club had begun to respond to the specific needs of a growing female student body by sponsoring "Dr. Vant's Sex Talks" in Freshman Introduction Week and the Big and Little Sister Program. Dr. Ross Vant was an obstetrician and gynecologist who provided a set of lectures on sexuality for the "freshettes" every year throughout the decade. He supplied medical information and advocated chastity, often recommending track work as an outlet for sexual energy. The Big and Little Sister program matched "freshettes" with seniors in an effort to help them become adjusted to the university and to protect them from the "dangers of over-attentive upperclassmen."[18] Toward the end of the decade, the society also instituted programs that provided tutors for native high school students and sent volunteers to visit patients at the University of Alberta Hospital. The society had originally raised all of its funds from its own activities, but by the end of the 1960s it was sustained by a small budget from the Student Union.[19]

II

In order to understand the conflicting perceptions of gender which permeated the 1960s, it is necessary to be familiar with both the statistical reality and the pervasive social mythology of the period. Girls[20] who entered university between 1960 and 1970 were the products of a provincial society that was being rapidly transformed from rural and agrarian to urban and industrial. Between 1951 and 1966, the proportion of the Canadian population living in urban centres rose from 31.4% to 54%.[21] The overall standard of living was also rising and an increasing number of people were becoming affluent. Although Canada experienced an extremely large postwar baby boom, the birth rate started to fall at the end of the 1950s and continued to fall throughout the 1960s. Declining family size occurred in spite of the fact that during the decade women's age at first marriage also fell slightly from 22.9 to 22.6 years.[22] This trend towards smaller families could be attributed at least in part to the popularity and increased availability of the birth control pill; moreover, it was shadowed by a steadily expanding number of women, especially married women, who participated in the paid labour force. While only 11% of the female labour force was made up of married women in 1951, by 1968, 54.6% of women in paid employment were married.[23]

Although it is impossible to evaluate how much of women's increased labour force participation can be attributed to modern technology, Canadian society was inundated with a proliferation of new labour-saving appliances, "time-saving" products, and technical innovations after World War II. Home freezers, dishwashers, automatic washers and dryers, as well as a myriad of other small electric appliances and gadgets mechanized Canadian homes. Supermarkets made shopping easier and new chemical processes "improved" the quality and availability of food products. Other processes resulted in new, long-wearing, low-maintenance fabrics. As a result of these changes and corresponding commercial advancements, most middle-class Canadians in the 1960s led easier lives and had (at least theoretically) more leisure time than at any earlier date in the country's history. Much of this new discretionary time was spent in front of televisions. The university students of the 1960s were the first generation to be exposed to television and the uniformity of largely American television programming and advertising may have helped to mould them into a homogeneous group with a body of shared experiences.

The statistics and innovations discussed in the previous paragraphs suggest that the women who entered Canadian universities in the 1960s led an unruffled existence, living as they did in a period of increasing affluence, sexual autonomy, economic opportunity, and personal liberty. This assumption is not entirely false, but neither is it entirely true. The women who entered university in 1960 had grown up in the 1950s and had absorbed a set of gender beliefs that were at odds with the trends shown by these statistics. It was this conflict between the prevailing societal myths and the reality shown by the statistics that created the schizophrenic nature of women's roles during the decade.

The societal myths of the 1950s affected Canadian and American women by reinforcing traditional, sexually deterministic gender beliefs. A number of strong arguments were put forward after World War II in an effort to persuade women to leave the work force and return to the domestic sphere and their traditional roles as wives and mothers. While women were no longer openly considered to be inferior to men, their sexuality was understood to make them different, and this assumption was combined with Freudian psychology in order to bolster the traditional idea that women's societal roles were determined by their biological makeup. Women were encouraged to believe that "they could desire no greater destiny than to glory in their own femininity."[24] According to contemporary "experts" such as Marynia Farnham and Ferdinand Lundberg, modern women were in danger of losing this precious commodity and degenerating into the "psychopathology of feminism," riddled by penis envy and desiring only "to deprive the male of his power, to castrate him."[25] This sad state of affairs had come to pass because women had not paid heed to their sexually-determined natures and accepted their proper roles as wives and mothers. In Farnham and Lundberg's interpretation, this problem had been exacerbated by the current trend of giving women higher education and the possibility of careers. Careers, especially intriguing, demanding careers, were seen to pose a threat both to women and to society:

> Work that entices women out of their homes and provides them with prestige only at the price of feminine relinquishment, involves a response to masculine strivings. The more importance outside work assumes, the more are the masculine components of the woman's nature enhanced and encouraged. In her home and in her relationship to her children, it is imperative that these strivings be at a minimum and that her femininity be available both for her own satisfaction and for the satisfaction of her children and husband. She is, therefore, in the dangerous position of having to live one part of her life on the masculine level, another on the feminine. It is hardly astonishing that few can do so with success. . . . The plain fact is that increasingly we are observing the masculinization of women with enormously dangerous consequences to the home, the children dependent on it and to the ability of the woman, as well as her husband, to obtain sexual gratification.[26]

Women were advised that they would be able to find true happiness and fulfilment only if they corrected the errors of the past, stopped envying and emulating men, and accepted the fact that their destiny lay in "sexual passivity, male domination, and nurturing maternal love."[27] This "feminine mystique," as it was termed by Betty Friedan, substituted a new image for an old job, that of housewife.

> The suburban housewife—she was the dream image of the young American women and the envy, it was said, of women all over the world. The American housewife—freed by science and labor-saving appliances from the drudgery, the dangers of child-birth and

the illnesses of her grandmother. She was healthy, beautiful, educated, concerned only about her husband, her children, her home. She had found true feminine fulfillment. As a housewife and mother, she was respected as a full and equal partner to man in his world. She was free to choose automobiles, clothes, appliances, supermarkets; she had everything that women ever dreamed of.[28]

Since woman's role in society and her success in life was dependent upon her in-born biological abilities and her luck in finding, marrying, and keeping a successful man who was also a good father, the entire issue of women's higher education was called into question. The sex-directed society inspired an increased interest in a sex-directed curriculum. Lynn White Jr., the president of Mills College, was one of the most famous of a number of writers who proposed "innovations" to make women's higher education more relevant. In *Educating Our Daughters*, he began with the presumption that women and men should not receive the same education and went on to propose a program of studies which would have rung familiar chords for educators in the late eighteenth or nineteenth century. White believed that women needed to be educated in order to prepare them for their ultimate roles as wives and mothers:[29]

> a firm liberal education is of great help to a married woman. Her task is only partially to manage a house and keep the babies' noses' blown. It is also to foster the intellectual and emotional life of her family and community, while avoiding the pitfall of being just an uplifter. To this end she must have and develop, and continue to cultivate as an integral part of her being, interests and enthusiasms which will infect her children, her neighbors and even her husband. An education, no matter how obviously useful and plausible, which fails to give a young woman capacity for this is inadequate. . . .
>
> "Do you send a girl to college to learn how to have babies?". . . The answer is an emphatic Yes. Motherhood has its spiritual as well as its biological aspects.[30]

Thus, higher education supplied women with "the really superior equipment for marriage which a college can give";[31] however, White felt that contemporary programs should be adapted for women by removing unnecessary "masculine" courses and replacing them with essential "feminine" equivalents:

a firm nuclear course in the Family, but from it will radiate curricular series dealing with food and nutrition, textiles and clothing, health and nursing, houseplanning and interior decoration, garden design and applied botany, and child development.[32]

If this program was carefully supplemented by vocational instruction in ceramics, sewing, and flower arranging, women would emerge from a four-year college education properly prepared for their place in society.[33]

Although White's recommendations did not perceptibly alter the educational system, the gender beliefs upon which they were based left their mark on society. By 1959, Betty Friedan, who was investigating the widespread unhappiness of American housewives—"the problem which has no name"[34]—was appalled to find that female students at prestigious American colleges were no longer interested in academic success and careers; rather, they "behaved as if college were an interval to be gotten through impatiently, efficiently, bored but businesslike, so 'real' life could begin."[35] "Real life" meant marriage, a suburban house, a husband and children. These young women had absorbed the pervasive mythology of the feminine mystique; only after they had fulfilled its requirements did many conclude that it was ultimately constraining and oppressive.

The contradictions between these social myths, reflective as they were of underlying societal perceptions of gender, and the statistical reality of the period is indicative of the sex role conflict which was inherent, albeit perhaps unconscious, for young women entering college or university at the beginning of the 1960s. Narrowing the investigation of these themes to the University of Alberta campus during the decade allows an evaluation of contemporary responses and an opportunity to assess change.

III

At the beginning of the decade, the ramifications of the feminine mystique were fully in evidence at the University of Alberta. Reflecting the relatively low value placed on higher education for women, less than one-third of the full-time undergraduate population of the university was female. Throughout the early years of the decade, female students concentrated almost entirely on traditional female fields. In 1961–62, Harrington's statistics show women forming over 50% of the enrolment in only four faculties: Education, Household Science, Nursing, and Rehabilitation Medicine. Pharmacy rested on the borderline with a female enrolment of 47.8%, while Arts lagged farther behind at 40.7%.[36] All of these fields represented acceptable training for women, as they rested within the confines of traditional female cultural or service work and thus could be reconciled with women's future roles as wives and mothers. Women's reluctance to participate in (or their families' reluctance to support training in) the "masculine," career-oriented sciences or professions with their longer, costlier, and more demanding programs is reflected in extremely low participation ratios. In 1960–61, women formed only 0.3% of the students in Engineering, 0.7% of the students in Dentistry, 7.5% of the students in Law, and 7.9% of the students in Medicine (MD).[37] This type of statistical division implies that men attended university in order to prepare themselves for economically successful careers, whereas women congregated in fields which were traditionally poorly paid, but furnished them with skills that could be adapted to child-rearing, housekeeping, or part-time work.

The activities of the Wauneita Society during the early years of the decade corroborate both these statistics and the mythology. At the beginning of the decade, the Wauneita Society was a large and active group. Every girl who entered the university automatically became a member, and the vast majority of "freshettes" participated in the Wauneitas' elaborate initiation ceremony during Freshman Introduction Week. In 1960–61, this number had reached five hundred, and by 1961–62 the Wauneitas decided that they could no longer manage to initiate all the "freshettes" at once and so split the girls into two shifts. The society's records for 1960–61 indicate that the majority of the Wauneitas' activities centred on social ventures and the preparations that these entailed. Far more time was devoted to organizing invitations, serviettes, hostesses, kitchen helpers, food, and tea essence for various teas or for the Wauneita Formal, than was given to intellectual pursuits.[38] Even the few talks and debates which the club sponsored were completely divorced from the academic and intellectual milieu. When Wauneitas gathered, they listened to male experts give speeches such as "Romance, Realism, Rules: An Autopsy on a Live Issue,"[39] or debate topics such as "Resolved: That Wauneita is a Sex Cult."[40] Dr. Vant's annual sex talks may have provided young female students with their most directly relevant Wauneita experience. If the Wauneitas of the early sixties can be judged on the basis of their club objective, then it is obvious that they were not helping each other become better students, but rather to learn the skills which would help them become better wives. In this way, the Wauneitas appeared to be much like their American counterparts, young women who attended college as a prerequisite to marriage. In fact, the Wauneita Council attendance sheet for 1960–61 indicates that some women apparently attended university only until they were able to marry. Ruth Broadhead, a representative from the Nurses' Residence, was present at council meetings until November, at which time her name was crossed out and the word 'Married' was written through the remaining columns.[41]

If the Wauneita Society was representative of the feminine mystique in action, the views found in *The Gateway* showed that the majority of students were affected by these gender beliefs. Freshettes were portrayed as the very incarnation of female helplessness and naïvete, easy prey for voracious upperclassmen.[42] The university administration also held this view, for it took upon itself the responsibility of trying to protect female chastity by restricting social contact between students. Student residences were segregated and visiting hours between the sexes were strictly curtailed. Students were not allowed to have visitors of the opposite sex in their rooms and curfews limited the length of their after-class activities. By 1962, students began to complain that these rules were stifling as well as futile: "The early curfews can not be considered guardians of Pembinite chastity as any number of sleep-outs can be obtained without difficulty. Any extra-curricular sleeping can be done discreetly elsewhere by those who do now and who would then."[43] As a result, students began to agitate for coeducational residences where male and female students could mix more freely. In a guest editorial, Ann Geddes clarified this argument, asserting that "co-educational does not mean co-habitational," and indicating that precedent for this type of housing was not only present at other universities, but that many off-campus lodgings in Edmonton were already coeducational.[44]

*The Gateway* provides ample illustration that sex was a matter of interest at least to the men on campus. Women at the university were often portrayed as sex objects. Queen contests dotted the calendar and scantily dressed kicklines were used to popularize almost every university event. Girls at university dances were referred to as "unsuspecting blossoms"[45] or "enchantresses" who provoked "shrieks of delight . . . from the foam-flecked lips of the assembled males."[46] Moreover, in 1960 *The Gateway's* editorial staff was sufficiently enamoured of a superficially humorous list of the thirteen things that boys most liked to hear coeds say, that they reprinted it from *The Ontarian*:

1. Sure I do.
2. No, it doesn't make any difference when we get home.
3. Let's go Dutch.
4. My, but I'm cold.
5. Why bother. There's no one home here.
6. No I haven't seen the tower in the moonlight.
7. I get high as heck on one beer.
8. You don't think this bathing suit is too tight, do you?
9. Aunt Jennie left me two million dollars.
10. I know mother wouldn't mind your staying another week or so.
11. Chaperone? What chaperone?
12. We can move in with my family.
13. Yes.[47]

In 1960–61, one of the dominant themes in the newspaper was early marriage. Men in the Debate Club argued the resolution, "The woman's place is barefoot, pregnant, and in the kitchen,"[48] while *The Gateway* summed up the generally accepted beliefs about the purpose of higher female education:

> Rumors have it that most girls are here looking for a husband and frosh week is always a good time to find a husband, especially if one is a freshette. These girls must be given a note of warning. Most seniors are not the marrying kind.[49]

The casual tone of the excerpt and the fact that no one took the time to write to the editor and refute these allegations implies that there may have been some truth to the rumors. It may have been true that many of the seniors were not interested in marrying immediately, but they were known to become engaged. A brief note in the 14 November 1960 "Short Shorts" is entitled "Editor Succumbs" and informed the student body in a half-mocking, half-serious fashion that the editor-in-chief had been "strucken [*sic*] with the most terrible affliction known to man—engagement."[50] There were also expanding numbers of married students on campus, but they were mainly men, as societal expectations pressured married women to retire to the domestic sphere. This was reflected by the formation of a Students' Wives Club in October 1960. The introductory advertisement clearly indicates its domestic mandate. The club was formed ostensibly to "provide a means of social contact for out-of-town and local women married to University students," but prospective members were informed that "the club will be divided into several small special interest groups which will be practising the domestic arts, such as knitting and sewing."[51]

The first letter to the editor which dealt with the subject of early marriage took women's pursuit of the "MRS" degree for granted, only complaining that university women were not inclined to let the men "enjoy" themselves before they were married:

> During the process of ostensibly becoming educated, when in reality she is trying to acquire a future "meal ticket," the coed . . . acquires a thin veneer of sophistication and intellectuality . . . Look girls, the guy you marry isn't interested in how sophisticated you are, but in other things. So smarten up. Maybe the guy you go out with tonight will not ultimately become your husband, but for God's sake at least let him enjoy himself.[52]

The decision to construct a new Home Economics building focussed attention on the relationship between women's education and their search for husbands. Columnist Chris Evans made his opinions clear: "that a secondary school for the encouragement of better and younger marriages for unmarriageable females should be considered for its own building is an insult to professional faculties."[53]

The underrepresentation of women in the student body was tied directly to contemporary perceptions of women's societal roles. In the eyes of *The Gateway* staff, those women who did not attend university were absent for three reasons: parents did not want to spend large amounts of money funding educations which would probably never be used; girls could not earn enough from their summer jobs to be able to pay for their own university educations; and most significantly, teenage marriage was combined with the prevalent belief that because "men want to wear the pants and be the bread-winners, they need better jobs."[54] According to these young men, coeds who were still unmarried at age twenty were known to panic because of their fear of being branded with "the label of the greatest of ills imposed by our society—spinsterhood."[55] In a society which measured female success by relationships with men and then constrained these relationships further by allowing them to exist only under the sanctified covers of matrimony, it is not surprising that young women feared remaining single and being labelled failures.

The university's male orientation was reemphasized in *The Gateway's* advertisements. Since men made up the majority of the university population and were presumably interested in looking professional and obtaining good jobs, the vast majority of the advertisements for services and employment were aimed at them; as women presumably attended university in order to find husbands, advertisements aimed at them were invariably predicated on appealing clothing. In 1960–61, the only career advertisement which was uniquely female was for stewardesses. The advertisement made it clear that successful candidates' educations would matter less than their physical attributes.

To sum up the prevailing beliefs at the beginning of the 1960s, the perception of gender at the University of Alberta relegated women to participation in only a few sanctioned female fields of study, denigrated their commitment as serious academics, promoted early marriages rather than careers, and emphasized their roles as sex objects. The success of the traditionally-oriented Wauneitas and the lack of critical commentary in *The Gateway* indicates that these gender beliefs were largely unquestioned.

By the middle of the decade, the children of the baby boom started to enter university and university populations across the country skyrocketed. Between 1964 and 1967, the undergraduate student population at the University of Alberta climbed from 8,394 to over 10,213.[56] Proportionately more women attended university. In 1964, women made up 35.6% of the total undergraduate population, but by 1967, this figure had reached 38.4%. However, women were still mainly concentrated in the same traditional female areas of study which they had occupied in 1960. Pharmacy and Music joined Education, Household Science, Nursing, and Rehabilitation Medicine as faculties in which more than 50% of the enrolment was female. Arts filled the borderline position at 49.7%. Women's participation in traditionally male fields had risen, but almost infinitesimally in some areas. It had crawled to 3.1% in Dentistry, 0.7% in Engineering, and 10.3% in Medicine (MD), and 9.5% in Law.

In the mid-1960s, university students across the country experienced the "British Invasion" in popular music and fashion. They also learned the rudiments of social activism and protest. Premarital sex, free love, drugs, and "flower power" were all new issues that took root and bloomed in an increasingly liberal atmosphere. Some university women became involved in new radical organizations, such as Students for a Democratic University (SDU), and began to struggle against what they began to name as societal oppression. As a result, they also began to question their own role in society and the feminine mystique that defined it. Rising women's consciousness was accompanied by the first faint stirrings of feminist activism and occurred as the social sanctions stressing the necessity of female sexual purity were slowly beginning to be modified. These changes were reflected in increased sexual permissiveness in Canadian society.

Wauneita Society activities in the middle of the decade exemplify the struggle that traditional institutions underwent in adjusting to keep up with a society in transition. What is most striking about the club during this period is its continuity rather than its change. The Wauneita program for 1963–64 followed practically the same lines as its predecessor had in 1960–61. In 1967 the program was still essentially the same; new issues were simply slipped into this ready-made format. Throughout the period, the Wauneitas continued to hold teas and coffee parties, arrange luncheons, and act as hostesses or usherettes for university activities. The Wauneita Formal and the White Gift Party remained successful, as did Dr. Vant's Sex Talks. As one indication of social change, however, men were first allowed to attend Dr. Vant's lectures in 1965.[57] Current issues such as drugs, birth control, and women's jobs were scattered through a series of noon-hour talks that also included such traditional topics as etiquette, marriage, and college men's opinions of college women.[58] The resulting juxtaposition of subject material and interests created an odd combination of the old and the new, a means by which women attempted to reconcile what they had been taught as children with what was then occurring on campus. Perhaps the most telling judgment of the Wauneitas' conservative strategy was the fact that by 1966 their Formal Tea, which had drawn hundreds of girls at the start of the decade, attracted a total of only fifty-seven "freshettes."[59] The Wauneitas were not changing quickly enough to keep up with the times and the wider interests of women in transition. Women's roles had become less insular; marriage and domesticity, while still considered very important, were not necessarily the immediate goals or the most important priorities for university women by the middle of the decade.

In light of students' changing attitudes towards sexuality and autonomy, the administration's response to growing demands for coeducational residences and relaxed visiting regulations reflects a grudging acceptance of students' adult status in a society which placed less emphasis on female sexual purity. In 1963, Mrs. J. Grant Sparling, the dean of women, and A.A. Ryan, the provost, stated that they did not believe the existing rules forbidding visiting between male and female dorms needed revision. A student poll disagreed:

"The girls at Pembina want longer visiting hours, better and warmer club rooms, and more opportunity for male visiting. Boys in residence are 80% in favor of girls being allowed in their rooms during certain periods of the day . . . and night."[60] In 1964, this issue took on new importance as the university administration attempted to limit contact between the sexes in off-campus housing. A form letter from George Tauzer, director of housing, had been sent to all landlords registered with Student Housing Services, asking them not only to discontinue integration of the sexes in rental accommodations, but also to disallow off-campus students from entertaining visitors of the opposite sex in their rooms. These requests caused quite a furor among the students who believed that off-campus independence was an inalienable student right. This attempt to extend the power of *in loco parentis* was actually the last official attempt the university administration made to regulate female sexuality. By 1965, Lister Hall began to relax its curfew regulations.[61] In September 1966, *The Gateway* announced that the new tower at Lister Hall would be a coed residence and regulations would allow male and female students to visit in mixed lounges on each floor.[62]

By the middle of the decade, the sexual revolution had arrived on campus. Sex, especially premarital sex, replaced marriage as the topic of discussion in *The Gateway*. Sexual freedom for both sexes did not follow. The essence of the sexual revolution on campus appears to have been the legitimization of premarital sex, not so that women were less trapped by discriminatory societal norms, but so that men could obtain sex more readily. Newspaper articles such as "Greater Freedom Characterizes Sex Revolution,"[63] "Free Love is Good, if Equal,"[64] and "Premarital Sex Discussed: Should We or Shouldn't We?"[65] all presented premarital sex as acceptable, especially for couples who were in love. This new interest in sexuality was accompanied by (and perhaps influenced by) new developments in contraception. The Pill had arrived at the university. By 1964 women's chastity had become less of an issue, but the prevalent belief was that women could only enjoy sex if they were in love; whereas men could separate sex from love. In Adam Campbell's words, "females . . . due to some functional inadequacy (excluding those persons who are inherently evil) . . . find that physically pleasurable sex is impossible outside the love relationship."[66] Women who indulged sexually without the benefit of a long-term relationship were still open to censure. Beliefs like these put women in a double bind: they were told that premarital sex was permissable and that sex, in itself, was good; conversely, they were also told that respectable women could only enjoy sex if they were in love. Thus, looser sanctions against premarital female sexuality did not preclude the development of a new version of the double standard.

As the first faint sparks of feminism began to emerge on campus, the first hints of a traditional backlash also became obvious. At a time when some women were beginning to advocate the dissemination of the Pill to all university students[67] and others were exploring the feminine mystique with Myrna Kostash,[68] there was a disturbing countertrend which emphasized women's roles as sex objects.

The first feminist article appeared in *The Gateway* in 1964 when Myrna Kostash investigated the state of the feminine mystique on campus. This article is important, not only because it provides a glimpse into the women's movement in its formative stages, but also because it spawned the first of many antifeminist responses to women's rising consciousness. Kostash discovered that the feminine mystique was far less prevalent among university women in 1964 than it had been at the beginning of the decade. Although marriage was still a goal for most of the women that she interviewed, it was not a goal that had to be met immediately. Women were beginning to look for other things than the trinity of husband, children, and home. Education was becoming increasingly important as a means of personal fulfilment: "being a woman is more than being a housewife or sexual instrument. That's boring. I want to do something different, something exciting. I want to learn."[69] Women were also being affected by the increased relaxation of moral standards and the availability of reliable contraception. The most daring women could not only be sexually active, but also openly acknowledge their sexuality. According to one coed, the days of the sexually passive female were numbered: "I will accept passivity with a man in the sex act. I wouldn't want to completely initiate and direct our sexual relations, although there are moments in the sex act when I would want to take the aggressive role."[70] Even more important than this, however, was Kostash's discovery that all of the women she interviewed were saying basically the same thing: "As a woman, fulfillment will be obtained only when I have the integrity of an individual, not simply the function of a female reproductive organ with the implication of inherent inferiority."[71] Women were no longer dealing with a problem that was nameless; by the middle of the decade, they not only knew its name, but also were beginning to find its solution.

Kostash's article and women's increasing self-consciousness were obviously threatening to some men, for her article quickly spawned a response that can only be attributed to a fear of change. In "Masculine

Mystaque," [*sic*] Jon Whyte revamped all of the sexually deterministic arguments of the mystique and threw them back at women. In his view, modern women were unhappy because they were attempting to go beyond their natural limits and enter the world of men:

> because she is not suited to do everything a man can. . . . Book-laden and thought weary as the modern woman is, she can cope with neither the tedium of the business world because she is a woman, nor with the utility of managing a household because Betty Friedan told her so.[72]

Whyte believed that only exceptional women were capable of being successful in the business world; the average woman was far more suited to staying at home and washing dishes. This argument acted as a smokescreen for his deeper concern. Expanding women's roles might threaten the place of men in society: "we shall find that Orwell's major mistake in *1984* was to misname Big Sister."[73] The growing antifeminist bias of *The Gateway* was reflected in comments such as these and was supplemented by an increasing number of cheesecake photos which emphasized female form but served no logical purpose. Tensions created by the changing role of women appear to have been present in other Canadian universities as well, for a somewhat confused excerpt taken from the *Xaverian* in 1966 advises freshettes that "your plight, and it is exactly that, lies in establishing the best possible relationship with the male population" while simultaneously indicating that they also had to retain their freedom as individuals.[74] By no means were all of the women on the University of Alberta campus searching their souls. While budding radical feminists in the SDU were investigating the causes of women's oppression, other female students continued to participate in kicklines, queen contests, fashion shows, and pin-up calendars. The times and the gender beliefs were changing, but in many cases these changes were gradual.

The advertising strategy of *The Gateway* emphasizes the sluggish and uneven nature of change during the period. It remained a male-oriented newspaper and as a result, advertisements for men's clothing, services, and careers outnumbered those aimed at women by as much as five to one. Advertising aimed at female students did not recognize the changing role of women; instead, it rested on the traditional belief that women could be successful only when they had made themselves desirable to men. Fewer employment advertisements

*Table 3* Women as a percentage of the full-time undergraduate winter session registration by faculty at the University of Alberta, 1960–70[75]

| | 1960/61 | 1961/62 | 1962/63 | 1963/64 | 1965/66 | 1966/67 | 1967/68 | 1968/69 | 1969/70 |
|---|---|---|---|---|---|---|---|---|---|
| Arts | | | | | | | | | |
| | 40.7 | 39.3 | 43.1 | 43.5 | 46.7 | 49.7 | 49.4 | 50.0 | 51.8 |
| Ag/Forestry | | | | | | | | | |
| | 1.6 | 4.8 | 5.3 | 3.2 | 6.0 | 6.5 | 10.2 | 10.9 | 9.3 |
| Bus. Admin. | | | | | | | | | |
| | 3.8 | 4.5 | 3.7 | 4.5 | 4.9 | 5.9 | 5.1 | 4.4 | 5.1 |
| Dentistry | | | | | | | | | |
| | 0.7 | 1.2 | 1.8 | 1.6 | 3.6 | 3.1 | 2.7 | 2.5 | 1.6 |
| Education | | | | | | | | | |
| | 56.2 | 55.0 | 52.9 | 53.5 | 57.8 | 58.7 | 59.2 | 59.7 | 61.4 |
| Engineering | | | | | | | | | |
| | 0.3 | 0.4 | 0.2 | 0.4 | 0.5 | 0.7 | 0.4 | 0.5 | 1.0 |
| Home Ec. | | | | | | | | | |
| | 100.0 | 100.0 | 100.0 | 100.0 | 100.0 | 99.5 | 99.7 | 99.7 | 100.0 |
| Law | | | | | | | | | |
| | 7.5 | 0.0 | 5.6 | 4.9 | 8.2 | 9.5 | 11.2 | 9.8 | 10.7 |
| Medicine | | | | | | | | | |
| | 22.3 | 26.5 | 28.9 | 26.7 | 25.2 | 22.3 | 24.7 | 27.0 | 24.9 |
| Nursing | | | | | | | | | |
| | 100.0 | 100.0 | 100.0 | 100.0 | 100.0 | 99.6 | 99.6 | 100.0 | 100.0 |
| Pharmacy | | | | | | | | | |
| | 47.8 | 41.1 | 48.8 | 50.7 | 59.9 | 63.0 | 61.1 | 60.3 | 58.5 |
| PhEd. & Rec. | | | | | | | | | |
| | 16.8 | 19.0 | 24.5 | 30.7 | 41.5 | 39.9 | 37.5 | 38.6 | 30.1 |
| Rehab. Med | | | | | | | | | |
| | 100.0 | 97.5 | 98.3 | 97.1 | 96.7 | 97.8 | 98.4 | 95.7 | 96.5 |
| Science | | | | | | | | | |
| | 14.8 | 14.0 | 15.0 | 17.3 | 17.3 | 17.6 | 21.2 | 23.0 | 21.5 |

were sex-specific, but since the majority of these advertisements came from companies operating in male-dominated fields, employment opportunities for females did not appear to be expanding.

By the end of the decade, university enrolments had skyrocketed. In 1969–70, the full-time undergraduate enrolment at the University of Alberta had reached 14,905 and women formed 40.6% of the student body. Women formed more than 50% of the total in enrolment in seven faculties—Arts, Education, Home Economics, Library Science, Nursing, Rehabilitation Medicine, and Pharmacy—although their participation rates in nontraditional fields was largely static. By 1970, women made up 1.0% of the students in Engineering and slowly increased their representation in both Law and Medicine (MD) to 10.7% and 14.9% respectively. The vagaries of enrolment saw female students drop to 1.6% of the students in Dentistry in 1970, only to rise to 5.2% in 1971–72.[76] Women were attending university in larger numbers, but they were still concentrated in traditional female fields, which in turn indicated that they would still have to contend with jobs which paid less and held less status than those of their male colleagues.

Between 1968 and 1970, the Wauneita Society declined rapidly. This may be due in part to the fact that it continued to intersperse current women's issues with events which were decidedly out of step with the time. Women who were protesting against beauty contests and the degradation of women were not likely to find talks on charm, modelling, fashion shows, flower arranging, or table setting particularly enlivening.[77] While the society did make some valid contributions to the women's movement in 1969 by publishing an "utterly candid book on birth control"[78] and conducting a feasibility study which showed a need for a Students' Union day care, these steps were too few and too late. The club was representative of a type of women's organization that was entirely out of fashion and died a lingering natural death in the early 1970s.

The women's movement on the University of Alberta campus emerged in 1969. *The Gateway* had vastly increased its complement of cheesecake photos and sexist cartoons in 1967–68, but began to decrease them as the women's movement gained momentum. Radical feminist students condemned those others who chose to participate in kicklines and queen contests,[79] decried the commercialization of women,[80] and spoke feelingly of women's oppression;[81] however, many other women were content to settle for less strident tones. A *Gateway* article by Beth Winteringham in October 1969 is indicative of the gradual way in which many female students adjusted their interpretations of women's roles. Winteringham's interviews with the new female students in Law and Medicine highlighted the fact that they did not identify with the radical feminists, but saw themselves as women who believed that careers and families could be combined. The idea that marriage and motherhood were not all-encompassing goals for women was echoed in the rising number of married female students and/or female students with children. This modification of women's roles reflects a gradual but significant shift in gender beliefs over the decade. It also resulted in practical steps to address new concerns. Female students with children required adequate child care and an organization called Mothers on Campus was actively working to improve conditions for student mothers. Their efforts resulted in the decision to create a day care. At the beginning of the decade, women who had children (in or out of marriage) did not normally attend university, but by the end of 1969 motherhood no longer precluded an education.

The women's movement did not meet with unqualified approval from either men or women on the University of Alberta campus. Some of the women who were organizers were very radical and did not easily win converts, especially among men. The fact that queen contests continued in spite of disapproval from both the women's movement and the Students' Council indicates that not all women were ready to give up their traditional methods of attracting males. However, the most blatant disregard for the concerns raised about women's oppression occurred during Engineering Week in 1970, when the engineers not only brought in a stripper but also paraded a nude "Lady Godiva" through the central quadrangle on a horse. *The Gateway* reported this incident with photographs: one of a gaggle of engineers crowded around a shapely young stripper dressed only in dark panties; and the second, a profile shot of the naked rider which emphasized the size and curvature of her breasts. The caption which accompanied these photographic feats was "Engineers—out to prove something or are they just showing off their women?"[82] Considering the tenor of the times, this statement, like the activity which it described, was deliberately provocative and inviting of confrontation.

Subtly or openly, *The Gateway* often appeared to be on a collision course with feminists at the end of the decade. An article on Woman's Day describes it as "a day to bitch about male chauvinism, second-class citizenship and the inequality of treatment women encounter in society," while a photo caption for the same event proclaims "Not everybody was interested in women's liberation . . . but a surprisingly large number were."[83] More often, the staffers restrained their commentary to negative titles: "Women can't get both knowledge and family,"[84] or "Women's liberation doomed to failure!"[85] Letters to the editor showed some support for this anti-feminist slant. The old issue of sex-determinism was revived by Bill Klaus. His comments on women's liberation and its possible effect on the next generation could easily have been written in the 1950s:

> Working men cannot possibly have sufficient time to emotionally mature an under five-year-old child. Neither can working women. It therefore appears that the goal of the women's liberation committee is largely to sacrifice their children ... in order to "liberate" themselves (cop out of responsibilities).
> Congratulations! They do not have a maternal bone in their bodies. I welcome them to the world of men. They should shake hands with their boyfriends (no more "good lays"). ... Only they must remember that the world is sufficiently populated so that we can do without their emotionally crippled children.[86]

Although vehemently antifeminist polemics such as this cannot be taken to represent average sentiments, they were a manifestation of the schizophrenic conditions caused by a decade of change.

By 1970, corporate image management had not yet begun to catch up to societal change and this was reflected in *The Gateway*'s advertising strategy. While more employment advertisements than ever before were asexual, the profusion and size of clothing advertisements which were aimed at men indicated that advertisers still presumed that the university was a largely male institution. Men's clothing advertisements were aimed at selling the image of corporate success: the business suit. Conversely, women's advertisements were far smaller and less numerous than the men's advertisements; moreover, they were blatantly sexual and sexist. Leisure wear, not professional attire, dominated clothing advertisements. Women's advertising concentrated on "the body beautiful" and played on the belief that women's status depended on the males to whom they were attached and that women's bodies were their most important attraction. One Tampax advertisement even went so far as to promote the feminine mystique as a woman's birthright.

IV

The 1960s were a period of transition across Canada. University populations soared and students became a major force in effecting social change. Students at the University of Alberta were representative of students throughout the country. The students who entered the university at the beginning of the decade brought with them a complete set of gender beliefs which defined women as sexual creatures who found satisfaction in marriage, domesticity, and maternity. Higher female education was not considered important, and, rather unsurprisingly, women made up less than one third of the student body. By the end of the decade, women made up over 40% of the student body and had largely succeeded in loosening the bonds of the feminine mystique that confined them to a life of household drudgery. The women's movement had emerged to force women and men to question previously established gender beliefs and slowly begin the process of change.

An examination of the records of the Wauneita Society and the editions of *The Gateway* for this decade provides clear evidence of a transition in sex roles. Concerns over early marriage were replaced by concerns with premarital sexuality. By the end of the decade, premarital chastity had lost its sanctity and women were allowed to be sexual without risking social ruin. While a double standard still existed and women were more likely than men to be condemned for unrestricted sexual activity, women had gained a great deal of sexual freedom. The Pill helped women to control their reproductive capacities and further reduce the dangers of extramarital sexuality. New standards in clothing and deportment provided women with increased freedom of movement and action. Women's participation in political activism and social change inspired them to question their society and the roles that were assigned to them. Increased belief in the absolute equality of the sexes led some women to question the necessity of marriage, husbands, and children, replacing these traditional concerns with a belief in fulfilment through career. Other women placed increased importance on careers without denying their possible roles as wives and mothers. By the end of the decade, many women believed that women could do anything, be anything they wanted to be. Both men and women were affected by these new interpretations of women's roles, yet neither sex completely approved or completely condemned them. One group welcomed the changes eagerly and forecast a new and better country as a result of women's increased freedom; another group saw only doom and destruction coming from a movement which threatened the status quo and the patriarchal institution of the family. In spite of these diametrically opposed views, the atmosphere of the sixties was generally one of change and of liberation. The feminine mystique of the fifties was not completely dispelled by the women's liberation movement of the late sixties.

Between the pressures of reform and reaction, the gender beliefs which delineated women's roles were slowly modified and it is fair to state that many of Canadian women's advances in the ensuing decades can be traced to this exciting transitional period.

*Elaine Chalus is a graduate of the University of Alberta. She is currently completing a Ph.D. at Oxford University.*

Notes

1. Jonah R. Churgin, *The New Woman and the Old Academe: Sexism and Higher Education* (New York: Libra, 1978), p. 15.
2. See "Student Birth Control Booth Open for Varsity Guest Weekend," *The Gateway*, LVIII, no. 43, 20 February 1968, p. 1.
3. See *The Gateway* LI, 1960–61.
4. See *The Gateway* LVIII–LX, 1967–70.
5. Wauneita Society Agenda Book, University of Alberta Archives, Acc. no. 77–149–2; Wauneita Society Minutes, 1960–70, University of Alberta Archives, Acc. no. 77–63–61.1.
6. In 1967 Richard J. Needham of the Toronto *Globe and Mail* questioned the U of A's validity as a university in light of its "conservative" nature:

   I was puzzled to be told in Edmonton that the University of Alberta is "conservative." You can't have a conservative university any more than you can have a pregnant virgin. If it's conservative, it can't be a university. A university should and must be a hotbed of ferment and uproar and furious dissent. Like Simon Fraser University of Vancouver, it should always be in trouble of various kinds. That way, you know it's alive and the people in it are alive. A university that's sedate and orderly is a funeral home and you can't learn much in a funeral home.

   As quoted in University of Alberta student Rich Vivone's defence of the university, "The Grand Mortician and his flock of Living Dead," *The Gateway* LVIII, no. 23, 24 November 1967, p. 3.
7. The statistics used in this and other tables are taken from C.A. Harrington, *Students and Staff at the University of Alberta 1908–1985* (unpublished study, University of Alberta, August 1985), Table 2.
8. Dominion Bureau of Statistics (hereafter DBS), *Preliminary Statistics of Education* (Ottawa: DBS, 1961); DBS, *Survey of Higher Education: Part One: Fall Enrolment in Universities and Colleges* (Ottawa: DBS, 1970). Unless otherwise noted, all DBS statistics have been taken from the relevant year of the DBS, *Survey of Higher Education: Part One: Fall Enrolment in Universities and Colleges*.
9. Harrington, Table 2. Unfortunately, Harrington does not provide statistics for 1964–65. Special thanks to Dr. Susan Jackel of the Canadian Studies Program at the University of Alberta for acquainting me with this unpublished but invaluable piece of research.
10. DBS (1961), Table 8, p. 23.
11. Harrington, Table 2.
12. DBS (1963), Table 4, p. 28.
13. Harrington, Table 2.
14. *Report of the Governors of the University of Alberta, 1968–69* (1970), Table 9, p. 12 (hereafter *RGUA*).
15. Research encompasses volumes 51 through 60 of *The Gateway*. The number of editions per year vary from under forty in the early 1960s to almost seventy in 1969–70.

16. *Gateway* staff throughout the decade were predominantly male. The sole exception occurred in 1967–68, when Lorraine Minich was editor-in-chief. Since the university population was also predominantly male, the overwhelming majority of the advertising in the newspaper was intended for a male audience. In many editions, the ratio of male-to-female audience advertisements is over five to one. This imbalance was not significantly reduced as the number of female students rose. While this may be indicative of the invisibility or at least presumed passivity of female students, it may also be related to economic realities that provided male students with more highly paid vacation work and supported advertisers' belief in greater male purchasing power.

17. Excerpted from a *Gateway* newsclipping dated October 1911, Wauneita Society Papers: First Fact File, University of Alberta Archives, Acc. no. 77–63–61.

18. "Freshettes Flustered as Orientation Begins,"*The Gateway* LI, no. 2, 20 September 1960, p. 8.

19. In 1968 the Wauneitas obtained $3,050 from the Students' Union.

20. I use the term "girls" with purpose, for most young female university students were under the legal age. There is also a psychological side to this appellation, for it is not until articles on women's issues began to appear in the second half of the decade that the word "women" replaced "girls."

21. DBS, *Canada Year Book* (Ottawa: Queen's Printer, 1968), p. 194.

22. Alison Prentice, *et al.*, *Canadian Women: A History* (Toronto: Harcourt Brace Jovanovich, 1988), pp. 320–21.

23. *Report of the Royal Commission on the Status of Women in Canada* (Ottawa: Information Canada, 1970), pp. 55–56 (hereafter *RRCSW*).

24. Betty Friedan, *The Feminine Mystique* (New York: W.W. Norton & Co., 1963), p. 15.

25. Ferdinand Lundberg and Marynia W. Farnham, *Modern Woman: The Lost Sex* (New York: Harper & Brothers, 1947), pp. 159–60.

26. Ibid., p. 235.

27. Friedan, p. 43.

28. Ibid., p. 18.

29. Lynn White Jr., *Educating Our Daughters* (New York: Harper and Brothers, 1950), p. 48.

30. Ibid., pp. 68–69.

31. Ibid., p. 70.

32. Ibid., p. 77.

33. Ibid., pp. 62–87.

34. Friedan, p. 15.

35. Ibid., p. 154.

36. Harrington, Table 2. See also *RGUA*, p. 14. The earliest *RGUA* statistics that break down the student population by sex are for 1962–63.

37. Ibid.

38. Wauneita Society Agenda Book, University of Alberta Archives, Acc. no. 77–149–2.

39. Wauneita Society Minutes (1 March 1961), University of Alberta Archives, Acc. no. 77–63–61.1.

40. Ibid. (14 December 1961).

41. Wauneita Society Minutes (1960–61).

42. "Freshettes Flustered as Orientation Begins," *The Gateway* LI, no. 2, 20 September 1960, p. 8.

43. Anne Geddes, "Let's Go Co-ed," *The Gateway* LIII, no. 10, 2 November 1962, p. 4.

44. Ibid.

45. *The Gateway* LI, no. 6, 2 October 1960, p. 5.

46. "Cheers and the Charleston Bring Frosh Aboard," *The Gateway* LI, no. 3, 27 September 1960, p. 1.

47. As quoted in "Kupsch on CUP," *The Gateway* LI, no. 14, 11 November 1960.

48. Ibid., p. 2.
49. "Poll Reveals Frosh Play Midnight Football," *The Gateway* LI, no. 3, 27 September 1960, p. 4.
50. "Editor Succumbs," *The Gateway* LI, no. 14 , 11 November 1960, p. 2.
51. "Knit One, Pearl Two," *The Gateway* LI, no. 7, 14 October 1960, p. 2.
52. "Womanhood,"*The Gateway* LI, no. 7, p. 5.
53. "Lord Knows—We Tried," *The Gateway* LI, no. 36, 17 March 1961, p. 5.
54. "Twice the Sex for Girls," *The Gateway* LI, no. 18, 25 November 1960, p. 12.
55. "Reflections," *The Gateway* LI, no. 15, 15 November 1960, p. 2.
56. For 1964 statistics see *RGUA*, p. 14. See Harrington, Table 2 for 1967 statistics.
57. "Year-End Review," *The Gateway* LVI, no. 44, 17 March 1966, p. 14.
58. Wauneita Society Minutes, 4 July 1967.
59. *The Gateway* LVIII, no. 3, 28 September 1966, p. 7.
60. "Mrs. Sparling Doubts Dormitory Visiting Wanted. Students Disagree," *The Gateway* LIV, no. 7, 26 November 1963, p. 1.
61. "Year-End Review," *The Gateway* LVI, no. 44, 17 March 1966, p. 14.
62. "Co-ed Residence Proposed for Campus," *The Gateway* LVIII, no. 4, 30 September 1966, p. 1.
63. "Greater Freedom Characterizes Sex Revolution," *The Gateway* LIV, no. 8, 22 October 1963, p. 1.
64. "Free Love Good, If Equal," *The Gateway* LIV, no. 14, 15 November 1963, p. 6.
65. "Premarital Sex Discussed: Should We or Shouldn't We?" *The Gateway* LIV, no. 25, 7 February 1964, p. 1.
66. Adam Campbell, "Short and Sour," *The Gateway* LIV, no. 26, 14 February 1964, p. 5.
67. Ibid.
68. Myrna Kostash, "The Feminine Mystique," *The Gateway* LV, no. 9, 23 October 1964, p. 6.
69. Ibid.
70. Ibid.
71. Ibid.
72. Jon Whyte, "Masculine Mystaque," *The Gateway* LV, no. 10, 30 October 1964, p. 9.
73. Ibid.
74. "Freshettes," taken from the *Xaverian*. Cited in *The Gateway* LVII, no. 6, 7 October 1966, p. 5.
75. Statistics for the faculties of Divinity and Library Science have not been included although they are present in Harrington's survey. The statistics for Divinity are too sparse to be representative, whereas Library Science statistics do not begin before 1968–69 and therefore have been left out of this comparison.
76. Harrington, Table 2.
77. See Wauneita Society Minutes, 1968–70.
78. "At last, at last," *The Gateway* LX, no. 2, 12 September 1969, p. 1.
79. Women from SDU gathered to heckle the kicklines at the election rally, calling the participants whores, sluts, dogs, and pigs. See "Emotion Abounds in U of A Rally," *The Gateway* LIX, no. 48, 20 February 1969, p. 3.
80. "Smile, you're on . . . candid commercialization," *The Gateway* LX, no. 13, 3 October 1969, pp. c-2–3.
81. "Women are serfs . . . in a feudal society?" *The Gateway* LX, no. 27, 24 October 1969, pp. c-4–5.
82. *The Gateway* LX, no. 60, 10 February 1970, p. 3.
83. "Women's Day Prompts Discussion on Abortion, Wages," *The Gateway* LX, no. 55, 29 January 1970, p. 8.
84. A letter by Tom Peterson, *The Gateway* LX, no. 34, 14 November 1969, p. 5.
85. A letter by Lee "the Hat" Venables, *The Gateway* LX , no. 57, 3 February 1970, p. 5.
86. A letter by Bill Klaus, *The Gateway* LX, no. 56, 30 January 1970, p. 8.

MARGARET-ANN ARMOUR

# WISEST

An Initiative at the University of Alberta
to Encourage Women into the Sciences
and Engineering

Early in 1982, the late Dr. J. Gordin Kaplan, then vice-president, Research, at the University of Alberta attended a seminar on microprocessors. The room was packed; there was one woman in the audience. Already concerned by the low participation of women in careers in the sciences and engineering, Dr. Kaplan took action. WISEST, Women in Scholarship, Engineering, Science and Technology was established. The committee has about twenty members including academic staff, students, professional engineers, representatives from Alberta Education, the Alberta Women's Secretariat, and educators. The mandate of the committee is to initiate action to increase the percentage of women in decision-making roles in all fields of scholarship. To date, many of the studies and actions of WISEST have concentrated on the fields of science and engineering. This is appropriate since the figures for 1987 (the latest year for which they are available at the time of writing) illustrate not only the low percentage of women receiving degrees in these fields but also the marked decrease in this percentage as women progress from bachelor's to master's to doctoral degrees. Thus, although in 1987 53% of all undergraduate degrees were granted to women, in mathematics and the physical sciences the figure was 28.5% and in engineering and applied science, 12.2%. At the master's level, 45.1% of the total degrees awarded went to women, 23.4% in mathematics and the physical sciences and 11.1%

in engineering and the applied sciences. Women earned 28.6% of doctoral degrees, but only 13.0% in mathematics and the physical sciences and 5.4% in engineering and the applied sciences. Hence, there
is room for change.

Much has been written about why young women do not choose
careers in the sciences and engineering and many reasons have been
given as to why this is so.[1] First, it has been argued that there is something intrinsic to the nature of science as we practise it in the late
twentieth century which excludes women from the field.[2] Certainly,
when a group of school children and undergraduates were asked to
rate a range of subjects including engineering, physics, mathematics,
and chemistry on a variety of scales, such as hard/soft, masculine/fem-
inine, complex/simple, it became clear that they viewed science as
being fundamentally masculine, as defined by the cultural stereotypes
of masculinity.[3] Thus dominance and power are equated with science.
Descriptions of scientific endeavours may cast scientists as male, and
Nature, which is being studied, as female. Metaphorically, the goal of
the scientist is described as being "to penetrate the innermost secrets
of the female Nature." She is described as holding on to those secrets
and forcing the scientist to tease them from her. The ideal seemed to
be to have a dominance over Nature which allowed the scientist to
remain detached and objective while subjecting Nature to his will and
to his reason. It is now recognized, of course, that the objective and
highly rational scientific method of popular belief is a myth, there
being many social and cultural influences on how we "do" science,
and so many leaps of intuition which afterwards, in describing the
work, can be conveniently edited out as the rational process is
described. However, the popular myth remains and young women
tend to avoid the sciences.

Second, there are cited social, cultural, educational, and occupa-
tional barriers to women entering these fields.[4] Some examples of
these barriers follow. School children still perceive scientists to be
elderly males who work very long hours alone in the laboratory. To
some young women, such a career does not fit with desires to have a
family. As yet, young men do not see as great a conflict with their life
plans. However, there are signs that this may be beginning to change.
As well, the attitudes of parents, teachers, friends, and the media have
a strong influence on the choices young women make. To a young
woman's announcement that she plans to be a physicist, the reaction
may still be "But doesn't that need a lot of math?" The often subcon-

scious sense that young women are somehow more fragile than young men and therefore should not be academically challenged to the same degree is still prevalent.[5] "Don't worry, dear, you will probably never need it again" is not often said to a young man who has just failed a math exam.

We have seen that students, both boys and girls, perceive science to be masculine. They also believe that it is difficult; mathematics and physics are literally *hard* sciences. Curricula and texts have tended to promote this view by encouraging the teaching of science subjects in a different way from that of the humanities. Thus, theory is to be understood first, then general examples are presented, and, finally, specific examples. There has been a move to introduce so-called "girl-friendly" science.[6] Not only are concepts illustrated with examples which are more part of girls' experience, but also a topic is often introduced by showing its relevance to everyday life, thus increasing the motivation of the students to try to understand the theory. Not only does this approach make science more attractive to young women, it has been shown that science also becomes more interesting to young men.

Third, it has been suggested that women are not as good at science as are men.[7] Young women *can* do math, but it is hard to persuade them of that fact.[8] A WISEST study showed that over ten academic years, from 1970 to 1981, the average grade points of female students in mathematics and the other science departments at the University of Alberta were as high as or higher than those of their male peers.[9] In grade school a problem has been recognized which is not related to ability but which does affect performance. Girls' and boys' cognitive abilities develop at different rates and since the curriculum has traditionally been designed to suit males, females are at a disadvantage. Therefore, a range of teaching approaches which accommodate the differences in male and female cognitive styles is needed.[10]

Believing that women have a great deal to offer to the scientific and engineering disciplines, WISEST has initiated several programs to try to build bridges across some of these barriers. Being based within a university, much of our effort has been directed to university and senior high school students. We recognize that many young women have made choices by this time and that we are influencing a very small group. However, we are convinced that it is important to build bridges wherever the expertise and the opportunity exist. Some of the programs of WISEST are described below.[11]

## Summer Research Program for High School Students[12]

One of the barriers which has been identified as keeping girls from considering the sciences and particularly engineering as possible careers is their lack of knowledge of what a scientist or an engineer does. One of the ongoing programs of WISEST is intended to help to break this barrier. In the program, students who have completed grade eleven spend six weeks during July and August working in research groups at the University of Alberta. The girls work in the faculties of Science, Engineering, and Agriculture and the boys in the faculties of Home Economics and Nursing. The program has been in operation since 1984 and the numbers of participants has increased from ten students in 1984 to forty in 1991. It is unique in that the students join research groups and work on established research projects, rather than taking specially developed courses. In this way we are making use of existing resources.

A pool of academic staff at the university who are willing to take students has been developed. Students are recruited for the program through the science supervisors of the local school boards and directly through the WISEST office. Students are chosen using several criteria: in fairness to their university supervisors, they must show strong academic achievement in the sciences; they should be at least somewhat open-minded about their career plans and they should have extracurricular interests. Choosing the students has been described by a member of the selection committee as both an exhilarating and a depressing experience; exhilarating because of the genuine interest and quality of the students, and depressing because so many excellent students cannot be accepted into the program. Each student is paid the minimum wage for the six weeks' work. Funding for the program comes from a variety of sources each year, including the federal and provincial summer employment programs, provincial government departments, the Winspear Foundation, and the University of Alberta. The program is managed by a paid coordinator who works full-time from May to September. In addition to soliciting the research projects from supervisors and helping in the choice and assignment of students, the coordinator visits the students regularly in their laboratories and maintains close contact with supervisors. The coordinator also arranges weekly gatherings of all students at which time they tour the university, learn about the library system, hear about job trends, listen to men and women in nontraditional careers talk about their experiences, and share with the group a description of the work each has done during her stay at the university. Among the places that the students have worked are the Department of Zoology collecting and analyzing water samples from lakes in northern Alberta, the Department of Environmental Engineering studying the effects of various disinfectants on drinking water quality, the Department of Physics analyzing the distortions to the earth's magnetic force field which result from the burst of solar energy which produces the northern lights, the Department of Mechanical Engineering gathering data leading to the determination of the surface tension of various hydrocarbons, the Department of Chemistry synthesizing new compounds and in the Department of Microbiology studying the effect on fish of different strains of bacteria.

When asked to evaluate the program, the majority of supervisors have been very positive. Most faculty who have supervised students have done so for more than one summer and have indicated their willingness to continue to do so. All of the students have responded that they enjoyed the experience and have benefited from it. In a follow-up of students who were in the program in 1987, 1988, and 1990, 100% of the respondents were attending or planning to attend university. A large majority (86%) indicated that the WISEST program had influenced their choice of field. Moreover, 80% expressed their intention of continuing on to graduate studies or of entering a professional school on completion of their first degree. Not only does the program provide information about what scientists and engineers do, it also introduces the students to university life. Many of them who have gone to university a year later have commented on how much more comfortable they feel than their classmates who were not part of the program. They also know a staff member to whom they can go and talk over any problems they may have.

Perhaps the most rewarding aspect for the supervisors and coordinators of the program has been the surprise and delight expressed by the female students when they realize that "This is engineering (or science); it is important; *I can do it!*" Our experience with the program leads us to believe that it is successful both in encouraging young women into the sciences and engineering and also in increasing the likelihood of their being successful at university and continuing on to postgraduate studies.

Annual Conference

When asked to visualize a famous scientist, school children still most often describe an elderly man in a white coat who is extremely hardworking and intelligent, and who has worked most of his life alone in a laboratory with little time for family life or other interests.[13] Seldom is the first image that of a woman, especially of a woman with a so-called "balanced" life. To try to counter this perception and to help to answer questions about how a career and a family can fit together, a day-long meeting is held at the university each May for high school and undergraduate students. The meeting provides the students with the opportunity to meet and talk informally with women in a variety of nontraditional careers and to have "hands-on" experiences in the sciences and engineering. Titles such as "Invest in Your Future with RSPs: Rewarding Science Programs," "Science, Engineering and Technology: They are for Women Too," and "Choosing Your Career the WISEST Way" have been used. The format of the conference is a plenary session with a keynote speaker or speakers followed by small group sessions in which the students can question three or four women in nontraditional careers about the requirements of their work, the qualifications they needed, how they manage their career and their family, and why they chose their career. The small group discussions are facilitated by a teacher. Discussion continues over lunch and then there are a variety of hands-on activities for groups of about ten students. Each student participates in two of these activities. These have included working in the water resources laboratory of the Civil Engineering department, using a computer program to test the viability of a new product and how many need to be sold to make a profit, doing one of several experiments in the chemistry laboratories, making models of strands of DNA, exploring superconductivity, learning about the Hubble telescope, and examining plant cells. The day closes with a plenary discussion and wind-up. About one hundred students and forty women scientists and engineers have participated in each meeting.

One of the teachers who acted as a small group facilitator in 1990 was the principal of an elementary school. She felt that much younger children could benefit from a similar experience and so in February 1991, a day-long conference was held at the University of Alberta for 120 female elementary school students aged 9 to 12. The length of the small group discussions was shortened and group model building competitions were included but otherwise the format was very similar to that for the older students. Log books were prepared for each child so that she could record her experiences and reactions during the day. The younger children's enthusiasm and eagerness to try new things made it an exciting and exhausting day. The success of this first venture in 1991 has encouraged the planning of such a meeting annually.

University of Alberta Women in Science and Engineering (UAYs)

It has been shown that many young women who very successfully complete a degree in the sciences and engineering choose to move into a more traditional career rather than continuing on to graduate school.[14] These are the young women who are needed to fill academic positions in these fields and to help increase the proportion of faculty women. In what way can WISEST provide encouragement for female students in the sciences and engineering? The UAYs, an acronym for University of Alberta Women in Science and Engineering, is a mutual support group for all women in these fields at the university, including undergraduates, graduate students, postdoctoral fellows, and academic and technical staff. The group meets about once a month during the academic year and produces a newsletter, the *UAYs News*, also on a monthly basis. A mailing list of just over five hundred names has been developed. The names of students who have participated in the WISEST High School Student Summer Research Program are added to the mailing list each year. Each September the UAYs newsletter and a letter of invitation to the first meeting are sent to female graduate students and third and fourth year undergraduates in the faculties of Science, Engineering, and Agriculture and Forestry, and distributed to as many first and second year female science and engineering students as possible. Meeting notices are posted around campus. Meetings have included panel discussions on topics such as "Choosing a Graduate School and a Research Director," "Gender Role Development," and "Managing a Career and a Family." There have also been talks by visiting women scientists and engineers, including Dr. Rose Sheinin, a molecular biologist who is vice rector, Academic, at Concordia University in Montreal, Dr. Ursula Franklin, professor of Engineering, University of Toronto; and Dr. Marie Morisawa, professor of Geology, State University of New York at Binghampton. Informal pot luck suppers are followed by discussion. A buddy system has developed within this group. Students who have questions about a specific course they are taking are paired with someone who has already completed the course. The effect this group may be having is hard to measure, but it has the potential to provide the role models and the informal networking which may help to persuade some young women of the value of continuing their studies and of considering an academic career.

In addition, thirty-five graduate student members of the UAYs volunteered to be role models for the pilot project of the Stepping Stones Program organized by the Alberta government. The students visited schools in Edmonton to talk with grade eight classes (thirteen- to fourteen-year-olds) about their choice of career. In this way, young women who still have choices to make about their careers have an opportunity to talk with those who have already made these choices.


Conclusion

Why do the members of WISEST think it is important to encourage young women to consider careers in the sciences and engineering and give much time and effort to try to make it happen? There are several reasons. First, we believe in equal choice and opportunity for all members of our society. Therefore, we are trying to remove some of the barriers which narrow the choices and deny the opportunities. Second, it is projected that there will be a shortage of trained personnel for technologically related tasks in the next five to ten years, so that jobs will be available. These jobs will be replacing many of the traditional women's jobs such as switchboard operators and stenographers. Third, men have traditionally been expected to provide a good standard of living for their families; when it becomes wholly accepted that women can have careers which allow them to share this role, pressure will be lifted from men. For this to become reality, a considerable shift in social attitudes will be required. Finally, and perhaps most fundamentally, I believe that the sciences need women. To find solutions to the complex problems which face our society today requires a wide variety of approaches. This applies as much in the scientific and technological fields as it does in business, the social sciences, and the humanities. Women bring to the discipline a different set of values and perspectives and ask different questions from those presently being asked. They help to reestablish connectedness with Nature in place of dominance over Nature.[15] In doing so they will accelerate a process of change which is essential.

*Margaret-Ann Armour* is assistant chair of the Department of Chemistry at the University of Alberta. She has received numerous awards, including the YWCA Tribute to Women Award in the area of Business, Labour, Professions and Technology (1990) and the Distinguished Service Citation from the Science Council of the Alberta Teachers' Association (1992). Dr. Armour is vice-chair and convenor of WISEST.

Notes

1. See for example, R. Sheinin, "Women in Science: Issues and Actions," *Canadian Women's Studies* 5, no. 4 (1984), p. 70; A. Kelly, ed., *Science for Girls* (Milton Keynes: Open University Press, 1987); over 3,000 publications are listed in a bibliography on *Women in Pure and Applied Science* compiled by WISEST member Sheila Bertram, Faculty of Library and Information Studies, University of Alberta, Edmonton, Canada T6G 2J4, and available from her at a cost of five dollars per copy.
2. H.S. Astin, "Sex Differences in Mathematical and Scientific Precocity," *Mathematics Talent: Discovery, Description and Development*, C. Stanley, D.P. Keating, and L.H. Fox, eds. (Baltimore: Johns Hopkins University Press, 1974).
3. H. Wenreich-Haste, "The Image of Science," A. Kelly, ed., *The Missing Half: Girls and Science Education* (Manchester: Manchester University Press, 1981).
4. E. Fox-Keller, *Reflections on Gender and Science* (New Haven: Yale University Press, 1985).
5. R. Rosenberg, *Beyond Separate Spheres; Intellectual Roots of Modern Feminism* (New Haven: Yale University Press, 1982).
6. A. Kelly, *Science for Girls* (Milton Keynes: Open University Press, 1987).
7. See for example: A. Kelly, ed., *The Missing Half.*
8. L.A. Fox, *The Problem of Women and Mathematics* (New York: Ford Foundation, 1980).
9. A.M. Decore, *Vive la Difference: A Comparison of Male-Female Aacademic Performance,* Canadian Journal of Higher Education 14 (1984), p. 35.
10. J. Harding, *Perspectives on Gender and Science* (London: Falmer Press, 1986).
11. *wisest: An Initiative at the University of Alberta*, University of Alberta Publication, 1989.
12. WISEST *Student Summer Research Program*, University of Alberta Publication, 1988.
13. P. MacCorquodale, *Self-image, Science and Math: Does the Image of the 'Scientist' Keep Girls and Minorities from Pursuing Science and Math?* (Washington: National Institute of Education, 1984).
14. P. Codding, *Despite the Odds*, M. Ainley, ed. (Montreal: Vehicule Press, 1990).
15. U. Franklin, *The Real World of Technology* (Toronto: CBC Publications, 1990).

PAT RASMUSSEN

# Telling Our Story

## Women's Program and Resource Centre, 1981–1991

The Women's Program and Resource Centre (WPRC) provides non-credit courses for, by, and about women within the Faculty of Extension at the University of Alberta. In 1991, we celebrated ten years of operation. As the director from 1989–92, I take this opportunity to reflect on our processes, changes, and tensions. By telling this part of our story, I hope to make visible a seldom discussed part of our existence.

Describing my work and WPRC at first seemed like a straightforward task. I soon realized, however, that I did not want to recapture times, places, and names (partly because it would be a huge task, but also because I feared missing someone or something); instead I wanted to convey the subtle tensions and processes of the program. On the pages that follow I try to share these with you by giving some general background about the Women's Program and Resource Centre, by describing the program's location within the university and community, by discussing some issues of curriculum and development and looking at future directions.

How Did WPRC Come to Be?

Since the early 1960s, an ever-increasing number of women in Canada, the United States, and Europe have become aware of the inequities women experience every day in western society. During the 1960s women in Canada started challenging the status quo by expressing grievances about societal assumptions concerning women's roles. The Royal Commission on the Status of Women in Canada validated these grievances and stated that a change in society's prejudice against women could be achieved only through a continuing study of the position of women in society and continuing efforts to secure justice and equal opportunity.

In the 1970s and early 1980s women worked to rectify economic and social inequities. In the 1980s and 1990s women started questioning the validity and reliability of all human knowledge. Human knowledge, traditionally presumed to be value-free and universal, has been under close scrutiny. Feminist scholars and practitioners contend that "human" knowledge has been created through a patriarchal prism and as such serves to oppress. A current feminist project is to describe, analyze, and envision how women create knowledge in a way that includes a plurality of voices and yet does not fall into a relativist abyss.

During the 1960s and 1970s, at various western Canadian universities, credit and noncredit courses about women were being offered. At the University of Alberta, a few credit courses that focussed on women within the humanities and social sciences started to appear in the 1970s, and within the Liberal Studies Program, Faculty of Extension, only a sprinkling of courses for women appeared among its diverse, noncredit, general interest offerings. Examples of these included afternoon courses in liberal studies, study group on status of women, law and modern women, seminars for women going into management, and Second Look.

Hayden Roberts, director of Liberal Studies, recognized the emergence programs specifically designed for women. He noted that such programs were flourishing at other universities across Canada and the United States. In January 1980 Phyllis de Luna submitted a proposal for a Women's Studies Program in the Faculty of Extension at Hayden's invitation. Hayden tabled the proposal to the General Policy and Program Review Committee (GPPRC) in April 1980 but no recommendations were forthcoming. At a staff meeting in March 1980, the faculty to examine proposed programs within a broader policy about directions in which the faculty should expand, and set priorities into which each of the programs would fit. Hayden's submission about women's programming was made primarily to indicate intention.

Hayden continued working on the project and called together a group of women in Edmonton to discuss the feasibility of creating a program specifically designed for women. Those present at the 22 May 1980 meeting included Phyllis De Luna, Maxime Gerlach, Ann Hall, Cheryl Malmo, Helen Melnyk, Dorothy Richardson, Shirley Roessler, June Sheppard, Margaret Smith, Sharon Smith, and Hayden Roberts. Members of the group came from the university faculty, the full-time student body, the university senate, journalism and publishing, private consulting, and the general public. The purpose of the meeting was to explore the need and desirability of a more coherent and expanded program for women, on the part of the Faculty of Extension.

This meeting was significant for it called into question the merit and appropriateness of the original proposal that was submitted to GPPRC for consideration. Hayden concluded from the meeting that the scope of women's programming through the faculty must include course offerings plus outreach activities with a wide range of women's groups. He resubmitted a proposal for increasing women's programming in July 1980, which changed the focus from merely offering courses, conferences, and forums to a program with a strong community development perspective and social change mandate. He argued that a new academic position must be created and the incumbent should be a field worker/programmer/community worker.

Faculty of Extension Council approved the proposal in September 1980 and official university permission to recruit a supervisor of Women's Programs was granted 29 January 1981. Sandy Susut was recruited for a one-year term beginning July 1981.

As outlined in the revised submission to GPPRC, the general goals of expanded women's programming were to satisfy a wide and growing public interest in women's perspectives on current and historic issues, and in the roles of women in various aspects of contemporary life; and to lead to the acquisition of knowledge, skills, and attitude changes, for women and men, which would both increase the participation of women in public life and enhance the personal lives of women touched by the program. The kinds of activities which would emerge from the implementation of this proposed program would include counselling; providing a physical space for women's groups, that is, a women's resource centre; a public advocacy of women's interests; help to women's groups in such matters as fund raising; social animation, that is, working with community groups, community leagues, and volunteers in needs assessment and program planning, and the offering of extension courses of an academic and fairly conventional nature, plus workshops of a more practical nature.

With the passage of time and practice, these goals have been slightly modified. By 1991, goals were to provide a program of special interest to women which would increase awareness of women's position in society and which would provide women with lifelong learning opportunities and means for improving that position, individually and collectively. The emphasis on providing on-site counselling had been reinterpreted to mean providing information and referral via the resource centre.

The program grew rapidly in the first five years of operation. In July 1983, the program moved from a single small room in Corbett Hall to a large two-storey house in North Garneau devoted entirely to the Women's Program and Resource Centre. From 1981 to 1991, 14,800 women had participated in courses, conferences, workshops, and forums offered by the program. Another nine thousand women used the services of the resource centre. Participant evaluations of courses and conferences are generally very positive. Public recognition of WPRC goes beyond the borders of Alberta and Canada. Several delegations of women from Japan, China, Australia, Central America, and the United States have visited the house to learn about the program.

A major strength of the program is the multifaceted approach to lifelong learning. Although it was recognized at the onset that the program could not be all things to all people, efforts have continually been made to push the limits and be as inclusive of the needs of as many women as possible, to truly extend the services and resources of the university into the community and to encourage the university to broaden its commitment to serve the needs of women. An example is worth noting. In 1985, WPRC in cooperation with the coordinating committee for Women's Studies and the Women's Studies Program at Athabasca University, submitted a proposal to the secretary of state for the establishment of a Women's Studies Chair in Edmonton. Unfortunately, the proposal was turned down and the western regional chair went to Manitoba. However, a proposal for a credit program in Women's Studies and the Women's Research Centre came out of that initial activity. The Women's Studies Program started at the University of Alberta in the fall of 1988 and the Research Centre started earlier the same year.

The major limitations centred on the lack of resources dedicated to WPRC. Although much had been accomplished in ten years (1981–91), the work load and work-related stress for all women involved, particularly for the directors, has been extremely high. One thing we as women have learned is that we must look after ourselves and be mindful of creating organizational structures that do not exploit and drain us. High expectations for social change and equality, shortage of funds, and an ever-increasing plethora of feminist theory and research fuel the pressures on the Women's Program and Resource Centre. At WPRC, I wanted to learn, for my own sake and the sanity and health of the women I worked with, how to break the cycle of martyrdom and "crazy making." Describing and analyzing the structure and processes of our work is one place to start.

What Is the Resource Centre?

Not all learning happens in classrooms, in fact, probably most learning happens in an unstructured setting when a person is actively engaged in "finding out." Because so few resources existed in the university library, or public library systems to augment the courses being offered by the Women's Program, Sandy Susut started to collect a few materials for participants to borrow. From 1981 to 1984 a small collection started to form. With the official opening of the house in North Garneau 8 March 1985, bookshelves and floor space were dedicated to the resource centre. A special collection of periodicals, books, offprints, briefs, and ephemerals came into being. The resource centre helped in this process of self-directed learning and research. The formally stated objectives included: to collect and publish information about, for, and by women on women's issues and services available to women; to animate community action and community organization projects addressing the needs; to support women's groups; to publicly advocate on needs and issues; and to support the courses offered in the Women's Program.

Women donate books, papers, periodicals, and unpublished materials. Most women's groups make sure that a copy of their respective briefs are available in the centre for women to use, other people donate money for acquisitions, some via a monthly debit from their pay cheques, others, lump sum amounts. Together with membership fees and grants from government and foundations, the resource centre is able to purchase the most current materials on selected topics. Over time an interesting collection has evolved.

As early as 1982, the first consultations between Dr. Sheila Bertram, now dean of Library Science, and Professor Sandy Susut were held concerning computerization of women's resources. From these discussions grew the *Canadian Women's Periodical Index* which continues to be a major research-related project of the Women's Resource Centre. This periodical is published for the Canadian Research Institute for the Advancement of Women (CRIAW) in cooperation with the Misener/Margetts Women's Research Centre through the work of a team that includes Dr. Marilyn Assheton-Smith, Mair Smith, Pat Rasmussen, and others. It indexes the woman-centred periodicals of the resource centre and University of Alberta library.

The use of computer technology did not stop with this project. Funding received from the federal government's secretary of state, Women's Program in 1985–87 allowed all the books, offprints, bibliographies, and ephemerals in the resource centre to be entered on to an MTS SPIRES data base system. The database entitled "Womansource" is accessible to all MTS/University of Alberta users, anywhere in the world. The grant for this project funded the acquisition of materials, computer usage, and staffing (Mair Smith, Sheryl Ackerman, and Marg White) until the project was completed. Since 1987 financial donations from individuals have made it possible to systematically update "Womansource" to include all new acquisitions.

The number of women visiting the resource centre has increased dramatically since the centre began. Originally, the collection was meant to augment the programs offered by the women's program and any research projects associated with the centre. With the initiation of the Women's Studies program in fall 1988 a marked shift occurred. Suddenly university students enrolled in women's studies classes and cross-listed courses started using the centre. In 1991, about two-thirds of the library visitors were university students and about one third were women from the larger community and participants of the Women's Program. All women taking courses in the Women's Program, instructors, and volunteers received one year's free membership to the resource centre. Women from across Alberta visit the centre for reading material, for research purposes, or for referral to feminist doctors, lawyers, counsellors, and therapists.

The resource centre is not free of turmoil and constant problems. In many ways it is an administrator's nightmare. Funding has always been on a project-by-project basis, which is precarious at best, especially given some of the limitations inherent in the funding agreements. Staff turnover is endless and therefore the detailed administration of subscriptions and coding is constantly being taught and retaught.

The resource centre is coming of age at a time when resources for, by, and about women are desperately wanted and needed by more women than ever before. The mandate of the centre needs to be reexamined in light of current realities and we hope the mandate will be broadened to include support for academic programs such as women's studies. Such a mandate demands ongoing resources and a strong organizational commitment. Discussions about the future of the resource centre and how it fits on campus are just commencing.


Politics of Location

The Women's Program and Resource Centre exists on the interface between the university and the community, and in order to gain a deeper understanding and appreciation for the processes, changes, and tensions one may examine our location within the educational institution, academic disciplines, physical setting, and local women's community.

*Organizational Location*
The WPRC is part of the University of Alberta which is a large, traditional, bureaucratic hierarchy, with a president, board of governors, senate, and various vice-presidents at the helm. The faculties each consist of academic and nonacademic staff. The WPRC is one of sixteen program areas located in the Faculty of Extension. Extension's mission is to extend opportunities to the people of Alberta to engage in lifelong learning, based on the needs of individuals and society and the resources of the university.

Organizationally, Extension has a dean, a director for each program area, additional academics assigned to larger program areas and a number of nonacademic staff. Instructors are primarily hired on a course-by-course basis and many programs draw upon the volunteer commitment of many other individuals to work on advisory committees and special projects. Extension is not formally departmentalized although directors, like chairs in degree-granting faculties, have many administrative responsibilities and are responsible for their own budgets and the management of their respective program areas. The staff complement of Extension is not significantly different from other parts of the university. More men than women hold academic positions, currently three directors are women and twelve directors are men, while many more women than men hold support positions.

Interestingly, about two-thirds of the student body of Extension are women.

Women's voices are not equally represented within the decision-making processes of the faculty, however, to date little has been done to rectify these inequities. The recommendations of a recent university commission on equality and respect has sparked some activity in various faculties. In Extension, at the direction of Faculty Council and the dean, a task force was struck to consider issues of equity.

The organization of WPRC has changed only slightly during ten years. WPRC started with one part-time clerical position and one full-time term academic position. All other staffing is on a project-by-project basis including paid and unpaid staff. In 1986 the clerical position became a permanent full-time position and only recently has been reclassified as administrative assistant. It was not until 1 July 1990 that the position of director assumed a tenure-track, assistant professor status. Prior to July, the supervisor/coordinator/director (various titles reflect the administrative responsibilities and evolution of WPRC within Extension) were hired on a term basis. Many of these terms were twelve months long. The allocation of this tenure-track position symbolizes, at long last, a structural commitment by Extension to women's programming and at the same time makes the incumbent a legitimate member of the academic community. A brief summary of this hard won recognition of women's programming may provide insight into some of the politics of location.

During the past decade, a major review of all faculties on campus has been underway. Each faculty followed the prescribed process. For Extension this review process took approximately seven years to complete. During this time, with each academic staff resignation, one position was held in abeyance awaiting the results of the review. By 1990, four tenure-track positions were inactive temporarily. One of the recommendations of the final review report was that four specific programs within the faculty be given one tenure-track position each. WPRC was one of these programs.

When the final report was submitted to the president of the University of Alberta in spring of 1990, the winds of fiscal crisis and restructuring had arrived and academic positions had become rare commodities. Dean Foth of Extension made application to the vice president, Academic, Dr. Meekison, to reactivate and recruit for these four positions. Only two of the four positions were approved for reactivation and recruitment. The university administration highly recommended that recruitment be made at the assistant professor level.

Recruitment at the associate or full professor levels would require a special justification and vice president, Academic, approval. Dean Foth, after several discussions with Extension academic staff, decided to allocate only one position, to WPRC, and put the other position aside until internal decisions about levels of recruitment and other related issues could be made.

Finally, after years of arguing the merit of such a classification, a tenure-track position was allocated to women's programming. The WPRC advisory committee was overjoyed with the decision. The call for applications went out across the country immediately. Appointment of a tenure track assistant professor and director was made for 1 July 1990.

Meanwhile, tensions flared in the faculty among members of the academic staff about the decision to recruit for only the Women's Program. The dean did not have the unanimous support of the staff on the process of decision-making or the decision itself. The decision about the second position was tabled for Fall 1991 when the dean would be back from sabbatical. In April 1991 the Faculty of Extension lost three academic positions as a result of the university-wide restructuring (two positions left in abeyance following the review and one set aside awaiting faculty decision). Anger and frustration were voiced but little could be done.

Tensions and fears within Extension shifted due to the severe funding reductions of the base operating budget for the Faculty of Extension announced in February 1991 and the impending decisions about restructuring the operation of continuing education. Faculties of continuing education at other universities across Canada have experienced very severe funding reductions, in some cases spelling the end of their operations. The Faculty of Extension at the University of Alberta had not been fully severed but had to reduce its operating budget from 2.8 million dollars in 1990–91 to 0.9 million dollars in 1995–96. Emotionally and psychologically, members of Extension felt under siege. Tensions and work-related stress were high amid an atmosphere of uncertainty and ever-increasing demands for more programming, more revenue and fewer resources. WPRC was not untouched.

The base operating monies that Extension receives from the university pays for academic salaries and some central operating costs. For WPRC the director's salary and the costs of the office space were traditionally covered by the university. Revenue to pay one full-time support person and various temporary project staff had been generated through tuition fees, grants, and donations. Extension programs have operated primarily on a cost-recovery basis. Cutbacks meant that programs, such as WPRC, were expected to become completely self-sufficient, covering all costs including academic staff and facilities. Such a free enterprise model, and the values and ideology that underpin it, begs the question of the commitment of the university and the taxpayers of Alberta to continuing education and women's programming. Market driven programming contradicts the goals and objectives of WPRC. Living with such contradiction was painful, but is part of marginality. New theories are needed to guide our actions in the months and years to come.

Universitywide discussions about the role and structure of Extension were scheduled for Fall 1991. Nested in these discussions was a debate about the merit of noncredit, lifelong learning about the responsibility of the university to the citizens of Alberta. Women's programming was under scrutiny once again.

*Discipline Location*
Dramatic technological and information changes in the workplace during the past decade require that workers constantly upgrade their skills and knowledge. Ever-increasing and new demands are being placed on universities to be responsive to the needs of the workplace. Many of the programs within the Faculty of Extension at the University of Alberta are designed to help meet these demands. Noncredit courses, conferences, and self-directed study are some of the ways that new skills and knowledge can be readily acquired.

The merit of noncredit courses and programs is commonly viewed by members of the university community as secondary to the more serious, degree-seeking activities that take place in other faculties. The work of Extension is not well understood on campus, and historically has been severely criticized as having little academic merit. At the same time, the Faculty of Extension is highly visible in the general public and has a long-standing reputation for offering high quality, relevant, and timely programs for the people of Alberta.

Adult education, the theory and methodology of teaching adults, has flourished during the past fifteen years, but it is not widely recognized as a legitimate academic pursuit. Despite the emergence of many advocates of interdisciplinarity, a hierarchy of academic disciplines persists, with the "real" or "hard" sciences (physics, biology, and medicine) at the top, and social sciences and education—including adult education and women's studies—at the bottom. Such a hierarchy reflects the implementation of the current scientific paradigm and epistemological assumptions which underpin it. Although there are increasing tensions which suggest we may be at a threshold of a paradigm shift, operationally at this university the hegemony of science remains intact.

If one were to classify the Women's Program and Resource Centre in terms of its academic pursuits, a question implicitly asked when issues of academic merit and research are raised, adult education and women's studies would be the quick response. Academic marginalization may aptly describe the academic location of WPRC. One major implication of this marginalization has been the apparent need to constantly justify WPRC's existence. This drains energy (staff time and resources) which could be used for many other more positive and constructive purposes.

*Physical Location*
Physically located on the periphery of the University of Alberta campus, at first in Corbett Hall on the southern tip of campus and, since 1984, in a restored old two-storey house in North Garneau, WPRC sits at the nexus of the university and community.

Within the Faculty of Extension, since WPRC moved to Garneau, we have experienced a satellite status. In 1984–87 the majority of communications with the rest of the faculty were carried out by campus mail and telephone. In 1989 the Faculty of Extension, not including the various satellites, was moved from Corbett Hall and relocated in various temporary quarters across campus. This displacement served as a major incentive to incorporate new technologies into our everyday world of work. With the incorporation of computer technology, WPRC was less isolated and with facsimile and electronic mail, we could transfer information and correspond rapidly and efficiently within the faculty.

Computer technology has facilitated an easier flow of formal information, but informal information exchanges within the faculty remain highly fragmented. Committee meetings were about the only opportunity for informal get-togethers, and these existed for the academic staff only. Nonacademic staff did not have structured committees and therefore did not have similar opportunities to meet.

The Women's Program administrative office and the Women's Resource Centre reaped the benefits and comforts of being in a big old house. In many ways "the house" symbolized the unique character of WPRC—we were part of the university but also separate and apart.

The house had not been significantly altered from its days as a majestic home for the Layton family. Light fixtures, woodwork, and appliances remained intact. New bookshelves were added periodically to accommodate new acquisitions, and desks were moved around to accommodate the changes in our work. Women who visited the centre often commented about the warm, welcoming environment. Unlike a traditional office space, the "house," as it was affectionately called, had spaces for women to meet, read, and visit. Many a rally, conference, or workshop had been planned around the kitchen table.

Historically, when most of the faculty were housed in Corbett Hall, many WPRC courses, conferences, and forums were held in that building and many students came to recognize the building as the site for extension. Since the relocation in 1989 to temporary quarters, classroom space allocated to the faculty included a few rooms in various trailer complexes. The implications for students and teachers was far reaching. The general ambience of extension programming had been significantly altered and issues of comfort have emerged.

Classroom requirements for good adult education, not to mention feminist teaching-learning, are significantly different from the traditional lecture format used in mainstream academic teaching. In the new extension building, which opened in 1992, care was taken to construct classrooms which attend to these needs to create a positive energy and ambience.

*Relations with Other Women's Organizations and Groups*
There is no singular "women's community" just as there is no one feminist perspective. In general, diversity and ad hoc connections probably best describe the nature of the relationships between women's organizations in Alberta. Formalized agreements are sometimes created for the duration of cosponsored activities or particular undertakings, but few ongoing structural ties exist. WPRC's relations with women's groups and organizations, not unlike those witnessed among other women's groups, are horizontal as opposed to the vertical and hierarchical relationships within the faculty and the university.

On the University of Alberta campus from 1981 to 1991, several women's groups emerged. WPRC, one of the forerunners, relates primarily with two of these groups, Women's Studies and the Women's Research Centre. These three programs share feminist values and ideals but hold different mandates. The director of WPRC is an ongoing member of the advisory committees of Women's Studies and Women's Research Centre, and a member of the Research Centre sits on the advisory committee of WPRC. Although there is an interrelationship embedded in the structure of these groups, each program is busy staying afloat financially and meeting ever-increasing demands, leaving little time to collaborate, support each other, maintain clear communication lines and boundaries, and share resources. Given the current university restructuring, it may be timely for the three groups, along with other interested women, to examine our interrelatedness and take an active role in constructing our future.

From 1981–91, dozens of women's groups have emerged throughout the province of Alberta, each usually around a particular set of issues. Organizations such as Northwest Media Network, Celebration of Women in the Arts, Women's Collective, Women's Research Centre, Women of Colour, Changing Together, Abortion By Choice, Edmonton Women's Health Collective, Options for Women, and a variety of support and reading groups have rapidly emerged. WPRC has provided, and continues to provide, support to many emerging groups in the form of meeting space, administrative aid, photocopying, fundraising, cosponsorship and collaboration.

In 1981 WPRC was a pioneer in offering noncredit courses for women in the Edmonton area. With the emergence of many women's groups and organizations came the potential for duplication of services, unfriendly competition, and disputes of territoriality. In efforts to avoid duplication and disputes, WPRC directors, in consultation with the WPRC advisory committee, have gradually evolved a set of criteria which help guide the program selection and address a particular market niche. All courses must be university-level and based on a social-political analysis of the position of women in society. Also, all courses must help women develop individual and collective means of bettering their lives. All instructors must have a graduate degree, be well versed in adult education practice, and be able to foster active teaching-learning in the classroom. In addition, a good communication network with women's groups and other course providers is required. Such a network is largely dependent upon the personal relationships of the director.

In 1989–90, the Edmonton office of the Women's Program, Secretary of State, commissioned a study of the organizational development needs of women's groups in Alberta. Bonnie Hutchinson and Associates of Camrose carried out the research. The results indicated that fundraising is the number one organizational concern. Staff training and development were also identified. Since WPRC maintains a commitment to foster and support women's groups and to facilitate women's learning, it seems timely and appropriate that WPRC mount a project to help women's groups flourish and grow.

## How Is Learning Facilitated?

Two of the luxuries of being in the Faculty of Extension and involved in offering noncredit programming are flexibility and autonomy. Because general noncredit courses do not collectively constitute the ingredients for a degree, any course, forum, conference, and educational event can be added or subtracted at the discretion of the director, with guidance from the advisory committee. Courses are not entirely content-driven, and the power and authority traditionally embedded in the text and instructor can be removed with relative ease. Learners in the women's program learn for themselves. The emphasis is on acquiring, integrating, and understanding new information and skills in order to move forward both personally and politically. The rich knowledge and experience brought to courses by participants becomes part of the emerging curriculum.

The teaching-learning processes of WPRC are highly interactive and bring together women from a broad cross-section of society to a safe, supportive learning environment. For some women it is the first time in their lives to be together with other women in an noncompetitive and supportive way. The aim of the educational program is to encourage women to find their own voices and to develop a strong sense of self and other. Each women is believed to be on her own path and will take from each course as much as she can at the time.

As the curriculum designer who compiled the course offerings of the WPRC, I was increasingly conscious of the power and privilege that I held. Discussions of the politics of curriculum design were commonly located within the degree-granting Women's Studies programs, and only a few authors have pursued issues within noncredit Women's Studies curricula. Noncredit curriculum design aims to match the needs of women with the resources of the university, however, what topics are identified and transformed into courses is a political process and not merely an objective and systematic administrative procedure.

In my practice, I used a multisourced strategy to gather information, themes, and ideas for new courses, conferences, and forums. I gathered information from course evaluations, advisory committee members, individual women's requests, organizational requests, instructors, magazines and journals, newspapers from various Canadian women's groups, and from other adult educators. My process is reflective, exploratory, and intuitive. My own interests and interpretations of the world entered into the creation of courses, workshops, and projects. Questions are also raised about inclusion, perspective, and privilege in the work of WPRC.

From the beginning, it has been clearly stated that WPRC cannot be all things to everybody; it is here that some of the tensions lie. Understanding WPRC and our commitment to the women's movement, I started to ask what are our boundaries. For ten years our boundaries had been rather vague, shifting, and at times arbitrary. Perhaps the time is ripe to develop clear boundaries and work to maintain them, for the sake of the future existence of WPRC.


Future Directions

Looking into the future can be an opportunity to dream, and I believe that many rainbows lie ahead at the Women's Program and Resource Centre.

WPRC announced the Counselling Women Certificate Program, which combines feminist theory with the practice of counselling, which began Fall 1991. Successful completion of this program enables graduates to apply feminist approaches to counselling women. Students learn to think critically about the assumptions that underpin various approaches to counselling. Practical application is emphasized. Nurses, teachers, counsellors from shelters and sexual assault centres, crisis workers, social workers, teachers, vocational counsellors, and adult educators find the program timely and relevant. Our dream is to deliver the certificate program at a distance by 1993.

Throughout this article I have alluded to various new undertakings, such as broadening the mandate of the Resource Centre and working with women's groups concerning issues of organizational development. I dream of the resource centre becoming a women's library and part of a vast international network of university libraries. The centre also becomes a publishing and clearinghouse and guidance and support centre for women's groups.

Learning new ways of organizing ourselves and getting the work done while remaining sane and healthy are high on the agenda for WPRC in the 1990s. How to avoid perpetuating the creation of a feminist orthodoxy with its corresponding dogma is a challenge that faces us. Issues of friendship, leadership, and power will need to be talked about openly. Learning how to care for and not take care of each other will be a crucial piece of this work, both intellectually and emotionally. Thanks to continuing support of hundreds of women, WPRC will be able to face these challenges and make our dreams become reality.

*Pat Rasmussen* served as director of the Women's Program and Resource Centre from 1989–92. In 1992 she resigned her position. That post is now filled by Dr. Reinhilde Boehme. The resource centre was decentralized in 1993 and is currently housed in various locations on the University of Alberta campus.

PATRICIA ROOME

# Remembering Together

## Reclaiming Alberta Women's Past

"I remember" writes Molly Chisaakay. Her poem weaves together images of her northern Alberta childhood on the Assumption Reserve near High Level during the 1950s, her elders with their 'noghe wodihe' (wolverine stories), songs, and drums and her grandfather Alexis Seniantha, the Dene Tha' spiritual leader and presence behind their tea dances.[1]

I, too, remember. Pictures of my childhood float past as I remember my McCurlie relatives who had immigrated to Stettler, Alberta, from Scotland in 1906, my Ontario grandparents who homesteaded at Cochrane, and my adolescence spent in the postwar, oil boom town of Edmonton. While both Chisaakay the poet and I the historian wanted to link our personal stories to a collective past, attempts at bridging our separate experiences brought us face to face with an older dilemma. As Simone de Beauvoir observed in *The Second Sex*, unlike blacks or the working-class who make themselves subjects by trans-forming either whites or the bourgeoisie into "others," women do not say "we" except in feminist gatherings.[2] Thus when Molly Chisaakay took my women's studies class in 1985, she challenged me to listen to native women's stories: I encouraged her to explore feminism. Each of us hoped that in remembering together, the "I" could be transformed more frequently into "we."[3]

Finding answers to our questions about native, immigrant, and Canadian grandmothers became easier with the publication of a wider variety of Alberta women's stories. Read together they demonstrate that the history of Alberta women is no longer "a harvest yet to reap."[4] This essay explores these stories in the context of the international debate on the significance of "experience, difference, dominance, and voice" in writing about women's past.[5] In remembering together, our voices speak out against the myths and stereotypes of women embedded in western Canadian history and challenge the dichotomies which have circumscribed women's experience.[6] Writing women into Alberta's history began with a deconstruction of the frontier myth to expose the heroic pioneer's dominance and unmask the masculine image of the West. This project critiqued the work of generations of writers, politicians, and businessmen who have fed Canadians and Americans a monotonous diet of western narratives—ensuring that their tale with its male heroes would become an intrinsic aspect of our culture heritage.[7] Following in this tradition, *A History of Alberta* is dedicated "to the fur traders, farmers and financiers who have made Alberta what it is," for according to James Macgregor these men are "the players who have trod its stage."[8]

As long as this narrative of "stalwart men and incidental, unimportant women," held centre stage, the story of a woman's West remained suppressed. "The men are so dominant," argues American historian Susan Armitage, "that the women have been all but crowded off the stage."[9] When women appear they are confined by the script to minor roles as refined ladies, helpmates or "bad women"; while native women play the part of princesses or squaws. Similarly, when telling the native story the male version presumes to speak for everyone, argue Patricia Albers and Beatrice Medicine who see native women as "the hidden half."[10] Waiting in the wings as a silent challenge to this limited script are a completely different set of female characters whose stories speak to us about dignity, self-worth, and importance—whether the language is English, Ukrainian, German, or Dene Dhah.

Telling native women's stories strikes at the heart of the current debate over voice and power. In Alberta, as elsewhere in Canada, native and non-native scholars and writers have presented representations of native women. Historians Sylvia Van Kirk and Jennifer Brown, in their pioneering work of the early 1980s, demonstrated native women's economic importance to the fur trade and showed that in addition to her economic and political role, a native wife, a family, and a home created "many tender ties" for fur traders like Richard Hardisty or John Rowand of Fort Edmonton.[11] Unfortunately, other historians have been slow to follow Van Kirk and Brown's example, with the result that native women disappear again from western history after the treaties of the 1870s. Gerald Friesen, for example, employs a revisionist approach to the native experience and documented the revolutionary era from 1840 to 1900, but his lack of recognition that gender is significant to historical change makes his synthesis of western Canadian history flawed.[12] Another recent study *Alberta: A New History* also fails to give native women's experience serious treatment; but in contrast to Friesen, historians Howard and Tamara Palmer effectively incorporate recent scholarship on women into their new history.[13] A third book, *Peoples of Alberta: Portraits in Cultural Diversity* tells us little about native women's history, since the portraits privilege ethnicity and ignore native women's different experience.[14] Historians writing in the 1990s face the challenge of giving importance to gender in native people's history while at the same time neither sacrificing cultural difference nor ignoring the history of racism in their analysis.

Balancing gender, culture, and racism is a more familiar exercise for women anthropologists. Those who write from within a Marxist-feminist framework speak about native women's loss of status, power, and control over their sexuality in the transformation of their once egalitarian societies. *Chain Her by One Foot* is Karen Anderson's conclusion about the impact of colonization, technology, and capitalism on eastern native women of the Huron, Iroquois, and Montagnais cultures. On the west coast, although colonization came later, Tshimshian women's status also declined.[15] Directly relevant to Alberta is a case study of the northern Plains Indians—Teton, Dakota, Assiniboines, Gros Ventre, and Blackfoot—and the political economy of gender during the nineteenth century. Author Alan Klein examines the severe rupture of the traditional eighteenth century relations of production which followed the increased usage and dependency upon horses and the hide trade among the northern Plains Indians. The resulting decline in women's status was masked by "an era of unprecedented prosperity, crisis in provisioning the society; the rise of male dominated institutions; and incursions by whites."[16]

As the concept of private property gained acceptance among the Blackfoot in Canada, gender relations altered, allowing warriors who had acquired wealth, status, and power the luxury of owning numerous wives. A case study on the impact of trade, Christianity, and cultural conflict on Crowfoot's wives and daughters would complement Pamela White's doctoral dissertation, "Restructuring the Domestic Sphere," which examines the federal government's manipulation of gender relations and women's status among the Plains Indians.[17] The use of native women to promote cultural change and assimilation on Alberta's Indian reserves is a theme which also needs examination. Jacqueline Gresko noted that educating native girls in industrial schools became a priority only when the Department of Indian Affairs discovered devoted nuns who would work for low pay teaching native girls domestic science and the proper role of a Canadian wife. Government officials anticipated educated native girls would exert a powerful civilizing influence on their future husbands and prevent the young men from selecting wives "among the uneducated woman of their bands and relapse into barbarism."[18] Although native girls' education in Alberta has yet to be examined, as a result of the controversy surrounding the Lubicon Lake Indians' land claims, there is new research on the impact of development on Lubicon Lake women. *"Rupturing the Ties that Bind" Lubicon Lake Women and Their Society* documents the negative effect of resource development on Lubicon women, addresses the land claims dispute, and shows the rapid and destructive changes which are transforming gender relations and the Lubicon's traditional culture.[19]

Gender, tradition, and change are also explored by Beverly Hungry Wolf in *The Ways of My Grandmothers*. Growing up on the Blood Reserve at Cardston, Hungry Wolf remembers how native women were neglected and negatively represented in her textbooks whose authority she was taught to respect. Hungry Wolf came to believe that "the old-time Indian women were sold and treated like slaves, because that's what the books said." Generations of government and missionary propaganda "against our old ways" effectively isolated native women from the culture of their grandmothers. Hungry Wolf found her elders while dedicated to their traditions were initially very reluctant to share their knowledge. Sadly, they also had absorbed the attitude that "there was no future in this world for their children and grandchildren if they didn't put aside these old ways." Refusing to accept this denial of her heritage and recognizing the alienation which it produced, Hungry Wolf devoted herself to learning from her grandmothers by participating in all aspects of their lives from the sacred ceremonies of the Sun Dance to the everyday routine of setting up a tipi.[20]

Through historical research Hungry Wolf unearthed a surprising story of tribal diversity in native women's experience, finding examples of women's subservience, equality, and leadership. Her oral history and short portraits of her elders and their ancestors expose the stereotypes and speak to Blackfoot women about their proud and distinctive heritage."A Grandmother Who Went on War Raids" and "Running Eagle—Woman Warrior of the Blackfeet" are two of the nontraditional women she presents. On a personal level, Hungry Wolf's Sarcee aunt, Mary One Spot, shared fond memories of being raised the traditional way by her grandmother and astutely dismissed the brief time which she spent at the missionary boarding school for its focus on manual labour, not education.[21] Hungry Wolf considers her aunt fortunate for escaping the insidious influence to become "modern" which permeated her mothers' generation and hers. For these women Hungry Wolf collected and recorded the myths, legends, dances, and teachings of her grandmothers which she learned as a young girl but only recently has come to value. Her journey through the Blackfoot women's spiritual world is testimony of Hungry Wolf's respect for her people.

"My language is Cree, and so I would like to say, 'Nitawa acimowak nisimak' ('My sisters are great storytellers'). With strength and love, they speak for all of us, and in doing so they honour us," wrote well-known Metis author Maria Campbell in 1990.[22] Working from a strong storytelling tradition, Metis women join with the voices of their grandmothers and those of other native women to create a new narrative grounded upon women's diversity, spiritual power and leadership. In *Fifty Dollar Bride,* Jock Carpenter reconstructs the life of her own grandmother, Marie Rose Delorme, who was born into a White Horse Plains Metis family in 1870 and educated at the St. Boniface Convent. Delorme married a Norwegian adventurer named Smith who paid her parents fifty dollars for their seventeen-year-old daughter in 1877. Shortly after marriage the couple move to Alberta where they eventually homesteaded near Pincher Creek and where Marie Rose raised a family of seventeen children. When she died in 1960 her life had become an inspiration for her numerous grandchildren.[23]

Metis grandmother Victoria Belcourt Callihoo, a contemporary of Marie Rose Smith, was born at Lac Ste. Anne in 1861 and died in Edmonton in 1966. In contrast to Marie Rose, Callihoo married the son of Chief Callihoo of the Michael Indian Reserve, but like Smith she was a seventeen-year-old bride. She raised a family of twelve with her husband, a prosperous Villeneuve farmer. Callihoo's memoirs create the image of a strong and remarkable woman whose faith, as did Marie Rose Smith's, sustained her through many difficult years.[24] A third Metis woman, Cheechumn, the great-grandmother of Maria Campbell, comes to life in Campbell's autobiography where she represents Metis tradition, self respect, and identity.

Each of these three women are remembered by granddaughters whose lives bore little resemblance to those of their elders. *Halfbreed* recreates Campbell's childhood among the northern Saskatchewan Metis "Road Allowance People" and her troubled youth spent on the streets of Vancouver, Calgary, and Edmonton in the 1960s. "I want to tell you about the joys and sorrows, the oppressing poverty, the frustration and the dreams" writes Campbell, about being a "halfbreed woman in our country."[25] Unfortunately, too few Metis or native women have written about their lives for us to reconstruct a continuous tradition or explain the deterioration in spiritual and cultural identity between these generations. In place of a history we have only isolated voices—like those who speak out in the local histories of the Kikino and Elizabeth settlements, two of the Metis reserves created by the Alberta government in the 1930s. Kikino women remember female leaders like Mary Ladouceur, their community's midwife throughout the 1940s; postmistress Helen Calliou; and the first university graduate, Leona Rose Thompson. They also remember fighting against exclusion from their settlement's first council meetings in 1939. When Metis women earned political rights, the Elizabeth Metis Settlement became the first to have a female chairperson.[26] Although important to community and family, Metis women's voices are seldom heard in the demographic studies which have documented the development of Metis families, often for legal battles in Alberta over land claims.[27]

This silence allows scholars to ignore Metis women's historical role and contribution. In 1975 when Ted Brasser analyzed Metis art, he acknowledged the distinctive genre which Metis artisans created, but failed to comment on the artisans' gender, a curious omission since Metis women trained by Catholic nuns and native grandmothers overwhelmingly outnumbered men as the artisans.[28] Fortunately, curator Julia Harrison's recent study corrects this error by acknowledging that Metis women were the innovators whose art shows "an expressive individuality."[29] Even racism has had a different impact on "halfbreed women" as Maria Campbell explains: "the missionaries impressed upon us the feeling that women were a source of evil. This belief, combined with the ancient Indian recognition of the power of women, is still holding back the progress of our people today."[30]

*Writing the Circle,* an anthology of native women's writing, speaks forcefully of racism, women's oppression, and women's power. Two poems, "Brown Sister" and "The Uniform of the Dispossessed" by Emma LaRocque from the Alberta Metis community of Big Bay, explore these themes.

In *Those Who Know,* Dianne Meili, Victoria Callihoo's great-granddaughter, recreates stories of Alberta's native elders and celebrates the strength, leadership, and spirituality of seventeen women, such as Maggie Black Kettle, a Blackfoot who now teaches in Calgary at the Plains Indian Survival School, and Victoria McDonald, a Chipewyan elder from Fort MacKay.[31] These elders' stories show the importance of cultural memory and spirituality to native identity, demonstrate the relativity of time and historical change, and caution women historians to avoid simplistic generalizations. While race and culture are central forces in framing aboriginal women's experience, gender also features strongly, making a feminist perspective an important framework for giving native women visibility and voice.[32]

Although native women speak proudly about their spirituality as the source of their power, women historians in Alberta as elsewhere have tended to ignore the importance of religion.[33] Despite rich archival records, the voices of Alberta's Catholic and Anglican teaching sisters have not been recovered nor their contributions deeply explored. For example, the diaries of the Faithful Companions of Jesus (FCJ) at the Glenbow Archives describe their trip from Liverpool to Prince Albert and record their perceptions of the west. Together with the Grey Nuns they settled in Calgary in 1885, built a convent, and developed the Holy Cross Hospital. A similar process occurred in Edmonton in 1888, Lethbridge in 1891, and also in St. Albert. Reverend Mother Greene, the FCJ's Superior, lived in Calgary from 1885–1933 and became the first superintendent of the Calgary Separate School Board; while Calgary's St. Mary's Girls' School, established in 1909, graduated some of the province's first professional women and remained the only school for further education for Catholic girls in southern Alberta for many years. The FCJ's shared educational work with the Grey Nuns of Nicolet who operated a residential school at Standoff from 1898–1942 and staffed a hospital on the Blood Reserve. Reconstructing this story would demonstrate the teaching sisters' importance in our educational history and break the silence on native women's experience of education.

Recent studies on Franco-Albertan, Mormon, and Ukrainian women illustrate ethnic women's greater interest in exploring their religious traditions. Anne Gagnon discovered that the Catholic Church orchestrated the growth of religious nationalism among young Franco-Albertan girls in the 1920s at the Pensionnat Assomption, a private boarding school.[34] Maureen Usenback Beecher also sees religion and ecclesiastical practices as "the strongest binding force" for Mormon women who settled the Cardston area. Their belief in women's responsibility for their own salvation encouraged the growth of charismatic practices in the Female Relief Society which bonded the women together and helped them forge a new identity in Alberta. Mormon women historians have given the practice of polygamy a new reading by listening to women's voices speaking about feeling trapped between "two fires," those of the American government and those of their husbands.[35]

Like the Mormons, the Orthodox Church relied heavily on women such as the Sister Servants of Mary Immaculate, who came to Edmonton in 1902 from the Ukraine to operate the Ukrainian Girls' Night School, to preserve Ukrainian identity in the face of assimilationist pressures on the prairies in the early twentieth century. *To Serve Is to Love* tells the success story of these sisters whose numbers grew as they went from humble beginnings at their Beaver Lake Mission to establish convents in Edmonton, Mundare, Vegreville, and Calgary, and hospitals in Mundare and Willingdon. Eventually the Sisters expanded across the prairies to Toronto and the United States serving the Ukrainian community and providing careers for Canadian girls. Canadian Sisters achieved a considerable degree of independence as a result of their importance to community survival through their role in 'ridni shkoly' (part-time Ukrainian schools), which taught children in Alberta the Ukrainian language, culture, and history.[36]

Under the auspices of the Presbyterian Board of Home Missions and the Methodist Women's Missionary Society (WMS), Alberta's Protestant churchwomen also created missions with residential schools and hospitals in the northeastern Ukrainian communities. Although unmarried women missionaries had an important cultural influence on the isolated Ukrainian farm women, they failed to win many converts to the Protestant church as long as conversion meant denying ethnicity. Their missions' emphasis on assimilation backfired and, as Vivian Oleander concludes, instead strengthened the "identification between Ukrainian ethnicity and the traditional Ukrainian churches."[37]

Women's spirituality remains to be explored in the Alberta context. As the following examples illustrate, women sought and demanded respect as spiritual leaders. After the death of Doukhobor spiritual leader Peter Verigen, Anastasia Holuboff took 165 people to establish the "Lordly Christian Community of Universal Brotherhood," a communal village near Shouldice. From 1926 until the 1950s the "Lords" maintained residences, shops, a school, and a community and prayer home where Anastasia and the Doukhobors worshipped. Based on the memories of former village residents, John Friesen and Michael Verigin paint an unfavourable portrait of an autocratic and unpopular Anastasia and her leadership struggles.[38] Although Nellie McClung never knew Anastasia Holuboff, she also fought for acceptance of women as spiritual leaders and ministers in the United Church, a fight which women finally won in 1935. Because of the male monopoly on ministerial positions, McClung also adopted a different vehicle for addressing women and created "literature as pulpit," argues historian Randi Warne.[39]

Although often overlooking the importance of religion, historians have been fascinated with early pioneer women. These women left a rich legacy of letters and diaries which speak of diversity, but also similarity in experience. Lovisa McDougall, wife of a merchant, records her perceptions of Fort Edmonton in the 1880s in the letters which she sent to her Ontario family.[40] Monica Hopkins and Sarah Roberts wrote about their lives on southern Alberta ranches and homesteads, while Monica Storrs described her work as an Anglican lay worker in the Peace River region.[41] Along with women's writings which have appeared in *Alberta History*, these narratives speak about the impact of migration on women, identify women's motives for coming to Alberta, articulate women's roles in their new communities, and record their impressions of the Alberta landscape. Reading these accounts confirms historian Joy Parr's conclusion that "emigration is a sex-selective process experienced differently by women and men."[42] The documents which Susan Jackel includes in *A Flannel Shirt and Liberty* demonstrate that British gentlewomen sought a greater measure of freedom when they came to the Canadian west. Since women's voices are seldom recorded in standard historical documents, pioneer women's accounts remain an invaluable source for understanding women's experience.[43]

*The Last Best West: Women on the Alberta Frontier 1880–1930* assesses the complexity of women's lives in pioneer society. Partially a collective autobiography, Eliane Silverman's work is based on interviews with 150 women who helped her to document the texture of "lives lived so silently." By listening to women tell of their experiences of marriage, contraception, childbirth, growing up female, working on the farm, in the urban home, or building new communities, Silverman is able to reassess the historical significance of these women's lives. Pioneer women "perceived their lives within the private realm, rarely fitting even their paid labour into public context," concludes Silverman as she calls for "integration of the private world of women with men's public spaces."[44] In placing women into the written history of frontier Alberta and using women's own understanding of their lives, communities, and families, Silverman begins this process. We learn that women from different backgrounds acted as both agents for the retention of status quo and agents of change. Old patterns of deference in church going, child-raising, sexual relations, and employment remained; but in the west, as many woman became economically productive, the myth of "the lady" also became irrelevant and crumbled. Alberta pioneer women seized new opportunities, argues Silverman, and created organizations, challenged older educational and political institutions, and constructed new careers.[45]

Emigration became a freeing process for many women, and making one's own history through hard labour is a dominant theme of pioneer women's narratives, especially those written in later life. They often mock the image of leisured ladies epitomized by the expression "the fair, frail flower of Western womanhood." Writers Catherine Philip and Sheilagh Jameson explore the dichotomy between this image and the reality by focussing on the civilizing function performed by all women on the Alberta frontier. On the homesteads men knew the "tell-tale signs of a woman's presence—curtains on the windows and a clothesline at the back,"[46] concludes Philip. Women also refused to accept their culture's idealization of motherhood and large families. Many women preferred small families, while others attempted to limit family size by self-abortions or hired abortionists like Calgary's "Dr. Lovingheart" whom Philip found practised quite openly in early Calgary. Clearly many frontier women resisted cultural prescriptions and descriptions, relying instead on their own decisions about their labour and its importance.[47] Lacking a hospitable environment to flourish, the imagery of "the lady" never became a feature of the western Canadian cultural history; whereas the helpmate stereotype, an equally narrow and romantic ideal, became deeply embedded in our cultural identity. Casting pioneer women in the role as helpmates neutralized gender conflict in society, masked the inequality in pioneer families, and minimized many women's unhappiness with the status quo.[48]

Two books, *All Of Baba's Children* and *No Streets of Gold*, demonstrate the degree to which cultural difference isolated ethnic women from these stereotypes. Socialist writer Helen Potrebenko concludes that the bleakness of the pioneer life encouraged Ukrainian peasant women of her grandmothers' generation to consult witches as often as they sought council from their priests. Potrebenko recalls that her grandmother raised her children with an absentee husband, faced battering when her husband returned, and coped with the deaths of her children while managing to develop their frontier farm. Despite Albertans' hostility, Ukrainian peasant women built farms and persevered as they had in eastern Europe in previous centuries. Ironically these women are not the heroines of *No Streets of Gold*, that role is reserved for the more ephemeral Ukrainian-socialist female activists.[49] Writer Myrna Kostash also condemns the Ukrainian patriarchal family's repressiveness toward women. Kostash remembers rebelling at the Ukrainian pattern of female subservience, exploitation, and compulsory unpaid labour. But she recognized that her push for independence began with "baba" and the women of her generation who quietly tried to subvert patriarchal authority and to establish "female dignity and female legitimacy in the human collective, even as Two Hills represented it, from the subtle forum of the Hallowe'en Box social."[50]

"No culture, no language, no tradition" is Potrebenko's bitter conclusion about this in-between-generation who suffered "that terrible purgatory of acculturation in which immigrants exist for one or two generations and native people for over a hundred years."[51] Canada forcibly separated immigrants from their old ways and then prevented them from participating fully in the dominant culture, argues Potrebenko, who remembers her first day of school and her teacher's distaste for her foreign dress and "bad" manners. Potrebenko found identity in the socialist politics, Kostash turned to literature and feminism just as other Ukrainian-Canadian women chose religion, ethnicity, and nationalism.

Historian Frances Swyripa explores these relationships, concluding, in contrast to Potrebenko and Kostash, that ethnicity has been more important than gender in determining Ukrainian women's experience. *Wedded to the Cause* explores the "primacy of the group" and the contradictions imposed upon Ukrainian women who desire to improve their status as women and retain their "Ukrainianness" while being pressured into showing active commitment to a homeland.[52] Baba's image has grown in importance, explains Swyripa, because her food, embroidery, and Easter eggs are the cultural symbols that now define "Ukrainianness." At both the elite and grassroots level Ukrainian Canadians generated images of women to symbolize their Canadian ethnic identity. The peasant baba is portrayed in a sculpture, which Leo Mol created for the Ukrainian Cultural Heritage Village, as a submissive part of the Ukrainian pioneer family, while a different sculpture of a young, sexual woman titled "Madonna of the Wheat," by John Weaver, stands proudly alone at Edmonton's City Hall. Baba's triumph over the official community image of "Madonna of the Wheat" represents, Swyripa argues, the Ukrainian Canadians' alienation from their politicized organized community.[53]

Kostash would agree with baba's victory. As a young woman she also failed to identify with the ethnic establishment's views. "If the only way to be a 'real' Ukrainian-Canadian was to accept romanticization of our history, trivialization of our culture and piece-meal demands for restitution, then I refused it," explained Kostash in 1977.[54] In analyzing these tensions, Swyripa draws heavily upon Alberta sources to document women's importance in the politics of nation-building and the impact of conflicting claims of nationalism on the daughters of first-generation Ukrainian immigrants in the 1920s. While the WCTU and the WMS represent the forces "making her Canadian"—that is, cast in the image of the middle-class, Anglo-Canadian wife—the elite of the Ukrainian community worked at "keeping her Ukrainian." Ironically, both communities "adopted similar arguments and priorities" for women but differed in "the national ends." Swyripa concludes that "by encouraging general enlightenment and modernization among Ukrainian Canadian women, the intelligentsia promoted their integration into Canadian society"; but she also makes clear that expectations for women to be Ukrainian homemakers and patriots meant women continued to "operate outside mainstream parameters."[55] Others like Kostash abandoned their ethnic baggage in disgust and postponed a reconciliation with this past until a more liberal climate prevailed. Many simply accepted intermarriage and assimilation as the easier route to acceptance.

Despite Swyripa's persuasive argument, the sparse number of studies on women and ethnicity in Alberta makes it difficult to generalize from Ukrainian women's experience.[56] Although there is an extensive literature on the Hutterites, only a few studies make women their focus; however, using their experience to build an argument for ethnicity as the primary force in shaping women's lives would be difficult given Hutterite women's unique situation.[57]

*Defiant Sisters*, another study on women and ethnicity, advances a different thesis. Varpu Lindstrom-Best stresses the importance of class and gender in the lives of the independent and militant Finnish women who immigrated to Canada.[58] Alberta mining towns provided many examples to support her thesis. Finnish feminist-socialist Mary North who organized the Woman's Labor Leagues in the Crowsnest Pass belonged to a network of Finnish women activists.[59] As Helmi Milander from Nellie McClung novel *Painted Fires* demonstrates, Finnish domestics in Alberta also possessed a socialist and feminist consciousness which, combined with a sense of ethnic pride, helped them build networks and develop strategies for coping with domestic work. Lindstrom-Best draws the conclusion that for immigrant women from the more industrialized European countries the contradictions of class and their bonds as women were as central to their experience as ethnicity.[60]

Socialist-feminists who argue for the primacy of class, and feminists who believe gender to be more formative in women's experience choose feminism and the international suffrage movement as their literary battlefield.[61] In Alberta, historians reflected and contributed to the thesis that Canadian women suffragists were not radical; indeed they never planned a women's revolution because their commitment lay in promoting their bourgeois class interests often through alliances with men at the expense of solidarity with working-class, immigrant, or native women. At best the women whose ideas Carol Bacchi studies in *Liberation Deferred* were social reformers and "maternal feminists" whose conservative views on gender, class, and race make then unacceptable candidates for feminist heroines. Radicalism, Bacchi concludes, was confined to a few, usually socialist, women who we might observe were also guilty of racist thoughts.[62] Because Bacchi privileges class over gender in her analysis, her thesis by the 1980s represents a historiographic regression. Her numerous critics challenged the validity of her arguments by using examples of sexual antagonism and intimidation which they uncovered through research into local sources in regions which Bacchi ignored.[63]

Alberta material on the suffrage movement includes descriptive pieces by Sheilagh Jameson and Faye Holt, an essay by Paul Voisey focussing on the movement's conservative reform character, a comprehensive and balanced survey by Barbara Nicholson, and later revisionist work by Catherine Cavanaugh and Veronica Strong-Boag.[64]

The debate over the radicalism of early feminist ideology centres on whether the suffragist wanted political privileges primarily to change society based on a view of their superior maternal qualities, or whether they sought political rights based upon their belief in egalitarian principles. A recent essay on prairie women's long struggle for dower legislation sides with the revisionist thesis in concluding that women were committed "to justice and equality" while men resisted "any change in the power imbalance between the sexes."[65] Historians who try to interpret this early women's movement without any understanding of feminist theoretical work with its analysis of patriarchy as a pervasive system will find that they have missed the logic of the international debate.

Prairie women's historiography usually casts rural women and urban women as wary opponents with different "class" interests, rather than as collaborators in redefining the sexual politics in favour of women. Studies on Alberta women's organizations have generally accepted this analytical framework, although Cavanaugh's thesis shows a shared interest in property rights for women. Women's shared goals and the informal networking which occurred between the many organizations which proliferated in the first two decades of the twentieth century are seldom addressed; instead the United Farm Women of Alberta, the Alberta Women's Institutes, the Women's Christian Temperance Unions, the Local Councils of Women, and the Young Women's Christian Associations are interpreted along a rural/urban axis, using an analysis that future studies need to examine. [66]

Women's crusades on temperance and prohibition which the WCTU in Alberta spearheaded received early attention from several historians. In a comparison between the Saskatchewan and Alberta WCTU, Nancy Sheehan concluded that the Alberta WCTU "adopted a more progressive philosophy, opting to stress legislative and suffrage work, and to push for scientific temperance instructions in the public schools"; whereas Saskatchewan emphasized more "charitable and benevolent activities."[67] The nature of the WCTU, settlement patterns, and dynamic leaders in Alberta are the factors which Sheehan argues account for the difference. Focussing on the WCTU's promotion of education, Sheehan neglects the broader ideological context and leaves room for a closer examination of the Albert WCTU in light of new interpretations which show that evangelical feminism was the voice of the WCTU.[68]

Women's biography is a neglected aspect in the writing of Alberta women's past, although it is thriving elsewhere. In a recent essay

Kathleen Barry outlined the radical nature of "discovering the acting subject." She argues that, "like any other oppressed group, women live in the contradiction of actively and creatively constructing their own identity while the male-dominated society imposes a reductive, biologized identity upon them, thus remaking them into merely the products of drives and instincts." Such essentialist determinism robs women of the ability to take themselves and their group seriously as subjects of history. Feminist biography restores agency to women and allows its subject a quest plot, complete with self-conscious ambition and achievement.[69] My doctoral dissertation on Henrietta Muir Edwards, one of "the famous five," whose leadership created the Alberta Local Councils of Women probes her dreams and "passion for politics" which began earlier in Montreal in the 1870s and continued until the 1930s. Although older by twenty years, Edwards shared feminist politics with Irene Parlby, the UFWA president and later Alberta cabinet minister, whose useful life will be examined by Catherine Cavanaugh. Among the famous five, only Louise McKinney's life has not been studied, although neither Emily Murphy nor Nellie McClung have been the subject of recent biographies. "I knew I had a story to tell" wrote McClung as she began her autobiography *The Stream Runs Fast*. Despite her urge to title her story "Without Regret," McClung found looking back over her accomplishments painful for they did not fulfil the "vision I surely had for the creation of a better world."[70]

After Alberta women received the right to vote, feminism survived the disbanding of the suffrage movement and found a home among organized farm women and urban community leaders. These feminists cooperated on a wide range of issues, such as the matrimonial property campaign, the Persons Case, and peace work, while some entered politics to further women's agenda.[71] Calgary women were especially active in local politics in the 1920s and 1930s supporting a variety of political parties. Despite their parties' formal commitment to equality, Alberta women who identified with labour and socialist politics found it difficult to advance as politicians but easy to work for the cause as fundraisers and campaign organizers behind the scenes. Not surprisingly, Amelia Turner's socialism usually took priority over her feminism even though women were given a secondary status within the Labour Party.[72] Nor did women's political participation lessen during the Depression: in the Social Credit Party women played an important role as organizers and supporters. *Alberta Women in Politics*, a recent study prepared for the first Alberta woman Senator Martha P. Bielish, a Ukrainian Canadian who was appointed in 1979, examines the undocumented role women have played in the province's public life. "When I was nine years old, I wasn't even considered a person—now I'm the Lieutenant Governor!" exclaimed Helen Hunley in 1988, reflecting on the changes the women's movement and feminism have brought for women in politics.[73] As this survey shows, many themes remain to be explored, for the voice of the female politician speaks softly in our histories.

The voices debating sexuality, femininity, and marriage in the Alberta context are only slightly louder. Again, the literature is strongest on pioneer women. They viewed marriage as an economic arrangement and a necessity, Silverman argues, rather than a cataclysmic moment or the highlight of their lives.[74] While Alberta women dreamed about partnership in marriage, the legal system sanctions male privilege, property, and power. Keeping your family under control was one of these prerogatives, and many women experienced firsthand the many faces of male violence. Terry Chapman examined court records and analyzed a variety of "sex crimes" in western Canada. Since only a minority of abuse cases ever came to court, sources like local newspapers are useful to reconstruct many of the other stories of wife-battering and its prevalence across class and ethnic boundaries in Alberta. Occasionally, rape victims' testimony appears in their own words entered into the court records; for example, a young Hardisty girl told the court in 1913 during a preliminary inquiry into a rape charge that "the accused had trespasses upon her private property when he had intercourse without her consent."[75]

Alberta women's desire to control their own sexuality and limit reproduction took many forms. In the women's columns of western papers, women exchanged birth control information and lobbied for change through their organizations like the UFWA which passed a resolution in 1933 requesting that the federal government remove the ban on birth control. Few studies address these issues in the Alberta context, although *The Bedroom and the State* shows the need for a study on the Social Credit Government's sterilization of "insane" women.[76] Infanticide and illegitimacy have been studied by Leslie Savage, who examined the records of the Sisters of Misericordia, the Catholic nuns responsible for establishing a shelter and hospital for unwed mothers in Edmonton in 1900. In contrast to Montreal where unwed mothers and their children were hidden away in secrecy by the Sisters, Savage found frontier society showed a lack of interest in confining unwed mothers in an institution; instead the sisters reordered their priorities and addressed the community's urgent need for expanded health services. Although Andree Levesque's research shows unwed mothers in Quebec continued to be hidden away until the 1950s, in Alberta "unwed maternity was still a disgrace, but not such a heinous one as to require . . . disappearance behind convent walls."[77]

These studies suggest a more open society in Alberta where women could assert their claim for greater independence, a view which was also advanced by early feminists. By 1917 Henrietta Muir Edwards wrote: "The women of Alberta, except in dower rights, are more favored in regard to legal status than are those of any other province in Canada." In her opinion "the Government's appreciation of the work of women in standing shoulder to shoulder with their men folk in the development of their country, has been shown by giving them this premier place in the Dominion."[78] Given Edward's belief that women's work was the basis on which the province granted women greater legal equality, it is ironic that the unpaid and paid labour of women is one of the most neglected topics in Alberta history. From the existing literature we have only brief glimpses of women's experience of work.

Regardless of the diversity in individual situations, in general the family economy and a successful life depended on woman's work: gardening, cooking, cleaning, sewing, child-bearing and rearing. On rural farms they managed dairying and poultry production, and were often midwives, postmistresses, and teachers. Their work subsidized the wheat crop and often kept the family out of debt; yet the power structure was never equal. As Marjorie Griffin Cohen's work on women and dairying has demonstrated, capital expenditure usually went to farm equipment first and to the house or the dairy last. Thus farm women did not benefit adequately from increased productivity in order to compete with highly capitalized poultry and dairy farms. Cheese factories also were more productive and efficient than wives' part-time work. As a result farm women abandoned production to work for wages for their local hospital, school board, or town businesses to keep the family economy viable.[79]

These studies challenge us to move beyond the stereotypes, to reexamine the role woman played in the wheat economy and to develop new perspectives. Does Cohen's argument have relevance for Alberta, or did women's productive work on the farm remain important for a longer period of time? How did women cope with the Depression of the 1930s and the postwar oil boom? At present we can only speculate on this theme, for until rural women's economic contribution has been analyzed, we have at best a partial view of the changes industrial capitalism brought to agriculture. By disregarding the sexual division of labour, we also perpetuate the assumption that technology had the same impact on both sexes in Alberta.[80]

Young women entered a different labour market than their brothers. In Alberta many young women's employment choices were limited to domestic service. While poor pay, isolation, and sexual abuse discouraged young girls from entering domestic labour except as a last resort, some fought back by forming organizations like Calgary's 1916 Housekeeper's League or the 1936 Domestic Workers League.[81] Encouraged by the letters and editorials in the agrarian press, rural girls migrated to Alberta's growing cities after World War I hoping to find opportunity and an easier life. Instead of achieving financial independence and interesting careers, young women, Rebecca Coulter explains, using her case study of the working girls in Edmonton as an example, found their opportunities confined to low paying and menial work, prostitution and marriage. Yet despite these limited horizons, more girls aged fifteen to nineteen left for the city than rural boys because the girls found even a small salary and menial jobs in the service, clerical, and manufacturing industries preferable to domestic employment on neighbouring farms.[82]

A Calgary stenographer who recorded her impressions was part of a broader movement of women into female job ghettos as industrial capitalism in the first decade of the twentieth century created the feminization of numerous occupations such as clerical workers, bank tellers, teachers, nurses, food service workers, and telephone operators. Only a few studies, such as Elise Corbet's thesis which describes changes in government legislation and women's work in the 1920s, address these economic changes in the Alberta context. Many important developments like women's role in the 1921 teachers' strike for recognition of the Alberta Teachers Association await investigation. As the careers of Amelia Turner, Edith Patterson, and Mary Crawford demonstrate, teaching represented an alternative to marriage for many women despite its poor pay and discrimination. Women teachers and nurses understandably supported professional unions in Alberta; however in general women workers remained unorganized.[83]

With only a few exceptions, it is the masculine voice that speaks out in the written history of Alberta labour. Women are rarely the subject of lengthy study; instead they receive honourable mention for their support in a strike, a sentence on their wage inequality with men and brief recognition for the union auxiliaries which they organized. Although labour historian Warren Carragata attempted to comment on women workers, the lack of secondary studies on women workers prevented him from presenting a balanced history. We catch a glimpse of women's activism when the United Packinghouse Workers of America (UPWA) organized union locals at Canada Packers and Burns during World War II. Since female employees earned thirty-three cents an hour in 1939, a rate that was twenty cents an hour less than male employees, equal pay for equal work became a central issue, and the Edmonton UPWA local planned to strike in 1945 over the issue of wage disparity. Who protested this situation and pushed the union to work for change? What was women's role in the UPWA? To answer these questions involves making women workers in Alberta the subject of research, an approach adopted in a thesis on women's role in the oil industry.[84]

The prostitute, whom western narratives cast as their "bad woman" is the least understood worker. What were the private lives of these public women like? If some had a lesbian identity, others sought to earn a wage, and the ambitious were "capitalists with rooms." Prostitution on the prairies, but not prostitutes, received early attention in *Red Lights on the Prairies* and in an essay on Calgary. Initially the city attempted to hide prostitutes but under the influence of the reform movement, after 1910, it attempted to prosecute men and link prostitution to drug and alcohol abuse.[85] In an analysis of female crime in Calgary in the same period, Elizabeth Langdon found a direct correlation between the influx of young women into Calgary and the decline in prostitution. This change in the sex-ratio along with more economic opportunity for women to work outside the home meant prostitution became a less necessary alternative. She argues that a broader study of women's role in the Calgary economy would shed light on questions of crime such as theft, vagrancy, and assault.[86]

Despite Henrietta Edwards's optimism about Alberta, girls continued to learn "their God-given place in life" as mothers and wives through the school's introduction of home economics into the curriculum at a time when career women battled prejudice and underemployment.[87]

Although the early feminists and women's organizations which made women's education and career advancement a priority have received some study, the voices of women who attended the University of Alberta remain muffled.[88] In 1908 the University of Alberta's first female students organized the Seven Independent Spinsters club which evolved into the Wauneita Society, an organization which continued to serve female students until 1973. One of the University of Alberta's early graduates was Eleanor Dowding who, as Dr. Silver Keeping, had a distinguished career as a mycologist and professor in the Genetics department. Many more fascinating stories remain to be uncovered: a few examples would include women at the Calgary Normal School, the Ladies Teachers Association and country schoolteachers.[89] Despite their privileged position, professional women have not received any more recognition than other working women. By the 1920s Alberta's small population of women doctors, lawyers, architects, musicians, and artists struggled unnoticed. Although they were no longer a novelty, sexual discrimination continued and professional women's numbers declined by the 1950s.[90]

Professional cowgirls, like Florence La Due who won the fancy roping contest at the first Calgary Stampede in 1912, turned their riding skills into more famous careers. According to historian Mary Lou Lecompte, the first Calgary Stampede "not only established the first real cowgirl superstars, it established women's place in rodeo."[91] At a time when women were cautiously engaging in sports, cowgirls demonstrated greater physical achievement than was believed possible. Lecompte credits these athletes with preparing the public for women's involvement in competitive sports in the 1920s. In Alberta the Edmonton Commercial Graduates basketball team competed from 1926 to 1940, winning an incredible 96.2% of the 522 games they played.[92] Earlier in the Rocky Mountains, a serious climber from England named Gertrude Bentham achieved legendary stature after numerous spectacular ascents. Many other women climbers followed and the Alpine Club of Canada, formed in 1906 by Elizabeth Parker, became one of the first to allow women to join. Drawn by the freedom and opportunity to escape Victorian conventions of femininity, women accounted for a third of its 259 members in 1907 and by 1917 fifty percent.[93] A shared enthusiasm for adventure, exercise, and mountains led two Calgary teachers, the Barclay sisters, to establish the first North American youth hostel in the 1930s. Whereas the earlier women climbers and adventurers had money, these women sought to democratize the sport of hiking to encourage young women with limited means to participate.[94]

A recent study, *Useful Pleasures: The Shaping of Leisure in Alberta 1896–1914*, recognizes class and ethnicity as importance forces in shaping leisure, but ignores gender and minimizes the importance of the many Alberta women who organized climbing trips, literary clubs, libraries, art societies, box socials, and musical or theatrical productions.[95] The proud tradition of the MacLeod Women's Fortnightly Club goes unrecorded even though the club was home of the artist Annora Brown and helped Henrietta Muir Edwards organize the town's first public library. In contrast, the first Dominion Chautauqua superintendent, Nola B. Crites (later Mrs. Erickson) who organized the Canadian movement from her Calgary office in 1917 receives recognition in Sheilagh Jameson's history of the Chautauqua movement. Jameson shows that women worked in equal numbers to men as superintendents, directors, workers, and performers in the Chautauqua.[96]

Drama historian Moira Day has also chosen to tell the story of Alberta women and the development of theatre in the interwar period. Although men participated in the amateur productions staged by most communities, Day argues that little theatre wore a surprisingly feminine face. During 1932–33 over one hundred productions in rural Alberta communities were sponsored by women's organizations like the UFWA, Women's Institutes, and the Ladies' Aids. Into this situation came Elizabeth Sterling Hayes, a gifted drama educator from the University of Alberta's Department of Extension, who remained the moving spirit in little theatre from 1922 to 1937. Day also argues that rural communities did not need cultural missionaries since places like Grand Prairie produced creative and unique drama festivals.[97] Women played important roles as organizers, directors, actors, and playwrights; but as the familiar refrain goes, their accomplishments have been ignored. For instance, despite their importance as Alberta playwrights, Elsie Park Gowan and Gwen Pharis Ringwood are overlooked in the history of playwriting in English Canada.[98]

In searching for Alberta women before the 1950s, we find that differences in experience and power have given some women a voice and silenced many others; however, as the case of Elsie Park Gowan shows, even a middle-class urban woman from a privileged background could not speak loud enough to be heard by future generations. As a student at Ross Sheppard High School where Gowan taught in later years, I never studied her plays. We performed *The Importance of Being Earnest* and I was Gwendoline. Later, at the University of Alberta, I remained oblivious of the long history of the Wauneita Society. When I discovered the traditions, stories, and voices of grandmothers from my immediate community I followed a path Elsie Park Gowan knew well. "When I was a youngster growing up in Edmonton, all literature was from far away," she recalled. " A poem was what Mr. Wordsworth wrote about daffodils, a play was something produced in London and a book was always written about somewhere else . . . the world we saw reflected was never our own. But now we have books, plays and pictures that mirror our environment."[99]

Gowan spoke with a "distinctively Canadian" feminist voice, giving Alberta women character and presence in her plays. So also should the stories/histories our children read mirror women's experience and employ the sense of place that exists among Alberta women to bridge differences and create a dialogue. Thinking about the unwritten history of women mountaineers an Alberta poet concludes: "Stories keep us listening keenly, keep us community." By remembering together we reclaim our past and create a future.[100]

*Patricia Roome is completing a Ph.D. thesis on Henrietta Muir Edwards, a Canadian feminist. Patricia has been a member of the Humanities department of Mount Royal College in Calgary since 1974 where she teaches Alberta and Canadian history as well as Women's Studies courses. She is currently part of a team developing a Women's Studies program at Mount Royal College.*

This essay began when Howard Palmer requested that I give a presentation on writing Alberta women's history at the Alberta 2001 Seminar in Red Deer, June 1988. Although substantially revised from the earlier version, "Remembering together" still owes much to Howard's inspiration and memory.

Notes

1. See Molly Chisaakay, "I Remember," *Writing the Circle: Native Women of Western Canada*, Jeanne Perreault and Sylvia Vance, eds. (Edmonton: NeWest, 1990), pp. 30–31. For background on Chisaakay's people see Dianne Meili, *Those Who Know: Profiles of Alberta's Native Elders* (Edmonton: NeWest, 1991), pp. 3–11. See also Patricia Moore and Angela Wheelock, eds., *Wolverine Myths and Visions: Dene Traditions from Northern Alberta* (Lincoln/Edmonton: University of Nebraska Press/University of Alberta Press, 1990). K. Abel, "'The Drum and Cross': An Ethnohistorical Study of Mission Work Among the Dene" (Ph.D. diss., Queen's University, 1984); and "Prophets, Priests and Preachers: Dene Shamans and Christian Missions in the Nineteenth Century," Canadian Historical Association, Historical Papers (1986), pp. 211–24.

2. For a discussion see Kathleen Barry, "Toward a Theory of Women's Biography: From the Life of Susan B. Anthony," *All Sides of the Subject: Women and Biography*, Theresa Iles, ed. (New York: Athene, 1992), p. 32.

3. For the debate on appropriation of Native stories see Leonore Keeshig-Tobias, "Stop Stealing Native Stories," *Globe and Mail*, 26 January 1990. See also Emma LaRocque, "Preface or Here Are Our Voices—Who Will Hear?" in *Writing the Circle*, pp. xvi-xxx.

4. Linda Rasmussen, Lorna Rasmussen, and Candace Savage, *A Harvest Yet To Reap: A History of Prairie Women* (Toronto: Canadian Women's Educational Press, 1976). For an early bibliographic survey see Patricia Roome and Leslie Robinson, eds.,

"Alberta," *Communique* IV, no. 2 (Autumn 1980), where pages 97–99 are devoted to sources on women. An excellent recent analysis is Susan Jackel, "Canadian Prairie Women's History: A Bibliographic Survey," *CRIAW Papers*, no. 14 (1987). See also Merrily K. Aubrey, *Sources for Women's History at the Provincial Archives of Alberta* (Edmonton: Alberta Culture and Multiculturalism, rev. ed., 1988) and *A Guide to the Holdings of the Glenbow Archives* (Calgary: Glenbow Archives, 1992) sections on "Women" and "Women's Organization."

5. See Ruth Roach Pierson, "Experience, Difference, Dominance and Voice in the Writing of Canadian Women's History," *Writing Women's History: International Perspectives*, Karen Offen, Ruth Roach Pierson, and Jane Rendall, eds. (Bloomington and Indianapolis, Indiana University Press, 1991), pp. 79–106.

6. On this theme see Gisela Bock, "Challenging Dichotomies: Perspectives in Women's History," *Writing Women's History*, pp. 1–24.

7. For a detailed discussion of the frontier myth and its evolution in early fiction see Patricia Roome, "'Images of the West' Social Themes in Prairie Literature" (M.A thesis, The University of Calgary, 1976), Chapter 1. See also R. Douglas Francis *Images of the West: Response to the Prairies* (Saskatoon: Western Producer Prairie Books, 1989). For a fictional deconstruction see Anne Cameron, *The Journey* (San Francisco: Spinsters/aunt lute, 1986) which carries the dedication ". . . . and for all the little girls who always wanted to be and never could grow up to be cowboys."

8. James G. MacGregor, *A History of Alberta* rev. ed. (Edmonton: Hurtig Publishers Ltd., 1981), p. 11.

9. Susan Armitage, "Through Women's Eyes: A New View of the West," *The Women's West*, Susan Armitage and Elizabeth James, eds. (Norman and London: University of Oklahoma Press, 1987), p. 7.

10. Patricia Albers and Beatrice Medicine, eds. *The Hidden Half: Studies of Plains Indian Women* (Washington D.C., University Press of America, 1983).

11. Sylvia Van Kirk, *"Many Tender Ties" Women in Fur Trade Society 1670–1870* (Winnipeg: Watson and Dwyer, 1980). Jennifer Brown, *Strangers in Blood: Fur Trade Company Families in Indian Country* (Vancouver: University of British Columbia Press, 1980). On the princess/squaw syndrome see Rayna Green, "The Pocahontas Perplex: the Image of Indian Women in American Culture," *Massachusetts Review* 26 (Autumn 1975), pp. 703–13.

12. Gerald Freisen, *The Canadian Prairies: A History* (Toronto: University of Toronto Press, 1984), Chapter 7.

13. Howard Palmer with Tamara Palmer, *Alberta: A New History* (Edmonton: Hurtig Publishers, 1990). Occasional comments like "some men and women became shamans because of their special gifts" also create a religious presence for Native women.

14. Donald Smith, "The Original Peoples of Alberta," *Peoples of Alberta: Portraits in Cultural Diversity*, Howard and Tamara Palmer, eds. (Saskatoon: Western Producer Prairie Books, 1985), pp. 50–83. Other sources on Alberta native peoples are also silent on women. See Hugh Dempsey, *Indians of Alberta* (Calgary; Glenbow-Alberta Institute, 1978). The published material on Native women is so sparse that a recent bibliography did not include a heading on women. See Hugh Dempsey and Lindsay Moir, *Bibliography of the Blackfoot* (Metuchen, N.J. and London: Scarecrow Press, 1989).

15. Eleanor Leacock, "Montagnais Women and the Jesuit Program for Colonization," *Rethinking Canada: the Promise of Women's History*, 2nd ed., Veronica Strong-Boag and Anita Clair Fellman, eds. (Toronto: Copp Clark Pitman Ltd., 1991), pp. 11–27. Karen Anderson, "A Gendered World: Women, Men, and the Political Economy of the Seventeenth Century Huron," *Feminism and Political Economy*, Heather Jon Maroney and Meg Luxton, eds. (Toronto: Methuen, 1987), pp. 121–38. Karen

Anderson, *Chain Her by One Foot: The Subjugation of Women in Seventeenth Century New France* (New York: Routledge, Chapman, Hall Inc., 1991). Jo-Anne Fiske, "Colonization and the Decline of Women's Status: The Tshimshian Case," *Feminist Studies* 7, no. 3 (Fall 1991).

16. Alan M. Klein, "The Political Economy of Gender: A Nineteenth Century Plains Indians Case Study, *The Hidden Half: Studies of Plains Indian Women*, pp. 143–73.

17. Pamela M. White, Restructuring the Domestic Sphere: Prairie Indian Women on Reserves: Image, Ideology and State Policy 1880–1930 (Ph.D. diss., McGill University, 1987).

18. Jacqueline Gresko, "White 'Rites' and Indian 'Rites': Indian Education and Native Responses in the West, 1870–1910," *Western Canada Past and Present*, A.W. Rasporich, ed. (Calgary: McClelland and Stewart West Ltd., 1975), pp. 163–81. For a British Columbia example see Jean Barman, "Separate and Unequal: Indian and White Girls at All Hallows School, 1884–1920," *Rethinking Canada*, pp. 215–33. For general studies see Kevin J. Carr, "A Historical Survey of Education in Early Blackfoot Culture and Its Historical Implications for Indian Schools" (M.A. thesis, The University of Calgary, 1968); Kathryn Kozak, "Education and the Blackfoot" (M.A. thesis, The University of Calgary, 1971); Joan Scott-Brown, "The Short Life of St. Dunstan's Calgary Indian Industrial School 1896–1907," *Canadian Journal of Native Education* 14, no. 1 (1987), pp. 41–49.

19. Rosemary Brown, "Rupture of the Ties that Bind: Lubicon Lake Women and Their Society" (M.A. thesis, The University of Calgary, 1990).

20. Beverly Hungry Wolf, *The Ways of My Grandmothers* (New York: Quill, 1982), pp. 109. See also Gretchen M. Bataille and Kathleen Mullen Sands, *American Indian Women: Telling Their lives* (Lincoln: University of Nebraska Press, 1984). Chapter 7, "Traditional Values in Modern Context: the Narratives to Come" discusses Hungry Wolf's work.

21. Hungry Wolf, *The Ways of My Grandmothers*, p. 53.

22. Quoted in *Writing the Circle*, back cover.

23. Jock Carpenter, *Fifty Dollar Bride: Marie Rose Smith—A Chronicle of Metis Life in the Nineteenth Century* (Sydney, BC: Gray's Publishing, 1977). See also the story of a mixed-blood woman who grew on the Bar U Ranch near High River. Ida S. Patterson, ed., *Mountain Memories: The Life of Emma Magee in the Rocky Mountain West 1899–1950* (1983).

24. See Victoria Calihoo, "Early Life in Lac Ste. Anne and St. Albert in the 1870s," Alberta Historical Review 1, no. 3 (Autumn 1953), pp. 21–26. Grant MacEwan, "Victoria Callihoo: 'Granny,'" in . . . *and Mighty Women Too* (Saskatoon: Western Producer Prairie Books, 1975), pp. 190–99. I was unable to locate the following reference: The Calahoo Women's Institute, com., *Calahoo Trails*, Mrs. K. Dalheim and Mrs. M. Keer, eds. (Calahoo Women's Institute, n.d). For brief references to the mothers of Metis leaders Jim Brady and Malcolm Norris see Murray Dobbin, *The One-And-A Half Men* (Vancouver: New Star Books, 1981), Chapter 1 "Extraordinary Families." On the Iroquois roots and problems of the Michael Indian Reserve see Robert Hunter and Robert Calihoo, *Occupied Canada: A Young White Man Discovers His Unsuspected Past* (Toronto: McClelland and Stewart, 1991).

25. Maria Campbell, *Halfbreed* (Toronto: McClelland and Stewart, 1973), p. 2. See Bataille and Sands, Chapter 6, "The Long Road Back: Marie Campbell."

26. Bill Miller ed., *Our Home: A History of Kikino Metis Settlement* (Edmonton: Alberta Metis Association, 1984). Elizabeth Metis Settlement Association Council, *Elizabeth Metis Settlement: A Local History* (Friesen Printers, 1979?), p. 7.

27. For a recent study see T.C. Pockington, *The Government and Politics of the Alberta Metis Settlements* (Regina: Canadian Plains Research Center, 1991). On demography, Trudy Nicks and Kenneth Morgan, "Grand Cache: The Historic Development of an

Indigenous Alberta Metis Population." *The New Peoples: Being and Becoming Metis in North America*, Jacqueline Peterson and Jennifer S.H. Brown, eds. (Winnipeg: University of Manitoba Press, 1985), pp. 163–81; also Joe Sawchuk, Patricia Sawchuk, and Theresa Ferguson, *Metis Land Rights in Alberta: A Political History* (Edmonton: Metis Association of Alberta, 1980). For a biased and poorly written study of the East Prairie Metis Colony see Paul Driben, *We Are Metis: the Ethnography of a Half-breed Community in Northern Alberta* (New York: AMS, 1985). When Driben did field research in East Prairie in 1970, he conducted interviews with all the men who owned land in the colony but writes that his "conversations with women and children were limited to those of the informal variety." Despite this Driben includes a large section on "kinship, socialization, and social control." See his preface and his explanation that his anthropological research methods minimized bias.

28. Ted Brasser, "In Search of Metis Art," *The New Peoples*, pp. 221–30. See also "Metis Artisans," *The Beaver* (Autumn 1975), pp. 52–57 which might be more appropriately titled Metis women artists.

29. Julia Harrison, *Metis: People between Two Worlds* (Vancouver: Glenbow-Alberta Institute and Douglas McIntyre, 1985).

30. P. Campbell, *Halfbreed*, p. 168. See Janet Silman, comp., *Enough Is Enough: Aboriginal Women Speak Out* (Toronto: Women's Press, 1987) and Dolores T. Poelzer, *Own Words: Northern Saskatchewan Metis Women Speak Out* (Lindenblatt and Harmonic: Saskatoon, 1986). On the importance of a woman's organization and men's resistance see Marlene M. Doxater, "The Metis Women's Association of Manitoba," *The Other Natives* II, Antoine S. Lussier and D. Bruce Sealey, eds. (Winnipeg: Manitoba Metis Federation Press, 1978).

31. See Emma LaRocque, *Writing the Circle*, xxx, pp. 143–55. See also LaRocque, *Defeathering the Indian* (Agincourt: Book Society, 1975). Meili, *Those Who Know*, pp. 71–78; 179–84.

32. For a discussion of feminist literary criticism and its impact on redefining the canon and accepting stories from oral tradition as literature see Barbara Godard, "Talking About Ourselves: The Literary Productions of the Native Women of Canada," *CRIAW Paper*, no. 11 (Ottawa: Canadian Research Institute for the Advancement of Women, 1985)

33. See Ruth Compton Brouwer, "Transcending the 'Unacknowledged Quarantine': Putting Religion into English-Canadian Women's History," Paper presented to Canadian Society of Church History/Canadian Historical Association, Kingston 1991). On Catholic sisters, Quebec education, and feminism see Marta Danylewycz, *Taking the Veil: An Alternative to Marriage, Motherhood and Spinsterhood in Quebec, 1840–1920* (Toronto: McClelland and Stewart, 1987). See also Ruth Compton Brouwer, *New Women for God: Canadian Presbyterian Women and India Mission 1886–1914* (Toronto: University of Toronto, 1990), and Rosemary Gagan, *A Sensitive Independence: Canadian Methodist Women Missionaries in Canada and the Orient 1881–1925* (Montreal: McGill-Queen's, 1992). William E. Mann, *Sect, Cult and Church in Alberta* (Toronto: University of Toronto Press, 1955).

34. Anne Gagnon, "In the Promised Land: the Lives of Franco-Albertan Women at the Turn of the Century" (Ph.D. diss., in progress at the University of Ottawa). Anne Gagnon,"The Pensionnat Assomption: Religious Nationalism in a Franco-Albertan Boarding School for Girls, 1926–1960," *Historical Studies in Education: Revue d'histoire de l'education* 1, no. 11 (1989).

35. Maureen Ursenback Beecher, "Mormon Women in Southern Alberta: The Pioneer Years," *The Mormon Presence in Canada*, Brigham Y. Card et al., eds. (Edmonton: University of Alberta Press, 1990), pp. 211–30; Jessie L. Embrey, "'Two Legal Wives': Mormon Polygamy in Canada, United States and Mexico," *The Mormon Presence*, pp. 170–85. See also Maureen Ursenback Beecher and Lavina Fielding

Anderson, *Sisters in Spirit: Mormon Women in Historical and Cultural Perspective* (Urbana: University of Illinois Press, 1987). See Kimberly Jensen James, "Between Two Fires: Women of the 'Underground' of Mormon polygamy," *Journal of Mormon History*, no. 8 (1981), pp. 9–62.

36. Claudia Helen Popowich, *To Serve Is to Love: The Canadian Story of the Sister Servants of Mary Immaculate* (Toronto: SSMI, 1971); see also J. Skwarok, *The Ukrainian Settlers and Their Schools 1891–1921* (Edmonton: Basilian Press, 1959) and Sophia Senyk, "Ukrainian Religious Congregations in Canada: Tradition and Change," *The Ukrainian Religious Experience*, David J. Goa, ed. (Edmonton: Canadian Institute of Ukrainian Studies, University of Alberta, 1989), pp. 95–107; Frances Swyripa, "The Ukrainians and Private Education," *A Heritage in Transition: Essays in the History of Ukrainians in Canada*, Manoly Lupul, ed. (Toronto: McClelland and Stewart, 1982), p. 250.

37. Vivian Olender, "The Cultural Implications of Protestant Missions," Continuity and Change: The Cultural Life of Alberta's First Ukrainians, Manoly R. Lupul, ed. (Edmonton: Canadian Institute of Ukrainian Studies, p. 224.

38. John W. Friesen and Michael Verigin, *The Community Doukhobors: A People in Transition* (Ottawa: Borealis Press, 1989); see also John W. Friesen, "Pacifism and Anastasia's Doukhobor Village," *Alberta History* 41, no. 1 (Winter 1993), pp. 14–19.

39. Randi R. Warne, "Literature As Pulpit: Narrative As a Vehicle for the Transmission and Transformation of Values in the Christian Social Activism of Nellie McClung" (Ph.D. diss., University of Toronto, 1988); Mary E. Hallet, "Nellie McClung and the Fight for the Ordination of Women in the United Church of Canada," *Atlantis* 4, no. 2 (Spring 1972), pp. 2–16. On recent contributions of women see Edmonton Presbyterial United Church, *Women Called to Respond 1962–1987* (Edmonton: United Church Women Presbyterial, 1987).

40. Elizabeth M. McCrum, ed., *Letters of Lovisa McDougall 1878–1887* (Occasional Paper No. 1: Provincial Archives of Alberta, 1978).

41. Hilda Rose, *The Stump Farm: A Chronicle of Pioneering* (Boston: Little, Brown, 1928). Monica Hopkins, *Letters from a Lady Rancher* (Calgary: Glenbow Museum, 1981), with an introduction by Sheilagh Jameson (hereafter Jameson); Sarah Roberts, *Of Us and the Oxen* (Saskatoon: Modern Press, 1968); also published later as *Alberta Homestead: A Chronicle of a Pioneer Family* (Austin: University of Texas Press, 1971). W.L. Morton, *God's Galloping Girl: The Peace River Diaries of Monica Storrs 1929–1931* (Vancouver: University of British Columbia Press, 1979); also R.C. Moyles, *Challenge of the Homestead: Peace River Letters of Clyde and Myrle Campbell, 1919–1924* (Calgary: Alberta Records Publication, Historical Society of Alberta VII, 1988).

42. For example, see the four part series of Catherine Neil, "Recollections of a Sheep Herder's Bride," *Alberta History* 35, no. 2 (Spring 1987) for part I ending with part IV, vol. 36, no. 1 (Winter 1988). Doris H. Pieroth, "Peace River Journey, 1916," *Beaver* 71, no. 1 (February-March 1991), pp. 39–42; see also Joy Parr, "The Skilled Emigrant and Her Kin: Gender, Culture and Labour Recruitment," *Canadian Historical Review* LXVIII, no. 4 (December 1987), pp. 529–51.

43. Susan Jackel, *A Flannel Shirt and Liberty: British Emigrant Gentlewomen in the Canadian West 1880–1914* (Vancouver: University of British Columbia Press, 1982); see also Emma Curtin, "Two British Gentlewoman," *Alberta History* 38, no. 4 (Autumn 1990), pp. 10–16. Nanci Langford, "Women's Pioneering Narratives in Alberta/Saskatchewan during the Settlement Period" (Ph.D. diss. in progress, University of Alberta). See also Elizabeth Thompson, *The Pioneer Woman: A Canadian Type* (Montreal: McGill-Queen's University Press, 1991). There is a growing feminist literature on women's autobiography which should be consulted as well. See Helen Buss, "'The Dear Domestic Circle': Frameworks for the Literary Study of Women's Per-

sonal Narratives in Archival Collections," *Studies in Canadian Literature* 14, no. 1 (1989), pp. 1–17; Helen M. Buss, "Canadian Women's Autobiography in English: An Introductory Guide for Researchers and Teachers," *CRIAW Paper*, no. 24 (Ottawa: Canadian Research Institute for the Advancement of Women, 1991).

44. Eliane Leslau Silverman, *The Last Best West: Women on the Alberta Frontier 1880–1930* (Montreal: Eden Press, 1984), p. iv.

45. See an earlier essay by Eliane Silverman, "In Their Own Words: Mothers and Daughters on the Alberta Frontier," *Frontiers* (1977), pp. 37–44 and "Women's Perceptions of Marriage on the Alberta Frontier," *Building Beyond the Homestead*, David C. Jones and Ian MacPherson, eds. (Calgary: The University of Calgary Press, 1985), pp. 49–64.

46. Catherine Philip, "The Fair, Frail Flower of Western Womanhood," *Frontier Calgary: Town, City, and Region 1875–1914* (Calgary: McClelland and Stewart, 1975), p. 118. See also Catherine Philip, "Women of Calgary and District, 1875–1914" (M.A. thesis, The University of Calgary, 1975); Sheilagh Jameson, "Women in the Southern Alberta Ranching Community," *The Canadian West: Social Change and Economic Development* (Calgary: The University of Calgary, 1977), pp. 63–78.

47. Philip, "The Fair, Frail Flower," pp. 122–23; Eliane Silverman, "Women and the Victorian Work Ethic on the Alberta Frontier: Prescription and Description," *The New Provinces: Alberta and Saskatchewan 1905–1980* (Vancouver: Tantalus Research, 1980), pp. 91–99.

48. Sara Brooks Sunberg, "Farm Women on the Canadian Prairie Frontier: The Helpmate Image," *Rethinking Canada: the Promise of Women's History* (Toronto: Copp Clark, 1986); see also Carol Fairbanks and Sara Brooks Sunberg, *Farm Women on the Prairie Frontier: A Sourcebook for Canada and the United States* (Metuchen, NJ: Scarecrow Press, 1983).

49. Helen Potrebenko, *No Streets of Gold: A Social History of Ukrainians in Alberta* (Vancouver, New Star Books, 1977).

50. Myrna Kostash, *All of Baba's Children* (Edmonton: NeWest Publishers, 1987), p. 174.

51. Potrebenko, *No Streets of Gold*, pp. 300–01.

52. Frances Swyripa, *Wedded to the Cause: Ukrainian Canadian Women and Ethnic Identity, 1891–1991* (Toronto: University of Toronto Press, 1992). Her thesis is argued in an essay, "Wedded to the Cause: Ukrainian-Canadian Women," in *Canada's Ukrainians: Negotiating an Identity*, Lubomyr Luciuk and Stella Hryniuk, eds. (Toronto: Ukrainian Canadian Centennial Committee and University of Toronto Press, 1991), p. 240.

53. Frances Swyripa, "Baba and the Community Heroine: The Two Images of the Ukrainian Pioneer Woman," *Alberta* 2, no. 1 (1989), p. 77, and "From Princess Olga to Baba: Images, Roles and Myths in the History of Ukrainian Women in Canada" (Ph.D. diss., University of Alberta, 1988); see also Marie Lesoway, "Women in Three Households" Lupul, ed., *Continuity and Change*, pp. 115–23.

54. Kostash, *All of Baba's Children*, p. 3.

55. Frances Swyripa, "National-Building into the 1920s: Conflicting Claims on Ukrainian Immigrant Women," *Continuity and Change*, p. 142.

56. Krystyna Joanna Lukasiewicz, "Polish Immigrant Women in Alberta 1919–1939" (M.A. thesis, in progress, The University of Calgary). See Donna Mavis Minions, "Three Worlds of Greek-Canadian Women: A Study of Migrant Greek Women in Calgary Alberta" (M.A. thesis, The University of Calgary, 1984).

57. Susan Jane McKenzie, "Hutterite Women: Work and Assistance Patterns" (M.A. thesis, The University of Calgary, 1975); see also Karl Peter, "The Changing Role of Hutterite Women," *Prairie Forum* 7, no. 2 (Fall 1982), pp. 267–77.

58. Varpu Lindstrom-Best and Allen Seager, "Toveritar and the Finnish Canadian Women's Movement, 1900–1930," *The Press of Labor Migrants in Europe and North*

*America,* Christian Harzig and Dirk Hoerder, eds. (Bremen: University Printing Office, 1895), pp. 243–64; see also Allen Seager, "Class, Ethnicity, and Politics in the Alberta Coalfields, 1905–1945," *"Struggle a Hard Battle": Essays on Working Class Immigrants,* Dirk Hoerder, ed. (Chicago: Northern Illinois University Press, 1986), p. 312.

59. Varpu Lindstrom-Best, "I Won't Be a Slave: Finnish Domestics in Canada 1911–1930," *Looking into My Sister's Eyes: An Exploration in Women's History,* Jean Burnet, ed. (Toronto: Multicultural History Society of Ontario, 1986); see also *Defiant Sisters: a Social History of Finnish Immigrant Women in Canada* (Toronto: Multicultural History Society of Ontario, 1988).

60. For an assessment of McClung's novel, see Roome, "Images of the West," Chapter 3, pp. 87–91.

61. See Patricia Roome, "'Beware of the Suffragist': Class and Sexual Politics in the Historiography of the British Suffrage Movement" (unpublished paper, Simon Fraser University, 1989); and "Embracing the Janus Face: The Historiography of the Canadian and American Suffrage Movement" (unpublished paper, Simon Fraser University, 1989).

62. Carol Bacchi, *Liberation Deferred: the Ideas of English-Canadian Suffragists, 1877–1918* (Toronto: University of Toronto Press, 1983).

63. For a critique see Ernest Forbes, "The Ideas of Carol Bacchi and the Suffragists Halifax," *Atlantis,* 11 (Spring 1985), pp. 120–22; see also Ernest Forbes, "Battles in Another War: Edith Archibald and the Halifax Feminist Movement," *Challenging the Regional Stereotype: Essays on the Twentieth Century Maritimes* (Fredericton: Acadiensis Press, 1989), pp. 67–90.

64. Sheilagh Jameson, "Give Your Other Vote to the Sister," *Alberta Historical Review* 15, no. 4 (Autumn 1967 ), pp. 10–16; Paul Voisey, "The Votes for Woman's Movement," *Alberta History* 23, no. 3 (Summer 1975), pp. 10–23; Barbara Nicholson, "Feminism in Western Canada to 1916" (M.A. thesis, The University of Calgary, 1975); Catherine Cavanaugh, "The Women's Movement in Alberta As Seen through the Campaign for Dower Rights 1909–1928" (M.A. thesis, University of Alberta, 1984). Faye Reiniberg Holt, "Women's Suffrage in Alberta," *Alberta History* 38, no. 2 (Autumn 1991), pp. 25–31; Veronica Strong-Boag, "'Ever a Crusader': Nellie McClung, First Wave Feminist," *Rethinking Canada.*

65. Margaret E. McCallum, "Prairie Women and the Struggle for Dower Law, 1905–1920" (paper presented to the Canadian Historical Association, Kingston, 1991), p. 2.

66. For example see Carol Bacchi, "'Divided Allegiances': The Response of Farm and Labour Women to Suffrage," in *A Not Unreasonable Claim: Women and Reform in Canada 1880–1920* (Toronto: Women's Press, 1979), pp. 89–108. Leslie Robinson, "Agrarian Reformers: Women and the Reform Movement in Alberta 1909–1925" (M.A. thesis, University of Alberta, 1979); Elise Schnieder, "Addressing the Issues: Two Women's Groups in Edmonton, 1905–16," *Alberta History* (1990); M. Jane Schulten, "Starting from Scratch: Social Reform by Pioneer Women of Southern Alberta 1900–1919," *Lethbridge Historical Society Newsletter* 6 (November 1990), pp. 2–4; Nancy Sheehan, "Women Helping Women: The WCTU and the 'Foreign Problem' in the West," *International Journal of Women's Studies* 6, no. 5 (November 1983), pp. 395–411; Elise Corbet, "Women's Canadian Club of Calgary," *Alberta History* xxv, no. 3 (Spring 1977), pp. 29–36.

67. Nancy M. Sheehan, "The WCTU on the Prairies, 1886–1930: An Alberta-Saskatchewan Comparison," *Prairie Forum* 6, no. 1 (Spring 1981), p. 30, and "Temperance, the WCTU, and Education in Alberta, 1905–1930" (Ph.D. thesis, University of Alberta, 1980); and "The W.C.T.U. and Educational Strategies on the Canadian Prairies," *History of Education Quarterly* 24 (1984), pp. 101–19. See also R. McLean,

"A Most Effectual Remedy—Temperance and Prohibition in Alberta, 1874–1915" (M.A. thesis, The University of Calgary, 1969).

68. Marianna Valverde, *The Age of Light, Soap, and Water: Moral Reform in English Canada, 1885–1925* (Toronto: McClelland and Stewart, 1991). See also Sharon Cook, "'Continued and Persevering Combat': The Ontario Women's Christian Temperance Union, A Study in Evangelical Feminism" (paper presented to the Canadian Historical Association, Kingston, 1991, and Ph.D. thesis, Carleton University, 1990; same title).

69. Kathleen Barry, "Towards a Theory of Women's Biography," *All Sides of the Subject*, p. 24. See also Carolyn Heilbrun, *Writing a Woman's Life* (New York: Ballantine, 1988). For recent examples of Canadian women's biography see *Mary Kinnear, Margaret McWilliams: An Interwar Feminist* (Montreal: McGill-Queen's, 1991) and Terrance Crowley, *Agnes MacPhail and the Politics of Equality* (Toronto: James Lorimer, 1990).

70. Nellie McClung, *The Stream Runs Fast* (Toronto: Thomas Allen, 1945), pp. x–xi. See also McClung, *Clearing in the West* (Winnipeg: Thomas Allen, 1933); Catherine Anne Cavanaugh, "Irene Parlby: A Useful Life" (Ph.D. diss., in progress, University of Alberta). Earlier studies are Clare May Findlay, "The Honourable Irene Parlby" (M.A. thesis, University of Alberta, 1953); Barbara Cormack, *Perennial and Politics: The Life Story of Honourable Irene Parlby* (Sherwood Park: Professional Printing, 1968); and Una MacLean, "The Honourable Irene Parlby," *Alberta Historical Review* (Spring 1959), pp. 1–6; Patricia Roome, "Henrietta Muir Edwards: Woman of Two Worlds" (Ph.D. diss., in progress at Simon Fraser University); Byrne Hope Sanders, *Emily Murphy, Crusader* (Toronto: Macmillan, 1945); E. Harmon, "Five Persons from Alberta," *The Clear Spirit*, M.Q. Innis, ed. (Toronto: University of Toronto Press, 1973); Una McLean, "The Famous Five," *Alberta Historical Review* 10, no. 2 (Spring 1952), pp. 1–4.

71. Veronica Strong-Boag, "Pulling in Double Harness or Hauling a Double Load: Women, Work and Feminism on the Canadian Prairies," *Journal of Canadian Studies* 21, no. 3 (Autumn 1986), pp. 32–52, and "Canadian Feminism in the 1920s: The Case of Nellie McClung," in *The Prairie West: Historical Readings*, R. Douglas Francis and Howard Palmer, eds. (Edmonton: Pica Pica Press, 1985), also "Peace-Making Women, 1919–1939," *Women and Peace*, Ruth Roach Pierson, ed. (London: Croom Helm, 1989). For a revisionist view on McClung see Randi Warne, "Nellie McClung and Peace," *Up and Doing: Canadian Women and Peace*, Janice Williamson and Deborah Gorham, eds. (Toronto: Women's Press, 1989). See Rudy Marchildon, "The Person's Controversy: The Legal Aspects of the Fight for Women Senators," *Atlantic* (Spring 1981), pp. 99–113.

72. Sheila May Moore Johnston, "Giving Freely of Her time and Energy: Calgary Public Women 1910–1930" (M.A. thesis, The University of Calgary, 1987). Elise Corbet, "A Do-Gooder, Not A Suffragette: A. Maude Riley," *Citymakers: Calgarians After the Frontier*, Max Foran and Sheilagh Jameson, eds. (Calgary: Historical Society of Alberta, 1987), pp. 208–24; Heather Foran, "Annie Gale: Reformer, Feminist and First Woman Alderman in Calgary," *Citymakers*, pp. 196–207; Patricia Roome, "Amelia Turner: Alberta Socialist," *Citymakers*, pp. 225–56. See also Patricia Roome, "Amelia Turner and Calgary Labour Women," *Beyond the Vote: Women in Canadian Politics*, Linda Kealey and Joan Sangster, eds. (Toronto: University of Toronto Press, 1987) and Joan Sangster, *Dreams of Equality: Canadian On The Canadian Left 1920–1950* (Toronto: McClelland and Stewart, 1989).

73. Michael Palamarek, *Alberta Women in Politics: A History of Women and Politics in Alberta* (A report for Senator Martha P. Bielish, December 1989), p. 1. See also Sylvia Bashevekin, *Toeing the Line: Women in English Canadian Politics* (Toronto: University of Toronto Press, 1985).

74. Silverman, "Women's Perceptions of Marriage on the Alberta Frontier," *Building*

*Beyond the Homestead*, p. 61. For a study on gender using a life-cycle approach see Veronica Strong-Boag, *The New Day Recalled: The Lives of Girls and Women in English Canada 1919–1939* (Toronto: Copp Clark, Pitman, 1988).

75. Terry Chapman, "Women, Sex and Marriage in Western Canada 1890–1920," *Alberta History* 33, no. 4 (Autumn 1985), pp. 1–12; and "Sex Crimes in Western Canada 1880–1920" (Ph.D. thesis, University of Alberta, 1984) and "'Till Death Do Us Part': Wife Beating in Alberta, 1905–1920," *Alberta History* 36, no. 4 (Autumn 1988), pp. 13–22. On women, rape, and sexual crimes see Constance Backhouse, *Petticoats and Prejudice: Women and Law in Nineteenth Century Canada* (Toronto: Women's Press, 1991).

76. On western women's medical self help see Norah Lewis, "Goose Grease and Turpentine: Mother Treats the Family Illness," *Rethinking Canada*, 2nd ed. On birth control see Silverman, *The Last Best West*, Chapter 4, and Elise Corbet, "Alberta Women in the Twenties: An Inquiry into Four Aspects of Their Lives" (M.A. thesis, The University of Calgary, 1979). Angus McLaren and Arlene Tiger MacLaren, *Bedroom and the State: The Changing Practices and Politics of Contraception and Abortion in Canada 1880–1980* (Toronto: McClelland and Stewart, 1985).

77. Leslie Savage, "Perspectives on Illegitimacy: The Changing Role of the Sisters of Misericordia in Edmonton 1900–1906," *Studies in Childhood History: A Canadian Perspective*, Patricia T. Rooke and R.L. Schnell, eds. (Calgary: Detselig Enterprises, 1982) and "Infanticide, Illegitimacy and the Origins and Evolution of the Role of the Misericordia" (M.Ed. thesis, University of Alberta, 1982). See also Andree Levesque, "'Deviant Anonymous': Single Mothers at the Hopital de la Misericorde in Montreal 1929–1939," *Rethinking Canada*, 2nd ed.

78. Henrietta Muir Edwards, comp., "Introduction," *Legal Status of Women of Alberta as shown by Extracts from Dominion and Provincial Laws* (Edmonton: Department of Extension University of Alberta, 1917).

79. Marjorie Cohen, "The Decline of Women in Canadian Dairying," *The Neglected Majority: Essays in Canadian Women's History* 2 (Toronto: McClelland and Stewart, 1985), pp. 61–83. See also Marjorie Cohen, *Women's Work, Markets and Economic Development in Nineteenth Century Ontario* (Toronto: University of Toronto Press, 1988).

80. See Marianne Fedori, "Women, Technology and the Home: Some Reflections on Calgary Homemakers in the Interwar Years," *Alberta Museums Review* 10, no. 1 (Spring), pp. 14–17; and Angela E. Davis, "'Valiant Servants': Women and Technology on the Canadian Prairies 1910–1940" (paper presented to the Canadian Historical Association, Kingston 1991); see also Veronica Strong-Boag, "Keeping House in God's Country: Canadian Women at Work in the Home," *On the Job: Confronting the Labour Process in Canada*, Craig Heron and Robert Storey, eds. (Montreal: McGill-Queen's Press, 1986). For the America context see Ruth Schwartz Cowan, *More Work for Mother: The Ironies of Household Technology from the Open Hearth to the Microwave* (New York: Basic Books, 1983).

81. Norma Milton, "Essential Servants: Immigrant Domestic on the Canadian Prairies" (M.A. thesis, The University of Calgary, 1986) and "Essential Servants: Immigrant Domestics on the Canadian Prairies," *The Women's West*.

82. On the agrarian press see David C. Jones, "'We Can't Live on Air All the Time' Country Life and the Prairie Child," *Studies in Childhood History*; Rebecca Coulter, "The Working Young of Edmonton, 1921–1931," *Childhood and the Family in Canadian History*, Joy Parr, ed. (Toronto: McClelland and Stewart, 1983).

83. Hugh Dempsey, "Confessions of a Calgary Stenographer," *Alberta History* 36, no. 3 (Summer 1988). See Graham S. Lowe, *Women in the Administrative Revolution: The Feminization of Clerical Work* (Toronto: University of Toronto Press, 1987). On

Alberta see Corbet, *Alberta Women in the 1920s*. On nursing see Irene Stewart, *These Were Our Yesterdays: A History of District Nursing in Alberta* (Calgary: D.W. Friesen and Sons, 1979).

4. Anna Woywitka, "A Pioneer Woman in the Labour Movement," *Alberta History* 27, no. 1 (Winter 1978), pp. 10–16. Warren Caragata, *Alberta Labour: A Heritage Untold* (Toronto: James Lorimer, 1979), p. 133. See Donna Zwicker, "Alberta Women and World War II" (M.A. thesis, The University of Calgary, 1985); see also Patricia Dezutter, "Women in a Resource Corporation in the Boardroom, at the Typewriter, on the Rigs" (M.A. thesis, The University of Calgary, 1981).

5. Mary Murphy, "The Private Lives of Public Women: Prostitution in Butte, Montana, 1978–1917," *The Women's West*; James Gray, *Red Lights on the Prairies* (Toronto: Macmillan, 1970); Judy Bedford, "Prostitution in Calgary 1905–1914," *Alberta History* (Spring 1981).

36. Elizabeth Langdon "Analyzing Female Crime in Calgary 1914–1941," *Law and Justice in A New Land*, Louise Knafla, ed. (Toronto: Carswell, 1986).

37. Robert Stamp, "Teaching Girls Their God-given Place in Life: The Introduction of Home Economics in the Schools," *Atlantis* (1977). See Douglas Coats, "Calgary: The Private Schools, 1900–16," *Frontier Calgary*.

38. L.J. Wilson, "The Educational Role of the United Farm Women of Alberta," *Alberta History* 25, no. 2 (Spring 1977), pp. 28–36; Shelley Bosetti, "The Rural Women's University: Women's Institutes in Alberta From 1909–1940" (M.Ed. thesis, University of Alberta, 1983); see also Shelley-Anne Bosetti-Piche, "The Interest of Edmonton Club Women in Education, Health and Welfare 1919–1939" (Ph.D. diss., University of Alberta, 1991).

39. For the papers of the Wauneita Society and Dr. Keeping see *From the Past to the Future: A Guide to the Holdings of the University of Alberta Archives* (Edmonton: University of Alberta, 1992), p. 94. On teachers see Collette Alice Oseen, "Women teachers in Edmonton Public Schools 1940–1950" (M.Ed. thesis, University of Alberta, 1985).

40. Recent literature on professional women includes the following: Margaret Gilkes, *Ladies of the Night: Reflections of a Pioneer Police Woman* (Hanna: Gorman and Gorman Publishers, 1989); Mary Evangeline (Percy) Jackson, *The Homemade Brass Plate: The Story of Dr. Mary Percy Jackson* (Sardis: Cedar-Cott Enterprises, 1988). See Blanche Lemco van Ginkel, "Slowly and Surely (and Somewhat Painfully): More or Less the History of Women in Architecture in Canada"; and Erna Dominey, "Wallbridge and Irmie: the Architectural Practice of Two Edmonton Women, 1950–1970," *Society for the Study of Architecture in Canada Bulletin* 17, no. 1 (March 1991). For artists see Jennifer Hamblin, "The Career of Operatic Soprano Norma Piper Pocaterra," *Citymakers*, pp. 356–65 and Peggy Armstrong, *Janet Mitchell, Life and Art* (Winnipeg: Hyperion Press, 1990).

. Mary Lou Lecompte, "Cowgirls at the Crossroads; Women in Professional Rodeo, 1885–1922," *Canadian Journal of Sport History* xx, no. 2 (December 1989), p. 27; see also "Champion Cowgirls of Rodeo's Golden Age," *Journal of the West* xvii, no. 2 (April 1989). For two short studies by Calgary authors see Robert Stamp, "Rodeo Women in the Early Days of the Stampede," *Western Living* (July 1982) and Donna Livingston, "Cowgirls of the Wild West," *Glenbow* 5, no. 4 (August 1985), pp. 11–13. Unfortunately these writers speak mainly about America superstars and neglect the Canadian/Albertan competitors.

Elaine Chalus, "The Edmonton Commercial Graduates: Women's History, An Integrationist Approach," *Winter Sports in Alberta*, Elise Corbet and A.W. Rasporich, eds. (Calgary: Historical Society of Alberta, 1990), p. 69; see also Kathleen E. McCrone, *Playing the Game: Sport and the Physical Emancipation of English Woman*

*1870–1914* (Lexington: University of Kentucky Press, 1988) and "Class, Gender a[nd]
English Women's Sport c. 1890–1914," *Journal of Sport History* 18, no. 1 (Spri[ng]
1991).

93. Cyndi Smith, *Off the Beaten Track: Women Adventurers and Mountaineers in Weste[rn]
    Canada* (Jasper: Coyote Books, 1989), p. 18; see also R.W. Sanford, *The Canadian Alp[s:]
    The History of Mountaineering in Canada* (Banff: Attitude Publishing, 1990).

94. Betty Dahlie, "The Barclay Sisters," *Citymakers*.

95. Donald G. Wetherell with Irene Kmet, *Useful Pleasures: the Shaping of Leisure i[n]
    Alberta 1896–1945* (Regina: Alberta Culture and Multiculturalism/Canadian Plain[s]
    Research Center, 1990).

96. [S............ & .......... *Chautauqua in Canada* (Calgary: Glenbow-Alberta Institute]

97. [.........................................................] tiator of Alberta The[atre]

-35; Moira Day, "Th[e]
[19]14–1945," *Theatre His[tory]*
[wit]h Sterling Hayes an[d]
[University] of Toronto 1990); se[e]
[...]of Drama in Calgary,[...]

98. [...]n," *Theatre History i[n]*

99. [...]uction of one play se[e]
    [...]*Canada* 8, no. 1 (Spring
100. [...]*ected Plays and Prose b[y]*